A Future to Inherit

GENERATIONS

A History of Canada's Peoples

A Future to Inherit

Portuguese Communities in Canada

Grace M. Anderson and David Higgs

Published by McClelland and Stewart in association with
the Multiculturalism Program, Department
of the Secretary of State of Canada and the
Publishing Centre, Supply and Services Canada.

Government Catalogue No. Ci 44-1/1976

The Canadian Publishers
McClelland and Stewart Limited
25 Hollinger Road
Toronto, Ontario

Printed and bound in Canada
by John Deyell Company

Contents

Acknowledgements

We find it difficult to single out individuals among the many in Canada, Portugal, and the United States who have helped with the collection of information for this study. Maria de Sousa, José Carlos de Sousa and Domenico Raimundo must, however, receive special thanks for their contribution to our research. Grace Anderson is particularly appreciative of Jean Burnet's many insightful sociological comments on the manuscript at various stages. David Higgs thanks Olwen Hufton for a long friendship and for the inspiration of her analytical and compassionate work on French social history. We are beholden to Christine Purden and John Roberts for their help in preparing the manuscript for publication.

Various agencies of the Canadian government on all levels, at home and abroad, have kindly facilitated the completion of our task. We are grateful to Mario de Marinis of the National Ethnic Archives. The officers of Portuguese social clubs, voluntary agencies, consulates and the Portuguese clergy have been extremely generous in their assistance. Above all, we wish to thank the many Portuguese-Canadians who told us about themselves and who offered early photographs for this volume.

G.M.A.
D.H.

Editor's Introduction

Canadians, like many other people, have recently been changing their attitude towards the ethnic dimension in society. Instead of thinking of the many distinctive heritages and identities to be found among them as constituting a problem, though one that time would solve, they have begun to recognize the ethnic diversity of their country as a rich resource. They have begun to take pride in the fact that people have come and are coming here from all parts of the world, bringing with them varied outlooks, knowledge, skills and traditions, to the great benefit of all.

It is for this reason that Book IV of the *Report of the Royal Commission on Bilingualism and Biculturalism* dealt with the cultural contributions of the ethnic groups other than the British, the French and the Native Peoples to Canada, and that the federal government in its response to Book IV announced that the Citizenship Branch of the Department of the Secretary of State would commission "histories specifically directed to the background, contributions and problems of various cultural groups in Canada." This series presents the histories that have resulted from that mandate. Although commissioned by the Government, they are not intended as definitive or official, but rather as the efforts of scholars to bring together much of what is known about the ethnic groups studied, to indicate what remains to be learned, and thus to stimulate further research concerning the ethnic dimension in Canadian society. The histories are to be objective, analytical, and readable, and directed towards the general reading public, as well as students at the senior high school and the college and university levels, and teachers in the elementary schools.

Most Canadians belong to an ethnic group, since to do so is simply to have "a sense of identity rooted in a common origin . . . whether this common origin is real or imaginary."[1] The Native Peoples, the British and French (referred to as charter groups because they were the first Europeans to take possession of the land), the groups such as the Germans and Dutch who have been established in Canada for over a hundred years and those who began to arrive only yesterday all have traditions and values that they cherish and that now are part of the cultural riches that Canadians share. The groups vary widely in numbers, geographical location and distribution and degree of social and economic power. The stories of their struggles, failures and triumphs will be told in this series.

As the Royal Commission on Bilingualism and Biculturalism pointed out, this sense of ethnic origin or identity "is much keener in certain individuals than in others."[2] In contemporary Canadian society, with the increasing number of intermarriages across ethnic lines, and hence the growing diversity of peoples ancestors, many are coming to identify themselves as simple Canadian, without reference to their ancestral origins. In focusing on the ethnic dimension of Canadian society, past and present, the series does not assume that everyone should be categorized into one particular group, or that ethnicity is always the most important dimension of people's lives. It is, however, one dimension that needs examination if we are to understand fully the contours and nature of Canadian society and identity.

Professional Canadian historians have in the past emphasized political and economic history, and since the country's economic and political institutions have been controlled largely by people of British and French origin, the role of those of other origins in the development of Canada has been neglected. Also, Canadian historians in the past have been almost exclusively of British and French origin, and have lacked the interest and the linguistic skills necessary to explore the history of other ethnic groups. Indeed, there has rarely ever been an examination of the part played by specifically British – or, better, specifically English, Irish, Scottish and Welsh – traditions and values in Canadian development, because of the lack of recognition of pluralism in the society. The part played by French traditions and values, and particular varieties of French traditions and values, has for a number of reasons been more carefully scrutinized.

This series is an indication of growing interest in Canadian social history, which includes immigration and ethnic history. This may particularly be a reflection of an increasing number of scholars whose origins and ethnic identities are other than British or French. Because such trends are recent, many of the authors of the histories in this series have not had a large body of published writing to work from. It is true that some histories have already been written of particular groups other than the British and French; but these have often been characterized by filio-pietism, a narrow perspective and a dearth of scholarly analysis.

Despite the scarcity of secondary sources, the authors have been asked to be as comprehensive as possible, and to give balanced coverage to a number of themes: historical background, settlement patterns, ethnic identity and assimilation, ethnic associations, population trends, religion, values, occupations and social class, the family, the ethnic press, language patterns, political behaviour, education, inter-ethnic relations, the arts and recreation. They have also been asked to give a sense of the way the group differs in various parts of the country. Finally, they have been asked to give, as much as possible, an insider's view of what the immigrant and ethnic experiences were like at different periods of time, but yet at the same time to be as objective as possible, and not simply to present the group as it sees itself, or as it would like to be seen.

The authors have thus been faced with a herculean task. To the extent that they have succeeded, they provide us with new glimpses into many aspects of Canadian society of the past and the present. To the extent that they have fallen short of their goal, they challenge other historians, sociologists and social anthropologists to continue the work begun here.

Jean Burnet
Howard Palmer

[1]*Report of the Royal Commission on Bilingualism and Biculturalism.* General Introduction, paragraph 7.

[2]Ibid. Paragraph 8.

Introduction

In a recent survey of Canadian history, the Vancouver humorist Eric Nichol told his readers that the century since Confederation just WOULD NOT DO. Perhaps he meant that new characters had to be found for the story if it was to be attractive. Historians of the various cultural groups in Canada would certainly agree. Canadian history is just beginning to escape an excessive emphasis on the biographies of the famous: the *res gestae* of politicians, editors, and diplomatists. It has been written almost exclusively in the context of British and French decision-makers, with a strong tendency to overemphasize the development of Eastern Canada. But the increasing complexity of Canadian society obviously requires more than political and biographical history if its development is to be adequately explained. The existing history of immigrant groups has too often been written in terms of governmental attitudes to their arrival, or the attitudes of the established community towards newcomers, rather than from the viewpoint of the immigrants themselves. Together with studies of migration and intercultural relations, there is a need for histories of the internal development of those communities.

This book deals with the historical experience of one group of Canadians who are neither British nor French: those of Portuguese descent. Portuguese have been connected with Canada since the earliest days of the discoveries, but only in recent years has a large, urban concentration of Portuguese Canadians taken place. The history of their settlement in Canada is a subject of interest to people of both Portuguese and non-Portuguese descent. With the more accommodating climate of opinion to newcomers that has developed recently, new Canadians have encountered less pressure to change their ways than did those who came in the decades before World War II. Many Canadians now take an increased interest in the national mosaic. As a result of intermarriage, tourism, and an increasing interest in alternative ways of living, a widespread trend has developed to accept and experience the lifestyles of Canadians of differing cultural origins.

Our aim in writing this history has been to clarify the experience of the Portuguese in the Canadian environment and to show how they have come to settle in various parts of the country. Our subjects are those persons who consider themselves part of the Portuguese-Canadian community. Thus, we exclude some Canadians with Portuguese family names, whose connections with the Portuguese world ceased long ago. The criterion by which we define the Portuguese immigrant group is explained in the general introduction to a recent history of ethnic groups in British Columbia:

> The most important criterion of definition is neither ethnic origin nor mother tongue, but a conscious identification with a group at the time of arrival. It is this sense of belonging to a group whose roots are not in Canada that essentially differentiates the ethnic Englishman, American, Ukrainian, Pole, Italian or Japanese from the established Canadian.

This *conscious* identification is crucial. In Canada, it is officially stated that such identifications are welcomed, for they contribute to Canada's cultural diversity. But some ethnic group members, including some Portuguese, feel that emphasis on their origin merely makes them conspicuous and is not useful in helping them enter the more desirable positions in society. Conscious identification may often be familial and related to a region or town of origin rather than to a nation. Consequently, the manifestations of *Portuguesismo* – the Portuguese outlook – are as various as the origins of the people.

The student of any diversified and growing cultural group has special problems. The most obvious for the historian is the scarcity of written records, for few people write chronicles of their lives or keep archives. The drawback of oral history is that it is based on memories that are often dim or inexact, or on personalized versions of larger events. Moreover, perspectives tend to change over time: an immigrant family may explain its problems very differently in the first years in a new country than it would with the hindsight of twenty or more years. Reporting in community newspapers, as in the press generally, is often influenced by political or personal bias. We have tried to sift and evaluate our evidence carefully, but errors of fact and interpretation cannot always be avoided. We can only say that we have honestly tried to avoid the pitfalls in the nature of our evidence, and to seek out additional information where gaps exist. We hope that ethnic associations and individual immigrants will come to realize the value of their records, correspondence, and photographs and will deposit them with the National Ethnic Archives in Ottawa, in order to establish a permanent record of the growth of their community.

To gather information on the Portuguese in Canada, we combined systematic historical research and sociological interview techniques. First, we examined any written material that was available. A quantity of unpublished material was offered to us for use in the study, though in some cases this was to be considered confidential background information. We also studied theses on the subject written by Canadian students and collected other historical and sociological material from Portuguese sources.

For many Portuguese-Canadian communities, basic data were totally lacking. The data collection for this study therefore lasted nearly three years. It involved studies of communities from Victoria, British Columbia, to St. John's, Newfoundland; from isolated northern locations, such as Kitimat, to southern border cities such as Winnipeg. In most cases, research data and information were gathered by the authors and supplemented by directed research undertaken by advanced graduate students and by correspondence.

In the spring of 1976 we estimated that there were 220,000 Portuguese living in Canada who had arrived since 1953. An attempt was made to study every Portuguese area of settlement containing more than 2,000 immigrants. In addition, some smaller communities were selected for special study because of their unique characteristics.

The role of a few well established English-speaking Portuguese immigrants in directing the pioneers to prospective areas of settlement should not be underestimated. In southern Ontario, Manuel Cabral of Galt was very influential. He was a Portuguese American from New England and first arrived in Ontario in 1919. British Columbian communities are indebted to Captain Antonio Quintal from Madeira, who came to Vancouver in 1940. Other, more recent, arrivals were also influential. These include Manuel Lima, who was among the small group of immigrants who arrived and settled in Calgary in 1957.

These and many other individuals and community leaders directed the spearhead movements in establishing communities to which the streams of immigration would later flow. These movements gained momentum through chain migration. In each of the communities that we visited personally, we attempted to locate and to interview six of the earliest Portuguese settlers. In some cases, the earliest settlers had died, moved on to another community in Canada or in the United States, or returned to Portugal. But many were still living in the communities in which they had originally settled, or were encountered in areas where they had relocated.

The interview was guided by a series of open-ended questions. Since this study is largely exploratory and since most of the interviewing was conducted by highly experienced persons, the open-ended and flexible approach gave the best opportunity for following up unforeseen leads.

One basic objective of the research was to identify reasons for the location of Portuguese immigrants in specific localities. While our focus was necessarily directed to Portuguese-Canadian communities we anticipate that the approach we have developed may find wider application in studies of other immigrant groups.

In an attempt to find consistent patterns of Portuguese immigrant movement across the country, we studied mobility of the pioneers in geographic and occupational terms. We placed less emphasis on examining communities that have been analyzed elsewhere than on those where no material is available through other sources.

In addition to interviewing the pioneering settlers in a community, we made contact with community leaders and especially executive officers of various Portuguese associations (social, sports, and folkoric). We talked to outstanding entrepreneurs in each community about their careers and their knowledge of the immigrant settlements. Founders of newspapers and directors and producers of radio and television programs were interviewed. Social workers, educators and priests ministering to Portuguese communities provided valuable information.

Our rescarch in Canada was complemented by experience of conditions in the Azores Islands, Madeira and mainland Portugal, which added to our knowledge of differences and similarities existing in the cultural backgrounds of immigrants from various regions. We firmly believe that the historical and social background of ethnic groups before their arrival in Canada must be studied if the subsequent range of interactions with the new country is to be properly understood.

In short, information was gathered from as many sources as possible, given the constraints of time and financial resources. In some Canadian localities, regrettably, we were unable to locate any supplementary material; we hope that future research will concentrate more particularly on those regions. The bibliography at the end of the study provides an overview of work done to date on Portuguese immigration to Canada and we hope researchers in many disciplines will further explore areas that have been studied here from a broad perspective.

NOTES

1.   John Norris, ed., *Strangers Entertained* (Vancouver, 1971), p. 2.

PART ONE:

Origins of the Portuguese-Canadian Communities

ONE

The Early Portuguese Maritime Contacts with Canada

EARLY EXPLORATION

During the fifteenth century, Portuguese explorers undertook a series of voyages of discovery that took them to the shores of Africa, Asia, and, in time, South America. The main stimulus for these first explorations was the desire to find a route to the wealth of India and China, which had been known in Europe for centuries.[1] Marco Polo and others had told of the spices, gold, silver, porcelain and precious objects to be found in Asia, but access for the Portuguese to these treasures was hindered by other powers. In the Mediterranean, they were blocked by European rivals. In the Levant, they encountered the more severe opposition of the Turks and Arabs. Consequently, they began to seek an alternate route, a "back door" to these riches.

The main thrust of their exploration was along the African coast, but some speculated that a way could be found by sailing westward. It was rumoured that the Scandinavians had found new lands in the Atlantic and, with the growing realization that the world was a globe, there was increasing hope that a route to Asia could be found across the Atlantic. It was, however, an intimidating alternative, for it meant sailing into uncharted waters far from land. While there were vague reports of islands and mainland shores in the North Atlantic, the northern ice and fogs were very dangerous for the wooden vessels used by the explorers.

The discovery of Madeira and the islands of the Azores stimulated interest in Atlantic exploration. Madeira Island was discovered in 1419 off the African coast, and by 1425 settlers were arriving, drawn at first from the coastal region of the Algarve in Southern Portugal and then increasingly from the crowded lands in the north. A decade and a half later, seven of the nine islands of the Azores were being colonized by families from Northern Portugal and Flanders. Settlement was extensive by 1500. Both island colonies soon became launching bases for further exploration.

From Madeira, the African coastal route to the Indies could be explored. It also marked a convenient point of departure for the South Atlantic crossing to Brazil, discovered by the Portuguese explorer Cabral in 1500. In the coming centuries, Madeira was to provide many emigrants to Brazil and, in the twentieth century, to Canada. The Azores looked out on a less hospitable ocean prospect, being father north, but they were nonetheless a base for exploration and for emigration, first back to the Alentejo region of Portugal in the eighteenth century, and later to North America.

There has been considerable debate on the question of the earliest Portuguese crossing to North America. One Portuguese author has argued that the honour of the first landfall in North America after the Norsemen should go to the Portuguese.[2] It has been claimed that in 1452, acting on orders of Prince Henry of Portugal, Diogo de Teive set out from Lisbon with a Spanish pilot to explore far into the Atlantic. The results of this expedition, which reached the North American coast, were known to Christopher Columbus and a member of the Pinzon family; indeed, it was claimed that the latter urged Columbus to persist when he was on the verge of turning back. Other Portuguese historians have supported the thesis that Columbus had prior knowledge of winds and currents thanks to the Teive expedition, which had staged from Fayal in the Azores.[3] Bartolomé de las Casas, a sixteenth century historian,[4] stated that the Portuguese had made voyages to the American shoreline forty years before Columbus.

Portuguese association with Danish and English exploration is well known. Close relationships existed between Portugal and Denmark in the fifteenth century as a result of royal marriages. In 1426, Dom Pedro visited Denmark, and at this time he undoubtedly heard reports of expeditions to Greenland. Various Danes were received at the Portuguese court, and about 1470 two Portuguese nobles were in Denmark.

Sofus Larsen has assembled evidence to show that João Vaz Corte-Real and an unidentified compatriate accompanied an expedition led by an Icelander or Greenlander named Jon Skulason (there are various forms of the name) and that they wintered in Greenland in 1470-71.[5] They may have taken a further step and visited Labrador, returned to Greenland for a second winter, made another expedition or possibly visited Norway, and then returned to Portugal early in 1473 or 1474. This expedition, made at the request of the Portuguese king, was referred to at various times in the sixteenth century. On the 1537 globe of Frisius and Mercator, there are Portuguese inscriptions on the drawing of Baffin Island and, to the west and north of Hudson Strait, a reference to Skulason. On Hudson Bay is written: "The northerly strait or the Three Bretheren Strait, which the Portuguese tried to sail through to the Eastern lands and India and the Malucca Islands." On the basis of this evidence, one historian has concluded: "All in all, there can be little doubt that the two Portuguese visited Greenland, Labrador and Hudson Bay."[6]

Probes into the Atlantic continued. In January, 1474, Fernão Teles de Menses was given the right to exploit such islands as he might discover at a distance from the African coast. In March 1486, this concession was given to Fernão Dulmo, an official of Terceira, who soon entered into partnership with Afonso do Estreito of Madeira.[7] Nothing is known of the result of their efforts, but these arrangements were typical of the Portuguese system of encouraging private voyages of exploration in the hope of making new discoveries. In the desire to identify heroes among the explorers, and to satisfy nationalistic claims for primacy of discovery, some historians have failed to attribute sufficient importance to the slow accretions of knowledge which resulted from partial or unsuccessful ventures. Certainly the seamen of the late fifteenth century worked for a variety of patrons and were indifferent to "national" claims, as they would later be understood. There were also, presumably, generalized rumours to justify the repeated granting of patents of discovery.

In support of the argument for early Portuguese exploration of the North American shoreline, one can point to the large numbers of Portuguese names that survive, in Anglicized or Gallicized forms, on the Atlantic coast.[8] They bear excellent witness to the extensive investigations made by Portuguese fishermen in those waters. The major navigational points named by the Portuguese were of interest to sailors of other nationalities, and the designations became corrupted so that they would be pronounceable in other languages. They exist, then, in fairly obvious forms: *conceição* (conception) as Conception Bay, *caramellos* (ice-blocks) as Crémaillière, Frey Luis (the name of a Portuguese priest) as Freels, *bacalhau* (cod) as Bacalieu, and *farelhão* (cliff) as Farilham. The delineation line (*marco*) of the Tordesillas Treaty is reflected in the Mark Islands, Labrador, and in Cape Mark, above Miquelon Island off southern Newfoundland. Battle Island derives from the Portuguese for a small boat (*batel*); Cape Race is named after a point in Portugal's Tagus estuary. The name given to meeting places for vessels before the return voyage to Portugal (*esperas*) is recognizable in various -spare, -spear, or -spair place names. Other examples have been documented:

> The Portuguese kept within their demarcation, but, like other Europeans, could not resist the lure of gold, and so made efforts to exploit mines in Nova Scotia, where as a consequence there are a few Portuguese place-names: the Bay of Fundy (Rio Fundo: deep bay) [river], the basin of Minas, Blomidon (*promontório*), Mira, named after a river in Portugal, and perhaps Cape Tormentine (*tormentinha*, a squall).[9]

The most striking evidence is found in the name of Labrador. Very probably it originally referred to João Fernandes, a *lavrador* (farmer) of Terceira Island in the Azores.[10] His name appears in the Bristol (England) customs records as early as 1493 as involved in trade with Lisbon. There is evidence that João Fernandes and Pedro de Barcelos, a rich landowner from Terceira, made a voyage of exploration to parts of Greenland. Subsequently, the name *lavrador* was given to those areas of the island that they had reconnoitred. They may have also sighted the present Labrador. By accident, the name of Labrador shifted on the maps drawn of the northwest Atlantic: owing to variations in the primitive compasses of that time, seamen believed the "real" Labrador was that so labelled in earlier maps which in fact was Greenland, but by the seventeenth century cartographers had transferred this name to the Canadian coast. (Greenland was called then by its original, Norse name.)[11]

The Genoese explorer, John Cabot, who sailed in the service of Henry VII, was probably acting on information provided by Fernandes as a result of the Bristol connection. It has been suggested[12] that Fernandes and Barcelos, aware of the restrictions placed on their king by the Treaty of Tordesillas, approached Henry VII, who felt much less bound by that arrangement.[13] Santa Crùz, the chief cosmographer of the Spanish court and a man who had personal contact with the Cabots for more than twenty years wrote in his *Islario* of 1541:

> It was called the Labrador's land because a husbandman from the Azores islands gave tidings and information about it to the King of England when he sent Antonio (*sic*) Gaboto, the English pilot and father of Sebastian Gaboto, who was Your Majesty's Pilot-major, to explore it.[14]

Other experts on matters of exploration have accepted the thesis that Cabot had prior information from Fernandes before he set off on his voyage of discovery.[15]

While there is much conjecture about the Fernandes-Barcelos expedition, one possible viewpoint has been forcefully put by the historian and former Portuguese ambassador to Canada, Eduardo Brazão:

> Until some absolute contrary proof is brought forward, we shall continue to consider João Fernandes and Pedro de Barcelos as the real discoverers of North America in that vast region that overlooks the Atlantic, and which nowadays belongs to Canada.[16]

The main sources of the dispute over who first explored Canadian waters from 1490-1500 are the rather scant official documents and correspondence to be found in European archives and also the maps of the time. The maps of the sixteenth century obviously leave much to be desired by modern standards. An anonymous Portuguese map of 1471 seems to represent an approximation of the Newfoundland coast. The Reinel map, the map in the Museo Oliveriana in Pesaro, Italy, and others have been adduced as evidence, but it is hard to prove any case from them. Early cartographers used every scrap of evidence as they tried to discern the possible shape of distant land masses which in many instances they had never seen. They approximated distances without the benefit of Mercator's projection, and they were often reminded by their patrons of the political implications of their inscriptions.

Thus, the evidence is open to a variety of interpretations. The American historian Samuel E. Morison has particularly distinguished himself in denying the Portuguese claim to a place in the forefront of the discoveries in the northwest Atlantic. Criticizing the fragmentary nature of the documentary evidence, he has relied heavily on personal sailing experience in framing his argument. He himself crossed the Atlantic by sail and he concluded it was highly unlikely that captains would reach Newfoundland from the Azores, since they would almost certainly have sailed with prevailing winds. He also believed that the maritime technology of the time was ill-equipped for the crossing.[17] In fact, the technology was more competent than Morison suggests.[18] Prevailing winds do not always prevail, as is evidenced by the many thousands of voyages later made to the Grand Banks. At least two recent students of the maritime discoveries in Canadian waters, Lima and Brazão, are far from willing to accept Morison's conclusions.[19]

Perhaps João Fernandes did land in modern Labrador. There is more evidence in support of the part played by Portuguese explorers in Newfoundland. Their discoveries are linked to the name Corte-Real. The Corte-Real family were governors of the Azorean island of Terceira in the late fifteenth century, and they were probably informed of the explorations carried out from the port of Bristol in southwestern England. From the twelfth century on, there was much trade between Portugal and Bristol: ships left from the Bristol Channel for Portugal, where they took on salt, and then sailed to Icelandic waters to fish, returned to Portugal to sell this fish and to buy wine, oil, and salt, and finally returned with this cargo to Bristol. From 1490 or 1491 until 1498, two to four ships were said to sail annually to explore the Atlantic.[20] It is therefore extremely likely that some information about the voyages was exchanged. Between 1498 and 1502, prominent landowners and officials on Terceira organized expeditions to extend Portuguese claims in the North Atlantic. In 1498, Gaspar Corte-Real sighted Greenland but did not land on that forbidding coast. Some authorities claim that on this occasion he entered Davis Strait. At all events, he was sufficiently interested in the results of this voyage that in 1501 he returned with three ships of the type perfected by the Portuguese and known as caravels. The expedition crossed the entrance to Davis Strait and found a coast with many rivers. They sailed up one of these for some distance. On landing, they found pine trees, berry-bearing bushes, and some native people, whom they captured. There is no certainty of where this site might have been: one authority has suggested that it was Hamilton Inlet, and another that it was the eastern coast of Newfoundland.

This expedition was struck by misfortune: Gaspar Corte-Real and his companions disappeared, and only two of the three ships returned to

Portugal. In the spring of 1502, Gaspar's brother, Miguel, organized a search expedition to sail from Lisbon. The three vessels of this new flotilla fanned out to widen the search along the coasts of Newfoundland, after agreeing on a rendezvous on August 20, 1502, in a bay which is generally thought to be St. John's harbour, Newfoundland. On the appointed day, only two ships appeared; like Gaspar, Miguel and his men were never seen again. In 1503, a third brother of the Corte-Real family wished to renew the search, but King Manuel refused to give him permission to go. Two ships did, however, set sail and explored the waters around Newfoundland. Nothing was ever found of the two missing vessels, and it is probably safe to discount the theory put forward by Delabarre that the Dighton Rock inscription in New England shows that Miguel became an Indian chief and that he was alive in 1511.[21]

There is debate also on the question of who set down the first coastal settlement along Canada's Atlantic coast. Traces of early, perhaps Iberian, settlement have been found at Ingonish on northern Cape Breton Island. According to a decree of King Manuel I of Portugal, dated March 13, 1521, João Alvares Fagundes or his agents landed in 1520 somewhere on the Atlantic coast between the Spanish claims in Florida and those of Corte-Real in Newfoundland. From the descriptions and the similarity of one of the reported places to an Indian name, it seems that the territory in question lay between Penobscot, Maine, and Sable Island off Nova Scotia.[22] L.A. Vigneras accepts that Fagundes discovered the southern coast of Newfoundland between Cape Race and Cape Ray, but feels there is no sure evidence that he explored Cape Breton or penetrated into the St. Lawrence.[23]

In 1570, Francisco de Sousa wrote a book about Madeira called the *Treatises of the New Islands*.[24] De Sousa's account gave more accurate details of southern Newfoundland and northeastern Nova Scotia than did maps or other documents of the time. Even more importantly, de Sousa reported an attempt to found a civilian colony. He described "Portuguese who came from Viana do Castelo (in northern Portugal) and the Azores to people the New Codfishland, some sixty years ago." He went on: "Forty-five or fifty years ago a party led by a nobleman from Viana set out in a big ship and a caravel to populate this very cold land." He described a bay where the natives were friendly. Having lost their ships, the Portuguese stayed there. They reported that "many valuable things, walnuts, chestnuts, grapes and other fruits and good earth" were to be had. There were several married couples from the Azores in the company. The geographer Sauer, who has written several books on the period of the early discoveries, thinks that the bay and the vegetation in the de Sousa account suggest the Annapolis lowland of the Bay of Fundy, a name itself derived from the Portuguese *Baía Funda* (Deep Bay).[25] Another possibility, which a Canadian archeologist is investigating, is that the landing was at St. Ann's Bay, Cape Breton. In any event, the colony did not survive long.

Only de Sousa's account attests to its existence, and he is imprecise about the date, which he puts at about 1510-1525.

King Sebastian of Portugal sent a letter to the *corregedor* (magistrate) of the Azores, Gaspar Gerraz, on May 4, 1567, in which he asked for the nomination of a man suitable to hold the post of civil governor of the Newfoundland captaincy. This shows at least a sporadic interest in establishing a claim to sovereignty. A document dated January, 1568 (once again, put forward long after the events related), spoke of a land called Barcelona, named after Diogo and Manuel de Barcelos, where cattle were said to have been released (presumably the *gado do ramo grande*, which is the typical breed of the Azores). A number of scholars have related this exploratory activity of 1567-68 to Sable Island or Prince Edward Island. Lima suggests that Barcelona was more likely Sable Island, and that it was the same as the "Sam Johâ" marked on the 1502 Reinel map.[26] Sable Island seems to have appeared in a variety of forms on early maps; and it was sometimes reported twice, in different places. French explorers also showed an interest in Sable Island. In 1598, the Breton Marquis de la Roche put down settlers there who found cattle. According to his historian, the lawyer Marc Lescarbot, these cattle had been released on the island by a nobleman of the time of Francis I.[27] Samuel de Champlain also found cattle on the island during his voyage of 1613, but instead of invoking ancient knights, he stated that they had been left there by the Portuguese.

DEVELOPMENT OF THE FISHERIES

By the first decades of the sixteenth century, the Portuguese interest in an alternative Atlantic route to Asia was on the decline. Increasing numbers of Portuguese vessels were bringing home spices in the annual India Fleet that sailed around the African coast. Atlantic exploration was costly in men and sparse in achievement. Like the English and French, the Portuguese had oriented some of their efforts to the northwestern Atlantic, but they found only icy waters and a desolate coast.[28] The opinion of the North Atlantic held in Lisbon was relayed to the Emperor Charles V of the Holy Roman Empire in a letter from the king of Portugal and the infante Dom Luis in 1541. "The codfishland where the French are going is so cold, the bad weather so persistent, that we have lost fleets there."[29] Indeed, King João III refused to authorize new expeditions to Labrador because of the many Portuguese vessels already lost.[30]

There was, however, one major attraction to Canadian waters: codfish. For centuries, cod was a staple of the Portuguese diet. Salted and dried, it was highly portable and served as an important source of protein; it was long known as "the faithful friend" (o fiel amigo) for its nutritious value. Portugal had always shown a keen interest in new sources of this commodity. Thus, when explorers returned with stories of fabulously rich fishing grounds in the coastal waters of Newfoundland, their reports were received with great enthusiasm.

In 1501, João Fernandes was involved in a venture that set sail from Bristol to investigate the fisheries. The take of fish was sufficiently substantial that by October, 1506, the Portuguese king was giving a grant of permission on cod-tithes. An Englishman, John Rut, wrote from St. John's on August 3, 1527, that his companions had "found eleven saile of Normans, and one Britaine, and two Portugall Barkes all a-fishing . . . . "[31]

In his classic history of the codfisheries, H. A. Innis concluded that the Portuguese were probably fewer than the French at that time, although they were very significant.[32] Around 1550, in Aveiro alone, there were as many as 150 ships equipped for the Newfoundland codfisheries.[33] The Portuguese had salt which was readily available to them in the homeland. They brought this with them and supplied the English with some of their needs; they also traded wines, marmalade, biscuits, and food. Initially, the Portuguese, French, Basques, and English fished in coastal waters and landed for water, bait, and food; they also hunted the now extinct great auk. The Portuguese concentrated on the Avalon peninsula. An account of their activities was recorded by an English merchant, Anthony Parkhurst, who became interested in Newfoundland after a visit to the fisheries in 1565 and made various subsequent voyages. From 1575 to 1578 he fished there, buying salt from the Portuguese and getting information from them. In 1578, he reported fifty Portuguese boats in the area with an average weight of sixty tons per vessel. They preserved their fish "green" or simply salted, and fished from April to July. Parkhurst also encountered Portuguese when he explored the coast of Cape Breton.

In the first half of the sixteenth century, men of different European nations fished the waters of Newfoundland fairly amicably. But with the growing tension between Elizabethan England and Spain, violence and piracy developed. The English in particular took advantage of their distance from authority and their superior strength (their vessels were larger than those of other nations) to prey on other fishing expeditions for supplies. With the annexation of Portugal by the Spanish crown in 1580, and the subsequent hostilities between the English and the Spanish, the Portuguese found themselves increasingly harried, particularly in St. John's harbour, which – like the Basques and the French – they used as a fishing base. In 1582, they suffered from the piracy of Richard Clarke; and some Portuguese, most probably from the Azores, were among the fishermen who accepted Sir Humphrey Gilbert's proclamation on August 5, 1583, that Newfoundland was the property of Queen Elizabeth I.[34]

Columbus said that Portuguese sailors discovered shoals and islands by watching the flight of birds, and it was by this method, noting the diving birds, that they identified the Grand Banks.[35] Cod on the Banks were generally larger than those found in the coastal waters off Newfoundland. But the advantages of the larger catch were offset by the fact that ice conditions restricted fishing activity mainly to the summer months. In addition, fogs on the Banks increased the risk of collision with icebergs; they were responsible for the loss of many individual dories (*barcas*).

Anthony Parkhurst's famous letter to Richard Hakluyt, written in 1578, gives interesting information on the ships used in the fisheries:

> But of Portugals there are not lightly above 50 saile, and they make all wet in like sorte, whose tonnage may amount to three thousand tuns, and not upwarde. Of the French nation and Bretons are about one hundred and fiftie sailes, the most of their shipping is very small, not past fortie tunnes, among which some are great and reasonably well appointed, better than the Portugals but not so well as the Spaniards, and the burden of them may be some 7,000 tunne. Their shipping is from all parts of France and Brittaine, and the Spaniards from most parts of Spaine, the Portugals from Aviaro and Viano, from 2 or 3 parts more. The trade that our nation hath to Island maketh, that the English are not there in such numbers as other nations.[36]

With gathering hostilities between England and Spain, fewer Portuguese ships came to fish in Newfoundland waters; and when the mid-Atlantic Azorean resistance to the Spanish occupation ended, their absence became even more marked. Some still came, up to the end of the sixteenth century: in 1598, fifty set sail from Viana do Castelo and Oporto. There were, however, fewer landings in coves along the coast between Bona Vista and Cape Race, where the Portuguese had been in the habit of going ashore.[37] According to D. W. Prowse in his *History of Newfoundland*, from 1614 to 1620 there were violent clashes between English and Portuguese fishermen, in which the English had the upper hand.[38] Outnumbered and suffering heavy losses from plunderers, the Portuguese abandoned both the coastal fisheries and the Grand Banks. By the time that Portuguese independence from Spain was regained in 1640, the English had established a firm grasp on the codfisheries. Ships from Portugal, Spain, France, and Ireland were fishing there in November and December of 1676, according to one of the Newfoundland planters.[39] But most of the cod then consumed in Portugal and Brazil was caught, cured, and transported in ships from ports based on the southwestern coast of England. The Portuguese bought salted cod from the English as part of a complex of Atlantic trade which involved slaves, salt, oil, wine, and other products.[40]

As a result of this evolution the Portuguese had little first-hand knowledge of British North America throughout the eighteenth century. There were a few Portuguese in the United States at the time of the War of Independence because of their use of the Atlantic shipping routes, particularly some shipwrecked sailors whose descendants lived in Robinson County, North Carolina. Certainly there was some interest in North America in Portugal, as witnessed by the publication in Lisbon in the 1790s of a book which seems to be a modified translation of an English original. It described conditions in Canada as very difficult. Nova Scotia was said to be so cold that people remained shut up in their houses,[41] and spent much money on brandy and wool in order to keep warm. Fishing was necessary to provide food, as there was little agricultural activity. The author concluded that "to establish colonies in such conditions is to work against all rational ideas of colonisation."[42] Of the French Canadians, he observed they were jovial and hospitable, and in Quebec and Montreal especially happy and sociable, which made them better able to survive the bitter winters. In general, the book presented a forbidding picture of what is now Eastern Canada.

By 1800, Portugal was importing large quantities of dried salt cod. From 1796 to 1820, for example, the sums spent annually on this fish fluctuated between 1,293,000 cruzados and 4,942,750 cruzados, a very substantial sum for the time. Much of this fish originated in Canadian coastal waters. In Portugal, there had been a decline in the fishing industry on the coast and rivers because of the heavy burden of seigneurial and civil taxes. There was therefore a strong interest in redeveloping Portuguese participation in this important trade. In 1813, the geographer Sebastião Francisco de Mendo Trigozo read a learned paper before the Portuguese Academy concerning the discoveries and commerce of the Portuguese in North America.[43] He described the sixteenth century voyages of discovery and drew the attention of his audience to the possibilities for a return to similar endeavours at a time when the Portuguese economy faced serious difficulties.

In October, 1835, a new company was established at Lisbon with the name *Companhia de Pescarias Lisbonense* (Lisbon Fisheries Company).[44] In that year, six or seven schooners with English and Portuguese crews were sent to Canadian waters from the home base of Ericeira, on the coast northwest of Lisbon, which was well-suited for outfitting vessels for a long voyage. For over twenty years, Portuguese sailors set off from the small, whitewashed cottages of that picturesque village to fish for cod. The company was disbanded by a decree of April 27, 1857, but by then it had successfully re-established the connection between Portuguese fishermen and Canadian waters.

During the nineteenth century, there was rapid growth in the American Atlantic whaling industry, and ships began to put into the Azores to pick up extra crew. Many of the local men were glad to find a lucrative way to escape military conscription and the American captains prized the Portuguese seamen, not only because they had courage and energy, but because among them there were none of the seaboard fights that often caused injuries among American sailors.[45] These whalers learned some English, became familiar with Canadian waters, and heard about the settlements in New England. In this manner, men from Ponta Delgada and Horta, the two best ports in the Azores, as well as Porto Judeu and Praia de Vitoria fishing harbours, became the source of information about the continent to the west. In the second half of the nineteenth century, the fishermen, who have been described as "one of the most endearing working classes and

12

perhaps the most characteristically Portuguese,[46]" were the first to publicize the opportunities in America and Canada that were open to their fellow countrymen.

In the twentieth century, when codfishing off the North American coast again became important to the Portuguese, occasionally fishermen would come ashore to stay. They numbered perhaps 6,000 in 1935. In 1940, Jorge Simoẽs, a Portuguese journalist, travelled from Lisbon to Newfoundland with the White Fleet (so-called for its sails) and wrote an account of his experiences. He found St. John's unattractive in comparison with his own home city, describing it as "very sad and black" and cold. He said that he saw snow falling on the afternoon of June 12 (the Vespers of Saint Anthony of Lisbon). He thought the restaurants and beer parlours generally inferior to those of Lisbon and noted the lack of European-style cafés. He was, however, impressed by the numerous fruit shops and the varieties of imported fruit available. The local people seemed to him to be hard-working and trustworthy. To his surprise, the chief of the customs house was a teetotaller. The port translator for the Portuguese was Jack Pinto, son of a stonemason from Viana do Castelo and a mother from Galicia in Spain (where the local dialect is similar to Portuguese). For twenty-five years, Jack Pinto had been an interpreter, although the well-educated Simoẽs pointed out that as a result of translation from both Spanish and Portuguese, his language had become rather confused.

Simoẽs met three Portuguese residents in St. John's. One was a cook on a fishing sloop, who lived at the mouth of the Bay of Fortune, opposite Saint Pierre. He had two sons and two daughters, and he did not plan to return to Portugal. This man visited the Portuguese ship and spoke timidly, "searching with a visible effort to remember the proper words." After many years in Newfoundland, he was beginning to forget his native language. A second man, who worked at the American naval base, also was married, with children. He tried to teach some Portuguese "at least to the boys," but found this difficult. Both men were illiterate and had been brought up on ships. The third Portuguese was a carpenter who lived outside St. John's, and who had jumped ship in the 1920s. Simoẽs, writing for a Portuguese audience, described the three men as "truly denationalized. It is with difficulty that they speak the language of the motherland."[48]

Cod fishing by the Portuguese fleet continued without interruption during the two world wars, although the fleet was subject to stricter naval surveillance than in times of peace. In 1941, 3,000 Portuguese were fishing annually in Canadian waters with a large fleet which included its own fully-equipped hospital ship, the *Gil Eanes*, and a chaplain. With peace came a renewed demand for salted cod in Portugal and Brazil. Although the fabulous wealth of fish on the Grand Banks was gradually being exhausted through heavy fishing by increasingly mechanized fleets, the Portuguese remained true to the old methods. Although some persisted in laboriously laying hand-lines from dories launched from schooners, as the years passed the number of vessels carrying sail dropped. In 1973 the White Fleet included five schooners that carried dories, and thirteen that used gill-nets. There were also thirty-six Portuguese trawlers on the Banks. In all, the crews of the fleet numbered about 4,000 men.[49]

Until the early 1950s the annual arrival from Portugal of schooners, fishing from April to October, and trawlers, which fish twice a year, was the most important single link between Canada and the Portuguese world. From the reports brought back by the cod fishermen there was some familiarity in Portuguese ports like Aveiro, Figueira da Foz and Viana do Castelo with conditions in Newfoundland. These reports were perhaps not overly rosy, made as they were by fishermen who struggled hard and long with the sea to earn their living. Certainly the odd fisherman remained ashore in Newfoundland and the other Maritime provinces, but this did not result in other members of the family arriving from Portugal. As a result, the oldest contact between Portugal and Canada, deriving from an Atlantic economy which took shape in the fifteenth and sixteenth centuries, never produced a large Portuguese community. This was only to result from governmental initiatives which are discussed in the following chapter.

NOTES

1. These explorations have been described in the dramatic poem *Os Lusiadas* by Luis de Camões. The poem, first published in 1572, has become the national epic of Portugal.

2. Jaime Cortesão, "A viagem de Diogo de Teive e Pero Vasquez de la Frontera ao Banco da Terra Nova em 1452," *Arquivo histórico da Marinha*, I, 1 (Lisbon, 1933). The argument is based on a voluminous legal dossier compiled by the Pinzon family to contest the claims of Christopher Columbus and his descendants.

3. M. C. Baptista de Lima, "Deux voyages portugais de découverte dans l'Atlantique occidental," *Bulletin des Etudes Portugaises* (1946). Avelino Teixeira da Mota, "Portuguese navigations in the North Atlantic in the fifteenth and sixteenth centuries; a paper delivered before the university on the occasion of the unveiling of the statue of Gaspar Corte-Real in Saint John's on the 28th September, 1965," St. John's, 1965.

4. De las Casas was the Spanish author of the *Historia de las Indias*, written between 1527 and 1562 and published in 1576.

5. Sofus Larsen, *Discovery of North America Twenty Years before Columbus* (Copenhagen, 1924).

6. Trggvi Oleson, *Early Voyages and Northern Approaches, 1000-1632* (Toronto, 1963), p. 119.

7. Manuel Monteiro Velho Arruda, *Colecção de documentos relativos as descobrimento e povoamento dos Açores* (Ponta Delgada, 1932).
8. Evidence on this subject has been documented by M. A. Buchanan, "Notes on Portuguese place-names in North-Eastern America," in *Estudios hispanicos: Homenaje a Archer M. Huntington* (Wellesley, Mass., 1952), pp. 99-104.
9. *Ibid.*, p. 101.
10. Ernesto do Canto, "Quem deu o nome ao Labrador?" *Archivo dos Açores*, XII, Ponta Delgada, 1894, pp. 353-71. " . . . um obscuro e humilde lavrador dos Açores."
11. Heinrich Winter, "The Pseudo-Labrador and the Oblique Meridian," *Imago Mundi*, II (1937), 61-73.
12. See T. Layng, "Charting the Course to Canada," *Congresso internacional de história dos descobrimentos* (Lisbon, 1961).
13. By the Treaty of Tordesillas of 1494, the Portuguese were excluded by the papacy from areas of America allocated to the Spanish for development.
14. Layng, "Charting the Course to Canada," p. 4.
15. See, for example, T. P. Jost, "Portuguese Activity along the Canadian Shore at the Beginning of Modern Times," *ibid.*, pp. 271-84. "Voyages of discovery: Hugh Say alias John Day; the men of Bristol and João Fernandes," *The Cartographer*, IV, 1 (June 1967), 1-12.
16. Eduardo Brazão, *The Corte-Real Family and the New World* (Lisbon, 1965), p. 47.
17. Samuel Eliott Morison, *Portuguese Voyages to America in the XV Century* (Harvard, 1940). He states a "firm conviction" that preliminary work by the Portuguese made possible the successful first voyage of Columbus (page 5); but in this, as in his later works, he has consistently questioned Portuguese claims to any primacy in North American discoveries.
18. A. Fontoura da Costa, *A marinharia dos descobrimentos* (3rd ed., Lisbon, 1960).
19. Eduardo Brazão, *La découverte de Terre-Neuve* (Montreal, 1964); Manuel Baptista de Lima, "Deux voyages Portugais de découverte dans l'Atlantique occidental," extrait de *Bulletin des Etudes Portugaises* (Lisbon, 1946).
20. C. B. Judah, *The North-American Fisheries and British Policy to 1713* (Urbana, 1933), p. 18; David B. Quinn, *Sebastian Cabot and Bristol exploration* (Bristol, Historical Association, 1968), p. 4.
21. On the Corte-Real family, see the article by L.-A. Vigneras, *Dictionary of Canadian Biography* (Toronto, 1966), I, pp. 234-6; Henry Harrisse, *Les Corte-Real et leurs voyages au nouveau-monde d'après des documents . . .* (Paris, 1883); Brazão, The Corte-Real Family (Lisbon, 1965).
22. C. O. Sauer, *Sixteenth Century North America* (Berkeley: University of California Press, 1971), p. 49.
23. Vigneras, *Dictionary of Canadian Biography*, I, p. 303.

24. This volume was published in 1877 at Ponta Delgada from a copy of the manuscript that had been kept in a convent library.
25. Sauer, *Sixteenth Century North America*, p. 50.
26. Manuel C. Baptista de Lima, "A ilha Terceira e a colonização do nordeste do continente Americano no seculo XVI," *Boletim Instituto Historico da Ilha Terceira*, XVIII (1960), 5-37.
27. Marc Lescarbot, *Histoire de la Nouvelle France, 1608* (Toronto: Champlain Society, 1907-1914), I, pp. 44-5.
28. Lionel Groulx, *La découverte du Canada* (Montreal, 1966), pp. 33-45.
29. Charles Germain de La Roncière, *Jacques Cartier et la découverte de la nouvelle France* . . . (Paris, 1931), p. 170.
30. Henry Harrisse, *Découverte et évolution cartographique de Terre-Neuve* (Paris-London, 1900), p. 148, note 1.
31. Judah, *The North-American Fisheries*, p. 14.
32. H. A. Innis, *The Codfisheries: The History of an International Economy* (Toronto, 1940).
33. Antonio de Oliveira Freire, *Descripçam corografica de reyno de Portugal* (Lisbon, 1739), p. 55.
34. A Portuguese fisherman told Gilbert of wild cattle and pigs released by his countrymen on Sable Island some thirty years earlier, and Gilbert subsequently set sail to investigate. David B. Quinn, "Sir Humphrey Gilbert" in *Dictionary of Canadian Biography*, I (Toronto, 1966), pp. 331-6; D. B. Quinn (ed.), *The Voyages and Colonising Enterprises of Sir Humphrey Gilbert*, 2 Vols (London, 1950). The setting down of livestock at uninhabited places which might in future be colonized, or where Portuguese vessels in need of food might pass, was an established practice. The Portuguese had done so on a number of islands in the South Atlantic.
35. Buchanan, "Notes on Portuguese place-names," p. 101.
36. Richard Hakluyt, *Principall Navigations, Voiages and Discoveries of the English Nation* . . . (London [1589], 1965), pp. 10-11.
37. C. de la Morandière, *Histoire de la pêche française de la morue dans l'Amérique septentrionale*, I (Paris, 1962), p. 220.
38. D. W. Prowse, *History of Newfoundland from the English, colonial and foreign records* . . . (London, 1895), pp. 102-3.
39. Judah, *The North-American Fisheries*, p. 141.
40. Bentley Duncan, *Atlantic Islands, Madeira, the Azores, and the Cape Verdes in Seventeenth-Century Commerce and Navigation* (Chicago, 1972).
41. A. C. Ribeiro de Andrada, *Cultura americana, que contem huma relação do terreno, clima, producção e agricultura* . . . (Lisbon, 1799).
42. *Ibid.*, p. 12.
43. Sebastião Francisco de Mendo Trigozo, "Ensaio sobre os descobrimentos e commercio dos Portugueses em as terras Setentionaes da America," (lido na sessão publica da Academia do anno 1813), in *Memorias de Litteratura Portugueza*, VIII (Lisbon, 1856), pp. 305-26.

44. *Consilheiro* Jacob Frederico Torlade Pereira d'Azambuja, *Memoria sô-bre a pesca do Bacalhaõ* (Lisbon, 1835). Azambuja credited Basque fishermen from the environs of Bayonne, France, with the discovery of the Grand Banks. He thought that they were attracted by the whale hunts a century before the landing of Christopher Columbus and that very probably Portuguese fishermen followed them (p. 3). He wrote his pamphlet in favour of Portuguese fishermen and small companies which deserved to be relieved of the burden of taxation (p. 34). On the subject of early nineteenth century Portuguese fishing off Newfoundland, see further Mathew H. Warren, *Lecture on Newfoundland and its fisheries with statistics; before the Mechanics' Institute at St. John's, March 14, 1853* (St. John's [1853]), pp. 24, xvi.

45. João de Serpa, *A industria piscatoria nas ilhas Fayal e Pico* (Coimbra, 1886).

46. Guilherme de Sousa Ottero Salgado, *Relátorio sôbre as pescarias nos mares dos Açores* (Ponta Delgada, 1935).

47. J. Simões, *Os grandes trabalhadores do mar* (Lisbon, 1942), pp. 168-70.

48. Simões, *Os grandes trabalhadores*, p. 17.

49. Gremio dos Armadores de Pesca de Bacalhau, Lisboa. *A pesca do bacalhau* (Lisbon, 1940), p. 15. A. J. Villiers, *The Western Ocean* (London, 1957); National Film Board of Canada, "The White Ship", 14 min. film, 1966; Shannon Ryan, "Newfoundland Cod Fisheries" (unpublished M.A. Thesis, Memorial University of Newfoundland, 1971). In 1973 the Portuguese Consulate in St. John's kindly provided information on the Portuguese cod fisheries.

TWO

Portuguese Migration to Canada

EARLY MIGRATION TRENDS

As we have seen, by the mid-twentieth century the Portuguese were a familiar presence in Eastern Canada, although a seasonal one. Despite the steady development of the saltfish fleet during the nineteenth century and its rapid growth after the First World War, there was no large settlement of Portuguese in Canada before the 1950s. There was, however, a trickle of Portuguese emigration to Canada over the centuries. Marie de l'Incarnation, writing to her son from Quebec City in 1668, told of the arrival of ships from Europe:

> The ships did not bring any maladies this year. The vessel just arrived was laden with a sort of mixed merchandise. There were Portuguese, Germans, Hollanders and others of I know not what nations. There were also Moorish, Portuguese and French women, and some from other countries. A great many girls have come and more are expected. The first woman to marry was the Moor, who wed a Frenchman. As for the men, they are men broken from the King's service that His Majesty wished sent to this country. They have all been put in Bourg-Talon [established by the intendant Jean Talon on land of the Jesuit seigneury of Notre-Dame-des-Anges west of the Saint Charles River] two leagues from here, to settle and people it.[1]

Portuguese names appear in French-Canadian legal records at the end of the seventeenth century. For example, Nicolas Dasilva (1698-1761), an illiterate stonemason in New France, complained about the confiscation of his land, though at the same time he protested his devotion to Louis XIV.[2] Montreal judicial archives of 1693 show that Pedro da Silva was paid twenty sols for the transport of a bundle of letters from Montreal to Quebec. This was the first known mail service between the two towns.[3] Mgr. Tanguay's French-Canadian genealogical dictionary gives some interesting information on the family of Pierre Da Silva (1647-1717). Pierre was from Lisbon and signed himself Pedro Dasylva; he was also known as Le Portugais and described in official documents as *bourgeois*. At age thirty-three he married a seventeen year old *canadienne* with the attractive cognomen of *Jolicoeur* ("Pretty Heart"). Between 1682 and 1706 they had at least two daughters (Marie-Madeleine, Marie-Anne) and seven sons: Pierre, Jean, François, Nicolas, Dominique, Jean-Marie and Jean-Baptiste-Marie. His sons also had large families: Pierre had two children, Jean seventeen, Nicolas thirteen, Dominique fifteen – he was married three times – whereas Jean-Marie had thirteen children from two wives, just as did Jean-Baptiste-Marie. All Pedro's children seem to have married partners of French descent with perhaps one exception, Barthèlemi Roza, husband of Marie-Anne, who may have been Portuguese. At all events, the Da Silva family made a substantial contribution to the demographic dynamism of New France, and the family name is to be found in French Canada in the nineteenth and twentieth centuries.[4]

Possibly the Portuguese names found in French Canadian records before the Conquest were "marranos," Christian converts from the Portuguese Jewish community of Bordeaux, which existed during the seventeenth and eighteenth centuries.[5] (Officially, Jews were excluded from the French colonies on April 23, 1615.) Bordeaux had strong links with the Atlantic trade, and one of the major Sephardic merchants of the city, Gradis, had interests in Canada. Another possibility is that the Portuguese were part of the organized emigration of artisans, or that they were serving in French regiments sent to the colonies and subsequently settled here. At all events, this Portuguese immigration to New France was small and soon lost its conscious identification with the Portuguese world.

The Dominion census of 1871 counted only 829 Portuguese and Spanish, lumped together under one heading. By contrast, in that year there were 788 Portuguese arrivals in Boston, Massachusetts.[6] The low level of Portuguese immigration to Canada at this time largely reflected the fact that the main outflow of Portuguese emigrants in the nineteenth century was to Brazil, the great Portuguese-speaking nation of South American. North America did attract Portuguese immigrants, especially from the Azores, but the vast majority went to the United States as contract labour. As an offshoot of the whaling industry large communities formed in New England by 1900, and this trend continued through the century. In 1973, it was estimated that 150,000 Portuguese Americans lived in the state of Massachusetts alone.[7] There were smaller communities in Connecticut, Rhode Island, New Jersey, central and southern California, and Hawaii.

In part, Canada did not attract Portuguese immigrants before World

War I because at that time Canadian immigration officials indicated a preference for northern Europeans. For example, in 1901, the Commissioner of Immigration at Winnipeg, W.F. McCreary, said he hoped to see more settlers from the British Isles, Germany and Scandinavia rather than from other European nations with more rapidly growing populations. In 1901, the Minister of the Interior, Clifford Sifton, stated that nothing had been done to encourage Italian railway workers at the time.[8] However, it was not lack of government encouragement that explains the virtual absence of Portuguese immigration to Canada but rather the attraction of Brazil, a country with the same language, and where many decades of migration had established familial and regional contacts which absorbed the Portuguese emigration of the time.

The Portuguese who came to Canada prior to 1939 were too few to constitute an easily traceable movement.[9] Probably many entered Canada for only short periods of time to work in the east coast fishing industry. Indeed, this movement was simply an extension of New England communities. In any event, no clear concentrations of Portuguese Canadians emerged. They were too scattered and disorganized even to be known to the Portuguese authorities: a comprehensive survey of Portuguese settlement throughout the world published in 1941 made no mention whatsoever of Canada.[10]

During the Second World War it was difficult to leave Portugal, and only with peace in 1945 was there a renewal of emigration opportunities. From a Canadian Immigration Department file, the following figures can be given for the immediate post-war years:

YEAR	NO. OF PORTUGUESE IMMIGRANTS	NO. OF UNSKILLED
1946	38	–
1947	25	2
1948	51	9
1949	66	4 (1 farmer)
1950	87	6 (1 farmer)

Source: National Archives of Canada. R.G. 27/Box 292/ 1-26-65-1.

The Portuguese who came to Canada in the first half of the twentieth century were highly mobile people, many of whom had experienced life in countries other than Portugal before they came here. By 1951, according to the census for that year, this highly variegated and dispersed immigration of Portuguese nationals had reached a total figure of 1,028.[11]

REGIONAL ORIGINS OF PORTUGUESE IMMIGRANTS

Before considering post-war immigration to Canada, it is pertinent to trace the regional patterns of emigration from Portugal. These have had a significant influence on the particular concentrations of immigrants and the nature of the communities that have developed in various parts of Canada.

At the beginning of the twentieth century, the four main areas of emigration in continental Portugal were Vila Real, Aveiro, Viseu, and Coimbra. Up to the 1970s, the major areas of international emigration have continued to be in the centre and north of Portugal. Thus, while there are Portuguese in Canada from every part of continental Portugal, Minho, Tras-os-Montes, Beira Alta, and Beira Baixa are the most common districts of origin.[12]

The majority of Canadian Portuguese, however, come from the Atlantic islands of the Azores; the largest contingent originates in São Miguel and the second largest in Terceira. Between 1900 and 1920, the islands experienced a decline in population, but subsequently there was a steady increase. Rising demographic pressure in an underdeveloped area with scant industrial prospects and limited arable land led local authorities to seek possible destinations for emigrants. On the island of Madeira there was also a steady rise in population and a corresponding increase in the number of those who wished to emigrate.

Canadian statistics do not record the regional origins of immigrants, but figures compiled by the Portuguese Junta de Emigração for the period 1953-1964 indicate that 38.2% of Portuguese emigration came from the mainland, 59.8% from the Azores, and 2% from Madeira.[13] The growth of the Portuguese community in Canada has been very much a product of sponsorship and nomination and it is highly likely that these proportions have remained constant, if indeed the Azorean majority has not been accentuated.

It should be recognized that the local economies of the different areas of Portugal vary substantially. The central and northern districts have a high rural population and a heavy concentration of small businesses as compared with other parts of the country.[14] The Azores have primarily an agricultural economy. On São Miguel, farms are largely in the hands of big landowners and are operated by hired help; on Terceira, there is more small holding. Madeira has a variegated, semi-tropical agriculture. This economic background affects the availability of credit to would-be emigrants to pay for the journey, and it also influences the emigrants' expectations regarding settlement in the new country.

For both Azoreans and Madeirans, emigration to continental Portugal or to other European countries has tended to be uninviting. Despite the

21

labour shortage in the industrializing area of Portugal, especially in the triangle of Lisbon-Setubal-Santarem, salaries were not sufficiently higher than those in the islands to justify the familial and personal dislocation of migration. There is, however, some migration from the smaller islands to the larger, especially to work in the American base on Terceira. Many Azoreans have some experience of the mainland, or the Continent, as it is called by the Portuguese: those with professional attainments are often trained either in Lisbon or Oporto; others may have been sent there to complete their military service. In general, though, there are no clear trends in movement between the two areas, and each island of the Azores group has tended to have a fairly closed and immobile society. The exception is the steady chain migration which takes Azoreans to North America, in recent years to Canada, and to Toronto in particular. Madeirans also look westward across the ocean rather than to Portugal for the possibility of improving their material prospects. Traditionally, their sights were focused on Brazil, and later on Venezuela, but familial links have brought many to Canada. In short, emigration from the Portuguese Atlantic Islands to Europe is marginal, comprising less than one per cent of the total Portuguese migration to other nations on the continent.[15]

Although the vast majority of the Portuguese in Canada comes from the Azores, the mainland, and Madeira, there is also a small inflow of emigrants from Macao, a Portuguese enclave close to Hong Kong. The population is mainly Chinese in extraction. Most of them have no knowledge of the Portuguese language, and their everyday business is conducted in either Chinese or English.[16] There are, however, bilingual families constituted by intermarriage between Chinese and Portuguese-speaking persons. Marriage has provided a familial network that has brought Chinese-speaking and some Portuguese-speaking residents of Macao to Canada, especially to Vancouver, but also to Winnipeg and Toronto. However, Macaoan immigrants to Canada associate mainly with Canadian and Chinese circles, and rarely with the Portuguese community.

There is a section of the Canadian Goan community which has a closer identification with Portuguese culture than do the Macaoans. Goa and adjoining territories were under Portuguese rule until their occupation by an invasion launched from India in 1961. Christianity had a profound impact on Goan society, as had the Portuguese language, at least among the land-owning and high-caste Baktaras. Goa had also been the source of a considerable emigration to English-speaking areas of Africa and to other parts of India during the nineteenth and twentieth centuries. There are therefore Canadian Goans who have Portuguese family names but no connection with Portuguese language or customs. Others, on the other hand, have received professional education in Portugal, and are fluent in Portuguese and conversant with Portuguese concerns. Like the Macaoans, however, the Goans are a small group, and only a minority associates with the Portuguese. Goans tend to be concentrated in Toronto and Montreal and Macaoans in Vancouver and Toronto, the numbers probably being only a few hundred in each community.

MIGRATION SINCE 1950

Between 1950 and 1969, the pattern of Portuguese emigration to other countries changed substantially, and this had a direct impact on migration to Canada. Brazil's immigration policy was changed in the 1950s, thereby diverting a large number of Portuguese to other destinations and this trend continues to the present time.[17] France emerged as the major receiving country, particularly during the 1960s, and by 1974 more than 800,-000 Portuguese lived there.[18] Some migrants came to Canada after a period of work in France, and these individuals generally preferred to settle in French-speaking areas of the country.

Official figures of the Portuguese Emigration Service showing the order of preference, or more exactly of destination, for emigrants during the period 1950 to 1969 are presented in Table 1. Other data indicate that, between 1956 and 1960, about 10% of emigrating Portuguese came to Canada (see Table 2). These statistics can be regarded as conservative. Clandestine emigration of persons without passports (such as young men avoiding military service, or categories of workers which the government wishes to retain) and illegal immigration of persons without official entry or work permits are worldwide problems. With the increased efforts of many governments to control and limit immigration in the mid-1970s, they are likely to become even more acute. Sudden shifts in the European labour force, the rapid turnover of foreign workers in response to short-term industrial needs in the Common Market, and movements of migrants to tertiary destinations add to the difficulty of collecting reliable statistics. Notwithstanding these qualifications, in the past two decades Canada had clearly emerged as a preferred destination for Portuguese emigrants, especially those from the Azores Islands and mainland Portugal. Unlike the United States, Canada has not been the migration target of "black Portuguese" (Bravas) from the Cape Verde Islands.

Table 3 indicates that frequently there is a considerable discrepancy between the numbers reported by Portugal as emigrants and those reported by Canada as immigrants. An overview and discussion of the problems associated with available statistics will be found in the *International Migration Review*, Portugal and North America issue, 1977.

The large-scale immigration to Canada from Portugal was a result of governmental initiatives. The reasons for the encouragement of this immigration differed in Ottawa and Lisbon, however. In the early 1950s it was widely known abroad that Canada was actively seeking agricultural workers. In June, 1951, the Department of Labour in Ottawa received a telegram from the High Commission in London stating that the British managing director of a Lisbon firm had entered into informal contact

23

TABLE 1
PORTUGUESE EMIGRATION TO CANADA AND OTHER PRINCIPAL DESTINATIONS, 1950–69

Country	No. of Portuguese Emigrants	% of all Portuguese Emigrants
Canada	61,755	5.5
France	489,813	43.5
Brazil	310,594	27.6
U.S.A.	82,867	7.3
Venezuela	73,554	6.5
Germany	45,474	4.0
South Africa	21,986	1.9
Argentina	12,377	1.1
Other	37,509	3.3
Total	1,135,929	100.0*

*Percentage column does not add because of rounding.

Source: Antunes, "Vinte anos de emigraçao portuguesa," p. 314.

TABLE 2
NUMBER OF PORTUGUESE EMIGRANTS TO CANADA COMPARED TO THE NATIONAL TOTAL: 1956-60

Year	Total Portuguese Emigration	Number of Portuguese Coming to Canada
1956	27,017	1,612
1957	35,356	4,158
1958	34,030	1,619
1959	33,458	3,961
1960	32,318	4,895
Total	162,179	16,245

Source: Pereira, "A emigraçao portuguesa no decénio de 1951-1960," p. 219.

TABLE 3

PORTUGUESE EMIGRATION TO CANADA*

Year	Data from the Emigration Board (Portugal)	Data from Canada Immigration**
1952	–	1,903
1953	179	555
1954	952	1,324
1955	941	1,427
1956	1,612	1,971
1957	4,158	4,748
1958	1,619	2,177
1959	3,961	4,354
1960	4,895	5,258
1961	2,635	2,976
1962	2,739	3,398
1963	3,424	4,689
1964	4,770	6,090
1965	5,197	6,505
1966	6,795	8,812
1967	6,615	10,478
1968	6,833	7,738
1969	6,502	7,182
1970	7,500	8,000
Totals	71,327	89,585

Estimated total of Portuguese Canadians born between
1953 and 1970   21,000
General Total   110,585

*Includes Portuguese persons coming from countries other than Portugal.
Source: Luis Augusto Martins, *Boletim,* Sociedade de Geografia de Lisboa, series 89, No. 7-9, July-Sept., 1971, p. 220. These statistics appear to have been adapted from figures of "Ethnic Origin and Country of Citizenship."

TABLE 4

IMMIGRATION TO CANADA BY MAJOR COUNTRIES OF LAST PERMANENT RESIDENCE, SELECTED YEARS, 1946–73

Portugal

1946–50	108
1951–57	8,115
1958–62	16,731
1963–67	32,473
1968–73	54,199
1946–73	111,626

Source: *Immigration and Population Statistics* (Green Paper on Immigration, Vol. 3) Ottawa: Manpower and Immigration, 1974, p. 32.

TABLE 5
POPULATION OF PORTUGUESE ETHNIC ORIGIN, CANADA AND PROVINCES, 1971

Canada	96,875
Newfoundland	340
P.E.I.	15
Nova Scotia	475
New Brunswick	195
Quebec	16,555
Ontario	63,145
Manitoba	3,815
Saskatchewan	275
Alberta	2,385
British Columbia	9,635
Yukon	25
N.W.T.	20

Source: *Immigration and Population Statistics* (Green Paper on Immigration, Vol. 3) Ottawa: Manpower and Immigration, 1974, p. 12.

TABLE 6
REFUGEES, DISPLACED PERSONS AND STATELESS PERSONS OF PORTUGUESE ORIGIN ADMITTED TO CANADA, 1947–67

1963	1
1964	10
Total	11

Source: *Immigration and Population Statistics* (Green Paper on Immigration, Vol. 3) Ottawa: Manpower and Immigration, 1974, p. 45. None of these persons appear in the statistics as Portuguese by country of birth; figures refer only to Portuguese origin.

TABLE 7
NUMBER AND LOCATION OF CANADIAN IMMIGRATION OFFICERS IN PORTUGAL

	Lisbon	Ponta Delgada (Azores)
1966	3	–
1967	3	1
1968	2	2
1969	2	2
1970	2	2
1971	3	–
1972	4	–
1973	4	–
1974	5	–

Source: *Immigration and Population Statistics* (Green Paper on Immigration, Vol. 3) Ottawa: Manpower and Immigration, 1974, p. 107.

with Canadian officials and railway representatives and proposed to re-
cruit two thousand farm labourers and woods-workers for Canada, for
which service he hoped to receive a commission. In the Immigration Department file the correspondence dealing with the offer contains a note,
"Would they make good Canadians?" The Librarian replied to the query
to the then Deputy Minister of Labour, A. Macnamara:

> It would be difficult to venture a guess as to citizenship possibilities.
> Portuguese farming methods are much inferior to ours. They should
> make as good citizens as other southern Europeans .... [19]

Laval Fortier, Deputy Minister of Citizenship and Immigration, in a letter of July 18, 1951, rejected the proposal:

> It has been our experience that private organizations operating in the
> migration field are primarily concerned with securing their commis-
> sion rather than in assisting the movement of suitable and desirable
> immigrants who will remain in Canada, and we would not be pre-
> pared to support a scheme involving remuneration to a private indi-
> vidual by the Canadian Government. [20]

He went on to suggest that it would be better to improve transportation
from existing sources of recruitment for immigrants rather than to add
new ones, and pointed out the complex and time-consuming procedure
required of prospective emigrants by the Portuguese authorities. While
this particular offer was rejected by the Canadian government it had the
effect of awakening interest in a new source of agricultural workers, and
discussions were undertaken in Ottawa with the Portuguese Embassy
about the possibility of recruiting.

At the same time that Canada was looking to Portugal for a solution to
its shortage of agricultural workers, Portugal was interested in finding
suitable destinations for the excess population of the adjacent islands. As a
result of this situation the first group migration of Portuguese to Canada
arrived in 1952. This has been described by one Portuguese writer on
emigration policy as "a typical example of state *dirigisme* in emigration."[21] Twenty persons, mostly from Terceira, were sent in the pilot
group. A year later, in late May, 1953, the Grace Line *S.S. Hellas* landed
110 men at the port of Halifax. These were mostly married men, sent with
the expectation that, once established in Canada, they would be joined by
their families.[22]

Many of these early arrivals had replied to advertisements in local
newspapers calling for agricultural workers. The majority were not, however, of rural background. Interviews indicated that among them, for
example, were a garage mechanic from Funchal, the capital of Madeira,
and a man from nearby Câmara de Lobos with experience as a net-maker,
carpenter, and banana grower. Both men decided to leave the island to
look for better economic prospects: the first had enquired about going to
Brazil and the second had filed for a United States visa when they replied

27

to the Canadian advertisement. They came to Canada because it happened to be the first country to accept their application. Since both had overseas relatives – the first in Brazil, the second in Brazil and Venezuela – migration was something of a family tradition for them.

Government initative remained important in starting new flows of migration, as in the Azores after the eruption of the Capelinhos volcano on Fayal in July, 1959. The governors of the autonomous districts of Horta and Angra do Heroísmo requested that Canada accept immigrant families from the devastated areas, and Canadian officials speeded up the processing of those concerned for humanitarian reasons. In 1959 and 1960, 100 families from Fayal and 50 from the neighbouring island of Pico moved to Canada. This was the second major influx of immigrants without family attachments to the existing community in Canada. It laid the basis for a chain of sponsored immigration to Canada from the two islands to complement that from Terceira and São Miguel, the most urbanized islands in the Azores group.

By 1961, the foundation was laid for a continuing characteristic of Portuguese immigration to Canada: the reconstitution of extended families. Parents, brothers, sisters, uncles, nephews, and other relatives were informed of Canadian conditions by those already established here and subsequently assisted in finding jobs and a place to live.

TABLE 8

IMMIGRATION TO CANADA, BY CATEGORY OF ADMISSION
AND COUNTRY OF LAST PERMANENT RESIDENCE (PORTUGAL)
1967–73

Year	Sponsored	Nominated	Independent	Total
1967	7,361		2,139	9,500
1968	5,220	1,912	606	7,738
1969	2,855	4,007	320	7,182
1970	2,619	4,673	610	7,902
1971	3,555	4,906	696	9,157
1972	2,873	5,505	359	8,737
1973	3,580	6,163	3,740	13,483
Totals	20,702	7,361 27,166	8,470	63,699

Source: *Immigration and Population Statistics* (Green Paper on Immigration, Vol. 3) Ottawa: Manpower and Immigration, 1974. Adapted from tables on pp. 40-43.

Family contacts appear more important as an explanation of Portuguese immigration than either individual enquiries made to Canadian immigration officers or the desire to escape the political situation in Portugal during the period 1950 to 1974.

The wish to remain near family members is also one reason for the concentrations of Portuguese in certain areas. In Toronto, for example, over 100 Azoreans from one small village on the island of Pico live in close enough proximity to enjoy frequent reunions. The social patterns of Portuguese families have been transferred almost intact, and the majority of new arrivals are part of family units already settled in Canada.

The major part of Portuguese immigration into Canada has taken place under the 1952 Immigration Act, which provides for the nomination and sponsoring of relatives as new entrants to the country.[23] Freda Hawkins has described the government's immigration program and its impact on numbers of Portuguese entrants during the 1950s:

> Immigration movements from Portugal for the next few years (from 1953 onwards) must be studied in the light of the then current shortage of heavy manual labour in Canada, and the persistent pressure from railway construction companies and agricultural groups for immigrant workers, coupled with the decline in immigration from our traditional source countries in 1955 and 1956. For the 1954 programme, at the request of the Portuguese Government, the Portuguese movement comprised 200 railway track workers for the R.F. Welch Company (1,000 Italian track workers had been recruited in 1953), 700 agricultural workers for mixed farms, and up to 50 tradesmen with all selection to be conducted in the Azores. In 1955, the approved movement consisted of 900 farm labourers and 50 tradesmen to be selected from the Portuguese mainland. In 1956 a similar programme was approved but with selection from the Azores. For the 1957 immigration programme, in line with a general expansion of activities, the programme included 2000 farm labourers (1000 from the Azores and 1000 from the Mainland) as well as 50 tradesmen. Subsequently a movement of 1000 track workers from the Azores for the R.F. Welch Company was also authorized in 1957 . . . .
>
> About this time (1957-58) serious doubts began to be felt in the Immigration Branch about the Portuguese movement. The Portuguese government was obviously making efforts to concentrate our recruiting activities in the Azores. At the same time there were increasing signs that the declining need for unskilled labourers in Canada would not continue to support the type of movements we had been accepting in Portugal. The several large movements of unskilled workers from the Azores showed signs of producing a disproportionate volume of sponsored immigrants (duplicating our experience in Italy).[24]

In 1959, the Minister of Immigration, the Hon. Ellen Fairclough, proposed an amendment to the Immigration Act that would remove brothers, sisters, and married sons and daughters of resident immigrants from

29

sponsorable categories; this proposal, however, generated a storm of protest and was subsequently withdrawn. Portuguese organizations were strongly represented in the protests. Indeed, the government's policy on illegal and sponsored immigration has been a regular concern of the Portuguese-Canadian press.

The claim is often made that Canadian conditions have been misrepresented to would-be immigrants by the Immigration Department. The Rev. A.J. de Melo, a parish priest in Toronto, referred to the problem in a newspaper interview:

> In the late fifties thousands of Portuguese immigrants were misled by Canadian authorities. At that time large numbers of agricultural workers from the Azores left their homeland lured by promising jobs on Ontario farms . . . . When they found Canadian farm machinery and techniques too sophisticated for their skills, they rushed to the cities after factory and construction work.[25]

In the early 1960s visitors to Canada frequently became immigrants but on November 3, 1972, new regulations came into force which did not permit a visitor to Canada to apply for the status of landed immigrant from within the country. Persons who came to Canada as visitors had to return to their country of origin to apply. At the same time, the process for appealing a deportation order was so time-consuming that it permitted an individual to remain in Canada for a number of years, during which time he or she could be earning wages.

Often, strong emotional bonds have led immigrant families to avoid the legal entry process. One moving case emerged in 1973, when the Federal Department of Manpower and Immigration launched a nation-wide adjustment of status program. Ninety-two-year-old Maria de Gloria Correia came forward at that time to register as an illegal immigrant and her story was reported by the *Toronto Star.*

> Mrs. Correia came here from Portugal in 1966 with Mr. and Mrs. João Maduoro. The Maduoros received landed immigrant status, but they were afraid to apply for Mrs. Correia, fearful her age and partial blindness would result in deportation. The bonds were too strong to take the risk.
>
> Through an interpreter, the old lady told her story. She first met the parents of João Maduoro when she was a girl of 16 in Portugal. João was only three years old at the time and the two became fond of one another.
>
> When Mrs. Correia married, she and her husband went to settle in Brazil. But when her husband died at the age of 30 leaving her without children of her own, she returned to Portugal and the Maduoro home.
>
> Mrs. Correia remained with the Maduoros for 41 years and when it came time for the family to come to Canada, they decided she must

come also. "She had no family back there at all," says Mrs. Maduoro.[26]

The period of large scale illegal immigration worked to the advantage of some travel agents in Portugal and Canada. For a fee of $200 to $300, they would coach prospective immigrants on the appeal procedure to be followed at the airport if immigration officers questioned their claim to visitor status. In the late 1960s and early 1970s, in all the main urban centres of Canada, immigration consultants were to be found who charged up to $1,000 to advise their clients on how to obtain landed immigrant status. Sometimes these individuals combined their advisory services with other businesses or jobs. One from central Toronto advertised in 1963 that he was "Notary Public . . . Procurations, Letters of Sponsorship and any other kind of Official Documents."[27] He had come from the Azores in 1957 and worked as an office cleaner, real estate agent, and travel agent before opening an immigration consultant's service. In 1970, the RCMP seized 1,400 files from his office and subsequently charges were brought of 24 cases of fraud involving money he received from visitors to Canada trying to obtain landed immigrant status. His trial resulted in conviction on three charges.[28]

In response to a crackdown on illegal immigration in March, 1973, forged work permits became a popular item sold by some immigration consultants. Permits are, however, computer filed and therefore easily checked. An anonymous source within the Toronto Portuguese community claimed that consultants, and their assistants in Europe and South America, were involved in a large scale operation of bringing people into Canada and subsequently providing them with jobs. The people involved were often unable to communicate in English, and some were illiterate in their own language. This is, of course, a perennial problem of first generation immigrants. Moreover, frustration at the lack of concern of government agencies can lead to participation in political protests.[29]

The growing numbers of illegal immigrants are fearful of deportation and therefore vulnerable to exploitation by the unscrupulous. In the opinion of one prominent Canadian labour leader, the Portuguese immigrant workers are "currently exploited more than any other ethnic group." Moreover, he estimates that "only five per cent of cases involving exploitation ever get reported." There seems to be some justification for this claim. A recent newspaper article cited the case of a middle-aged woman from Portugal who worked in one of Toronto unorganized clothing industry workshops: "For a total of 90 hours' work she was collecting $30 gross. An extreme case, perhaps, but there are others, only slightly less appalling."[30] A number of case workers with Portuguese and other immigrants feel that the Portuguese-language press is not doing enough to inform the immigrants of their rights, and to emphasize that confidentiality is guaranteed by the officials of the Employment Standards Branch. Many hope to see more political activity on the part of the Portuguese.

31

It is difficult to anticipate what Portuguese migration patterns will be in the mid-1970s. The withdrawal of the Portuguese from Africa will probably involve movements of population as settlers relocate. Fluctuating demand for labour in the most industrialized areas of the European Common Market may force many Portuguese workers to look farther afield for employment. Changes in the Canadian immigration regulations will affect the Portuguese the same as they will other immigrant groups. Whatever developments occur in these and other factors which govern Portuguese emigration, there is much evidence that Portuguese emigrants will continue to be enthusiastic about coming to Canada. With the increasing size and sophistication of the Portuguese community here, Canada has become known as a desirable destination.[31]

NOTES

1. Marie de l'Incarnation, *Words from New France*: the selected letters, trans. by Joyce Marshall (Toronto, 1967), p. 345.
2. P.N. Moogk, "The Craftsmen of New France," (unpublished Ph.D. Dissertation, University of Toronto, 1973), p. 314.
3. Frank W. Campbell, *Canada's Post Offices, 1775-1895* (Boston, 1972), p. x.
4. A genealogy of the Da Silva family appears in Cyprien Tanguay, *Dictionnaire généalogique des familles canadiennes depuis la fondation de la colonie jusqu'à nos jours* . . . (Québec, 1871-90), Vol. I, p. 158, vol. II, p. 243, vol. III, pp. 294-6. We are indebted to Dr. Peter Moogk of the University of British Columbia for this reference. John Dickenson in his researches into the Prévôté of Québec, 1666-1759, has found references to the family in a number of civil cases which he has pointed out to us. (Forthcoming doctoral dissertation in history, University of Toronto).
5. Zosa Szajkowski, *Jews and the French Revolutions* (New York, 1970), pp. 1-150; Stuart Rosenberg, *The Jewish Community in Canada: a history* (Toronto, 1970), I, pp. 18-19.
6. Portugal, Ministerio dos negócios estrangeiros, *Emigracão portuguesa . . . documentos* . . . (Lisbon, 1874), p. 241.
7. *Boston Evening Globe*, April 30, 1973.
8. Donald Avery, "Canadian Immigration Policy and the Foreign Navvy, 1896-1914," *Canadian Historical Association; Papers* (Ottawa, 1972), pp. 135-156.
9. The figures for immigrants received in Canada show a small but steady flow of Portuguese before World War II. Royal Commission on Bilingualism and Biculturalism, Book IV, *The Cultural Contribution of the Other Ethnic Groups* (Ottawa, 1970).

10. Sociedade de geografia de Lisboa, *Colónias portuguesas em paises estrangeiros* (Lisbon, 1941), p. 21.
11. Canada, Bureau of Statistics, *Census of Canada 1951* (Ottawa, 1953 and 1955).
12. M.L. Marinho Autunes, "Vinte anos de emigração portuguesa: alguns dados e comentários," *Analise Social*, VIII (1970), 351.
13. "A emigração portuguesa para o Canadá," *Communidades Portuguesas*, II, 6 (1966), 81.
14. Eugenio de Castro Caldas and Manuel de Santos Louveiro, *Níveis de desenvolvimento agrícola no continente português* (Fundação Gulbenkian, centro de Estudos de Economia Agrária, Trabalhos, Ser. A, 13 [Lisboa, 1963]).
15. Autunes, "Vinte anos de emigração portuguesa," p. 351.
16. "Macau continua a ser Lusitano, mas muito pouco," *Diário de Lisboa*, 26 August 1974.
17. Joel Serrão, *A emigração portuguesa* (Lisbon, 1971), pp. 25-50.
18. *Le Monde*, June 5, 1974.
19. Undated memorandum, Immigration Department, National Archives of Canada: RG 27/Box 292/1-26-65-1.
20. Correspondence, 28 June – 14 August, 1951. National Archives of Canada: RG 27/Box 292/1-26-65-1.
21. Gil Pereira, "A emigração portuguesa no decénio de 1951-1960," *Estudos politicos e sociais*, XI, 1 (1964), 205-45; Yves Leloup, "L'émigration portugaise dans le monde et ses conséquences pour le Portugal," *Revue de Géographie de Lyon*, XLVII (1972), 59-76.
22. Pereira, "A emigração portuguesa," p. 220.
23. Dependent immigrants are divided into two categories, sponsored and nominated. These meet less stringent entry requirements than independent immigrants. Sponsored immigrants are close relatives, members of an immigrant's immediate family; whereas nominated immigrants include more distant kin. Writing of sponsored dependants the Green Paper on Immigration, Vol. 2, states: "We consider ourselves duty-bound also to accept those close relatives who would normally be dependent on them in a society such as our own." (A Report of the Canadian Immigration and Population Study, *2 The Immigration Program*, Ottawa: Manpower and Immigration, 1975, p. 52, which is one of a series of studies popularly known as "The Green Paper on Immigration.") It is implied that the sponsoring person will be responsible for a life-time for those sponsored and that they will not necessarily be members of the work force. Therefore "no economic requirements are set." (Vol. 2, p. 53.) "The nominated category is a compromise, a hybrid between the independent and sponsored dependants categories. On the one hand it recognizes the legitimate desire of people in Canada to help relatives other than close family members, and in this sense it has a social and compassionate connotation. On the other hand it also takes account of the fact that the

great majority of relatives other than close family members will be entering the labour market and setting up separate self-sustaining family units . . . since immigrant relatives could expect assistance from their relatives in Canada, this support could take the place of the short-term economic factors; on the other hand, since the immigrant relatives would ultimately have to strike out on their own and establish themselves in the Canadian economy, they would be assessed under the long-term economic factors applicable to independent applicants." (Vol. 2, pp. 54-55) An excellent summary of selection factors for the three categories of immigrants is contained in Vol. 2 of the Green Paper, p. 59. See also *Office Consolidation of the Immigration Act*, Ottawa: Queen's Printer, 1968, and "Policy and Program, 1963-1971" in Freda Hawkins, *Canada and Immigration: Public Policy and Public Concern*, Montreal and London: McGill-Queen's University Press, 1972.

24. Hawkins, *Canada and Immigration*, pp. 49-50.
25. *Toronto Star*, March 2, 1970.
26. *Toronto Star*, September 29, 1973.
27. *Jornal Português*, July 23, 1971; *Toronto Star*, April 4, 1974. The whole question of travel agents and immigration consultants in Canadian immigrant history needs to be investigated. The *Toronto Star* described one consultant who previously held a variety of posts with the Immigration Department as "one of the few immigration consultants considered reputable in Toronto" (March 17, 1973). His maximum fee was reported to be $400, while other "consultants" charged much more.
28. *Toronto Star*, April, 1973.
29. *The Globe and Mail*, August 28, 1973, detailed the experience of a man suffering from injuries who had come from the Azores and was illiterate. He had joined a demonstration against the Workman's Compensation Board sponsored by the Marxist-Leninist Party of Canada.
30. *Toronto Star*, September 3, 1973.
31. Maria Beatriz Rocha Trindade, "Sobrevivência e Progresso de uma Aldeia Despovoada", *Revista da Sociedade de Geografia de Lisboa*, IX,35, July, 1973 and *Immigrés Portugais: Observation Psycho-Sociologique d'un groupe de Portugais dans la Banlieue Parisienne (Orsay)*, Instituto Superior de Ciências Sociais e Política Ultramarina, Lisbon, 1973, give descriptions of a village in continental Portugal which has been depopulated by emigrants to France and the subsequent transformation which occurred through the flow of remittances back to the hamlet. Although no parallel studies have been conducted regarding immigration to Canada and depopulated villages yet valuable insights may be gained through these available studies.

THREE

Growth of Portuguese-Canadian Communities

Economic opportunity is the major stimulus to Portuguese migration to Canada. Many of the immigrants themselves have described their single, overriding incentive as "dollar fever." Not only did it draw men initially, but it also prompted frequent moves in a constant search for better jobs.[1] Nation-wide interviews have confirmed these findings for the Portuguese communities scattered across Canada.

An immigrant we interviewed aptly summed up the views of many of his compatriots in these words:

> One of the nicest things at the beginning was the difference we noticed in the level of living. We could afford the same as a rich man back home in the old country. There, regardless of how much you work you can never get these things. Here, after six months, we bought our own home. There, we work for 10 years and still do not have anything to show for it. We now have a car. I got one after I had been here two years. Pretty nearly everyone has his own car. At first there was great frustration with the language – English sounded just noise. The eating habits were so different too.

For many of the first Portuguese immigrants to Canada, the process of emigration was a course of action which, once begun, was almost impossible to reverse. As soon as they announced to family and friends that they had made enquiries about emigrating, the men faced public skepticism and often strongly adverse reactions from their families. They were ridiculed by their relatives, and the village elders called them young fools. Some prospective emigrants weakened at this point and forgot the whole idea. A few came to Canada and returned almost immediately. But for a small band of hardy pioneers, the hometown opposition intensified their determination to make a success of the venture. Success became mandatory; and even when they encountered difficulties far beyond their deepest misgivings, pride forbade the admission of hardship or defeat. The mental picture of the ridicule they had suffered remained vivid for years.

In an article "Canada: Land of Opportunity?" M. Custodio Tavares vividly portrays the opportunities proferred to prospective Portuguese immigrants and the subsequent disillusions of many of them.

Canada! Land of a thousand opportunities. Offers of a country as big as Europe with a population as small as Portugal. And to poor people, those uneducated in this type of activity, came the project of saving and struggling to attain this golden goal: Canada. Unbuilt houses and split up families . . . all to finally get to Canada . . . .

Knowing of the immigrant's pride and his ignorance, there was no fear of this cheap labour force returning to its homeland . . . an immigrant will not return home a failure . . . .

Basically, the land of opportunity is the land of opportunists. In the name of liberty they commit wrongs. It is fundamental to distinguish between the myth and the reality.[2]

The economic and family life of the Portuguese in Canada during the modern period (post-1952) can be considered to fall into four distinct but overlapping phases:

1. The pioneer immigrant phase (1953-1959)
2. The urbanized immigrant phase (1960-1967)
3. The visitor phase (1967-1973)
4. The second generation phase (1965 to the present).

THE PIONEER IMMIGRANT PHASE

In the first phase of immigration, Portuguese men came to Canada either through application to the government for employment as farm labourers, or under the auspices of private labour contractors who recruited prospective railway section hands. Most immigrants regarded these jobs as temporary; primarily, they provided a means of paying for the ocean crossing and entering the country.[3]

Nearly all the immigrants interviewed in the present study who arrived in Canada during this early phase said they suffered extreme hardships for the first months or years of their stay. Of course, this is not universally true: some encountered few difficulties and adjusted easily to their new life. On the evidence, though, it appears that immigration was a harsh and trying experience for most.

Their problems began as soon as they disembarked in Halifax harbour. They found themselves in a totally unfamiliar situation, with which they were ill-equipped to deal. Language was the first major obstacle. Most of the newcomers had received primary education in Portugal and were therefore literate, but they had little academic or practical experience in learning other languages. Their unfamiliarity with either English or French made the most simple everyday transactions a trial: they had

36

difficulty finding accommodation, making travel arrangements, or even buying appropriate food.

The Portuguese government anticipated some of these problems and tried to make the transition easier by providing a booklet of instructions for the early immigrants. They were reminded, for example, that the importation of foods from Portugal was not permitted and that only one bottle of liquor could be brought to the new country. This in itself seemed a curious regulation to nationals of the country with the highest per capita wine consumption in Europe. When they landed in Halifax, they were to wear coloured labels on their coats to indicate their destinations: orange for Quebec, red for Toronto, blue for Vancouver, pink for Edmonton, beige for Ottawa. These markers were to be placed in the lapel to assist the immigration officers at railway stations but, upon arrival at their destination, the travellers should remove them so that they would not be conspicuous to "persons of few scruples who might take advantage of their inexperience."[4]

The booklet gave a list of organizations that could provide help to the new arrivals.[5] Foremost among these was the reception centre on rue Saint Antoine in Montreal, which provided a restaurant and rooms with bunk beds (the booklet noted: "The food provided, of Canadian type, is healthy"). In other cities, the YMCA was recommended. Some general observations about working conditions also were made, with the injunction that jobs should not be left at the beginning of winter since unemployment was widespread during that season and it would be difficult to find other work. Agricultural jobs were pointed out: tobacco at Delhi, Ontario, and at Joliette, Quebec; market gardening and fruit farming on the Niagara Peninsula. Work with wood and milk products was suggested. Contracts would be oral, with pay (1955) for the first month at $55, for the second $60, and with increases thereafter of $5 per month. Officially, it was not permitted to leave an agricultural job for the first year of Canadian residency. The immigrants were also informed that unemployment benefits were not available to those working in agriculture, fishing, and domestic service.

Although many of the Portuguese immigrants who came to Canada in the 1950s had not been employed in agricultural work before, their first employment experience here was on farms. Many had grown up on farms, but had left their rural villages in their early teens to find employment in service industries in the towns, prior to emigration. For the majority of the earliest arrivals, the process of allocating farm labourers was handled through immigration offices in major urban centres. One man recounted his memories of the experience. The immigrants were gathered in groups, and the farmers came to claim them. Since there was no common language between them, communication was confined to close scrutiny and gestures. Some immigrants were offended by the procedure, and a man we interviewed felt that his dignity was being compromised: "It was like a concentration camp or slave market. They looked and were thinking to

themselves, 'he's small, he won't eat much, or he's big, he will work.'"
Another Azorean remarked, "I was poor but I never had to work for
anybody else [in Portugal]." Because of this hiring system, relationships
between the immigrants and their employers often commenced in an
atmosphere of strain and tension.

The lack of farm experience caused substantial problems for farmers
and workers alike. One man was asked whether he could drive a tractor,
and because the job paid well, he replied that he could, though he had
never driven one in his life before. He feigned ignorance of the language
and the type of machine in order to be shown how to operate it. The
farmer gave him a demonstration, then left him to run it; and the immigrant nearly ruined the tractor in the process of learning to drive. After he
had mastered the machine, he left and went to work in another part of the
country.

Some men stated that the heaviness of the work made the first few weeks
burdensome, as they were not accustomed to it and had no muscles for the
task. Some had worked in village stores before they came to Canada, but
had registered with immigration officials as farmhands. Other men were
sent to dairy farms who knew nothing about cows or milking; some were
asked to deal with horses, though they never had before. A few became
violent when asked to do unfamiliar work. One pioneer, requested by the
farmer to saddle the horses, became so exasperated with his inability to do
the job that he flung the saddle down on the farmer's head. He then left the
farm and headed for city work.

After some time had passed – and no doubt government officials had
received many complaints from the farmers – Canadian interviewing
officers in Portugal began to examine the hands of workers for calluses.
But some immigrants passed even this test, having obtained calluses in
work totally unrelated to farming.

Not surprisingly, many immigrants arrived on the farms eager to move
on to city employment at the first opportunity. One farmer's daughter
recalls:

> I remember when my father had to hire immigrants because there
> was no local help to be had. But given a choice, he and all of our
> neighbours preferred local or native help, mainly because they were
> more reliable. In most cases the immigrant would just take off with no
> advance notice, leaving the farmer with no help just when he most
> needed it. They were often insolent and looked down on the farmer
> and his way of life. They put in time on the farm merely to fulfill their
> contract, which was their ticket over here. Often they considered farm
> work beneath their dignity, and worked accordingly. The govern-
> ment thought they were doing the farmer a favour by holding these
> immigrants to a contract to work on the farms, but in reality the
> scheme turned out to be nothing but a big headache for a lot of
> farmers.

One former Portuguese government official, now resident in Canada, comments:

> When Canadian government officials saw what happened to the imported farm hands they tried to stop the process. But the immigrants had already settled in Canada, brought out their families, wives, children, parents, brothers and sisters. They had encouraged other relatives to come and sometimes nominated them. Many of the single men who returned to the homeland on vacation married a local girl. Others arranged marriage by proxy and later brought the bride to Canada to join them.

Initially, on the farms changes in eating habits were a major problem. Both the type of food and the timing of meals were different from traditional Portuguese ways. In Portugal, the men were used to having a light breakfast, a substantial noon meal, and a very late dinner, a heavy meal, about 9 or 10 in the evening. Many of the immigrants who arrived in the 1950s lost thirty pounds weight in their first few months in Canada because of the change in environment and food and the nature of the work. Some related that when they rejoined their friends and fellow villagers, they had become so thin that they were no longer recognized. Men who had been assigned railway contracts usually received ample food, but it was seldom of a type that they enjoyed since they had previously lived on a predominantly fish diet.

One pioneer sent to British Columbia to work on a farm remembers clearly his early impressions and reactions to the new country. He crossed Canada by train, and in the course of the journey, he began to comprehend, to his dismay, how vast the land is. He had never crossed any land area larger than the island of São Miguel. He thought, "I will never forget how many miles the train has run; I'll never be able to return; I shall never see my parents again." To make matters worse, he had come to Canada against the expressed wishes of his family.

After a few months, he decided to change jobs, since he had heard that there were better employment opportunities at places where some of his friends were working. He went to the railway station, but it was the wrong one (both Canadian National and Canadian Pacific had stations in the town). Moreover, he took a local train, and it was going in the wrong direction. He spoke no English, and he quickly became lost, bewildered, and frightened.

> When we reached the end of the line . . . I said I wouldn't get out until I reached my destination. Three company men came and forced me out – I put up a good fight . . . . Now there was a man who gave us a place to sleep but no food . . . . I didn't know how to ask for it. The next day I got on the train going to Winnipeg. I had had nothing to eat or drink for twenty-four hours. People tried to talk to me but I didn't understand anything. Finally, I was taken to a hotel where I

ate only bananas for eight days. I went to a store and followed a man in there, but didn't know how to ask for anything, so I bought bananas and left. It was terrible, and I said to myself, "I'll die here." After two more days they took me to the unemployment office, with another Portuguese man. On leaving I said to the other man, "Do you know what street we are on?" "Oh no, I don't," was the answer. "Then, in that case we are lost and with this hunger of mine I will surely die . . . . I'll never see my father and mother again."

Finally, the two men found their way back to the hotel and waited a further two days until they were placed in employment on the railway. At that point, however, the two were separated, and the man we interviewed was without Portuguese companions for another six months. He had problems washing his own clothes, for this had always been done for him at home. He wanted to buy some soap, and eventually he made his needs known to the other workers. They directed him down the track one day after work, and he started walking to find a store.

I must have walked ten miles following that track. Ten miles! Finally I found the store, but when I came to return it was already late at night and I was tired. I sat down on the rail tracks and said to myself, "Should any wild animal come . . . oh . . . . " If a train had come I would have committed suicide. You see, I was depressed. After all, nobody cared about me. They all told me to "get lost." Those who worked with me couldn't care less about me. I didn't speak with them at all. If my father were there at that moment I would kneel before him and kiss his feet (he didn't want me to come here). Eventually, I managed to get home with soap and cigarettes. It had been already six months and I had not smoked a cigarette or washed my clothes with soap. Had it not been that my father said he would not pay any money for me to go visiting . . . I would surely have returned immediately after getting here – that is, providing I would have had the means to do so.

After some months, this pioneer received a letter from friends in another part of the country telling him how to take a train and join them, and then to take a taxi. He left soon thereafter and, on taking the taxi, found that he was charged $24 instead of the $2 he had been told to expect. He remarked, "Those who wrote home never told of the hardships they experienced, the conditions they had to put up with, the suffering they had to bear." No doubt they feared that their parents would write, "I told you so." Now he is settled in southern Ontario and no longer regrets his decision to emigrate; in fact, at a later date, he persuaded his parents to come to North America, though they chose to go to Massachusetts. He commented, "I still have a booklet I was given in English and Portuguese. The first thing which I'll never forget is the saying on the first page: 'Imigrar e travar uma grande luta,' a literal translation of which is: 'To immigrate is to put up a big fight.' This is the truth!"

It is, however, worth noting that although the majority recount tales of considerable initial hardship, unaccustomed work, discouragement, and food problems, many immigrants were welcomed to their new way of life by kind and considerate people. One man recalls that his employer's family treated him like a son. He was taught English by the farmer's wife, driven to the stores and the bank, and shown how to send letters home. He still regards this family almost as blood relations and visits them from time to time.

As we have noted, the cause of the majority of early problems was lack of knowledge of English. Frequently, Portuguese men found that they were able to comprehend French more readily; but word was passed around among the immigrants that "French is the language of Quebec, English is the language of the whole country." Often, then, even in French-speaking areas, it was English that they tried to learn first. One man recalled his chagrin on discovering, after some time of learning – as he thought – the language of the country, that his fellow workers had been teaching him Italian. Others found themselves working entirely with recently arrived Europeans and had no chance to gain a working knowledge of either English or French. In the early days of isolation, language classes were difficult to arrange. Also, the men arrived in from the fields or from work on the railway tracks too tired to be able to learn much.[6]

There were several cases, such as that of the pioneer in British Columbia, in which an immigrant did not have an opportunity to speak to anyone in his own language for six months or more. Eventually, when he met someone who spoke Portuguese, he had forgotten so much of the language that he had difficulty communicating at all. But such men constituted a very small minority.

A sense of utter helplessness was to many men the most devastating aspect of the language problem. Some thought the solution was to move to an area where fellow countrymen were working. For a small minority, the answer was to learn English or French as soon as possible. For many, the hope was to return to the homeland as soon as they were able, but this was not easily managed. Officially, their contracts lasted for at least a year. Usually they had borrowed the money to make the journey, and this must be repaid. Some were trying to support several persons in Portugal on perhaps $50 a month. One man summarized his situation as follows: "Had I known I was going to suffer so much I never would have come." Many others would have fervently agreed with this statement.

As soon as the men were able, they changed to more remunerative jobs. If one immigrant found a more remunerative position, he wrote home about it. News was traded in the home villages and towns, and addresses of compatriots arrived in the mail together with details of possible job opportunities. Often, the men felt themselves to be in a desperate situation and moved whenever they thought their circumstances could be improved, always bearing in mind the desire to earn enough to be able to return home. But these moves often were not found to be as lucrative as they had been led to believe. In their letters home, the men would report that their salary had increased but would omit saying that now they lost most of it in paying for room and board, which on the farm had been provided free. (On the railway, they were charged a nominal fee for board, but the food was ample and of good quality.) Again and again, the immigrants moved, trying to equal or surpass the record set by hometown men for earnings abroad and eager to justify their decision to emigrate. Some men went to northern construction sites or became loggers in the bush. A few reached their goal and remained; but the majority moved frequently, always searching for a job which would enable them to surpass their fellows and to feel that their decision to emigrate was vindicated. Most were obsessed by the tremendous desire to succeed. Their reputation and their esteem among relatives and friends were totally dependent upon success.

This obsession led to an entirely new set of problems, this time of the immigrants' own making. They would hear rumours of other jobs in another part of the country and would leave suddenly in the search for better-paid employment. In doing so, they would find themselves cut off from the security and assistance initially promised, because they had broken contracts. It became the pattern to leave jobs whenever better prospects seemed remotely attainable, without regard for the consequences. It was this impetuous pursuit of money and success that the immigrants referred to as "dollar fever."

The men frequently did not wait for their pay, although sometimes they wrote for it later. They seldom told their employers that they were leaving the area – they simply departed, usually with a friend, almost always to join a group of compatriots. Thus, overnight, farmers found themselves without the assistance they needed, usually at a very busy time of the year.

Often, individuals set out for new destinations without any comprehension of the distances involved. The letters of direction were often too complicated for them to understand, and sometimes they arrived to find they were too late to obtain the expected jobs. Often they did not reach the destination at all: they met someone on the way who persuaded them to remain in the town where they were changing trains, or they became lost en route and remained where they happened to stop. In any case, by the end of the 1950s the pioneers were, for the most part, moving towards the cities, especially the largest centres – Montreal, Toronto, and Vancouver.

Many of the young men who arrived to work on the farms or railways came as single persons. Among the married men, the majority left their wives and families behind in Portugal. Although there are no published studies on Portuguese immigrants in the 1950s, parish priests and social workers have emphasized that it was often several years before the women and children joined the men in Canada.

But a few women did come in the early years, with their husbands. These couples or families usually asked to be located in a city or town.

Often the home of one of the families would become a boarding house for several of the single men who worked in the locality. In some cases, the wife obtained work outside the home, in a private home or in a hospital, a garment factory, or a food processing plant. There was no evidence uncovered in this study of any single young women coming to Canada alone in these early years. When young women arrived, they had usually been promised in marriage and frequently the couple had been officially married by proxy while the bride was still in Portugal.

Sometimes a widowed mother was brought to look after young children in the home while the wife went out to work. Frequently one home became an informal baby-sitting centre for several families, thus freeing the other wives to work outside the home. Later, the usual pattern was for the single men to return to Portugal to select a bride, and usually this event precipitated the move from an isolated location into an urban area.

On arriving in the cities, the large majority of Portuguese immigrants found that, because of limited educational background, only a few occupations were open to them. *Networks of Contact* (Anderson, 1974) documents the channels of employment for Portuguese blue collar workers in Toronto. Subsequent research has confirmed that this pattern has been followed in many of the cities and towns across Canada.

One of the great attractions drawing Portuguese men to the cities was employment in the construction industry. Many Canadian cities were, and still are, expanding rapidly. The construction industry provides on-the-job training for remunerative semi-skilled trades such as "cement finisher" and "tile setter." Other areas of employment also became occupational specialties of Portuguese immigrants. Some men obtained employment in factories. Many obtained work in hospitals as housekeeping staff, or in the kitchens, or in cleaning jobs. The better educated who had related experience in the medical corps of the armed forces in Portugal prior to coming to Canada sometimes became medical orderlies.

When men arrived in the cities in the middle of winter and there were no suitable jobs for the unskilled, they would sometimes ask if they could wash dishes in a restaurant in return for meals. Of course, this undercutting of wages was resented by other workers. But at times the immigrants were desperate, and were afraid to ask for welfare when they had recently arrived in the country, especially if they had deserted a job before the initial work contract was completed.

Many immigrants showed considerable initiative in finding employment. One man told how he obtained a job for his brother-in-law, who could speak no English. He took his relative to a body repair shop and asked for a job, but was told that none was available. In desperation, he said to the owner, "Listen, he work for you for a week, no pay." The owner thought to himself, "Oh boy, that's a chance to see what he can do," and he decided to test him out (he intended to pay the man in any event). He pointed to a wreck that had been towed in and was considered to be a total write-off, and told the Portuguese immigrant to fix it. The

43

instruction was duly translated by his brother-in-law, who then inquired apprehensively, "Can you do it?" The immigrant said he thought he could and began to work. Each day, his relative would enter the body repair shop and ask the owner how the new man was doing, and translate messages between the two. At the end of the week, the car was well on the way to being restored, and the owner decided, "This boy is going to stay with me." The Portuguese is now considered one of the best men in the largest repair shop for automobile bodies in that city.

The immigrants who moved to the cities, together with the very few who had commenced working there, formed the nucleus around which the urbanized immigrant communities developed over the next decade.

THE URBANIZED IMMIGRANT PHASE

In the early 1960s, a new type of immigrant arrived from Portugal – the highly skilled technician and the white collar worker, articulate and with at least secondary school education. These immigrants wanted to settle directly in the larger cities. They came with their families or as single men who later brought over and married the sweethearts they had left behind in the homeland. Frequently, they learned either English or French before they left home. They were likely to open travel agencies, to qualify as real estate agents, to establish driving schools in the larger centres, and to provide some of the other services needed in the new urban Portuguese communities.

As soon as they were able, they purchased houses, for back in Portugal every family has its own home. Indeed, to save enough for a down payment and to own a house became a major preoccupation of the Portuguese community. The new immigrants were not discouraged by apparently substantial obstacles. A major problem was that housing costs were much higher in Canada than in the small centres in Portugal. In addition, the houses themselves were different, they were located in an urban setting and a climate quite unlike those known before, and the social and monetary situation was unfamiliar to the newly arrived immigrants. Despite these difficulties, many of them attained their objective. In 1969, 54 % of a sample of Portuguese blue collar workers in Toronto owned their own homes.[8]

With the steadily rising cost of housing and soaring interest rates, however, it has become increasingly difficult for Portuguese families, particularly in Metropolitan Toronto, to pay off mortgages. A social worker at the Portuguese Service Centre of the Mount Carmel parish has found her counselling taken up increasingly with family problems related to the strain of trying to meet large mortgage payments. This worker stated, "To Portuguese, home ownership is a symbol of security and they will sacrifice the privacy of their families in an effort to pay off their homes."

New arrivals, both single and in families, usually find accommodation within the Portuguese community. The rent they pay for their rooms often makes it possible for others to meet their mortgage payments. It is a widespread characteristic of the Portuguese and many other ethnic communities, and has been from earliest establishment in the cities, that the first arrivals to obtain houses provided lodging to those who followed. One man we interviewed said he lived in a house with seventy-three other Portuguese persons when he first came to Canada. Some men experienced considerable emotional stress from living in crowded conditions.

TABLE 9

HOUSING: TYPE OF ACCOMMODATION BY COUNTRY OF BIRTH (PORTUGAL) AFTER 3 YEARS IN CANADA, ENDING IN 1972

Boarding House	Apartment	Rented House	Own House	Other	Total
10%	30%	23%	29%	8%	100%

Source: *Three Years in Canada: First Report of the Longitudinal Survey on the Economic and Social Adaptation of Immigrants* (Canada Immigration and Population Study), Ottawa: Manpower and Immigration, 1974 p. 65.

Lipman[9] has documented the difficulties that many Toronto immigrants encounter in trying to meet mortgage payments.[10] Immigrants have tried to meet the challenge of home ownership in various ways. Women may work outside the home for the first time in their lives, in either full-time or part-time employment.[11] Men may supplement their income by volunteering for as much overtime work as possible, or by taking a second full-time job or part-time job.[12] Sometimes children are encouraged to leave school in order to earn money. In many cases, the only way that the family can retain its home through a difficult period is by having multiple sources of income.

One popular form of ancillary employment is worm-picking (*ir a minhocas*). A live bait company in Toronto is reported to employ 300 full-time and 400 part-time employees to meet the demand for live bait, primarily for the United States market; of these, 60% are said to be Portuguese. Women are among the best pickers; but often whole families collaborate in this extra fund-raising, including children who are still at school and husbands who are home from work. In 1968, a first-rate picker could earn $200 a week, and the average was $100 at the rate of $5.50 per thousand worms. This has now increased. Since 1974 pickers have been paid at least the minimum wage.

It's not particularly back-breaking work. It's more like you use a lot of muscles you don't ordinarily use, especially the ones in the back of your thighs. Once you get in shape you hardly notice it.[13]

The Portuguese have tended to look for houses in older parts of the city where their compatriots are already settled and costs are lower. In Montreal, Winnipeg, Vancouver, and particularly Toronto, there are clear areas of Portuguese concentration, some of them sections that were once considered blighted and have been restored by the immigrants. In the larger communities marked residential segregation usually occurs in the inner city. Often it is the reception area of the most recent arrivals. Businesses servicing this ethnic area have a tendency to remain although, after a number of years, many of the immigrants follow the native-born to the suburbs.

When a Portuguese family obtains possession of a house, its members soon begin to renovate. Typically, they paint the outside of the house in the bright colours familiar in the homeland. The possession of a bright, freshly painted house is part of the obsession to "make good" in their adopted country. Often, the Portuguese help each other in building and redecorating. When a house is to undergo major renovations, a work party of relatives and possibly a few friends is called on to assist on weekends. Traditionally, beer or home-made wine is served and a large meal is cooked by the women. At the end of the day, there is a party atmosphere in the home. Later, those who have assisted the owner feel free, in turn, to call for assistance when they have a project under way themselves.

Not all the Portuguese who arrived in Canada in the early 1960s fell into the pattern of settled community living. The men who came on their own were still highly mobile in employment and place of residence. They changed jobs readily across the country, moving from Montreal to Vancouver to Toronto, and then going to Kitimat for awhile. They travelled to and fro between the large centres and the isolated but lucrative work sites, and boarded where they could with Portuguese families.

When these men were in the city or among other Portuguese, their conversation inevitably gravitated towards jobs and pay. As one man put it, "I came out here to make a better life for my family, but it was such a struggle that in the process I forgot about my family and thought only about making money." In other studies of immigrant groups, it has been suggested that close family ties may be a hindrance to mobility,[14] but for the Portuguese the situation was reversed: mobility became a hindrance to family life. Year after year dragged on, while the children grew up in Portugal without the benefit of their father's presence. The women learned to be independent; they made all the decisions at home and waited for letters from their distant husbands. Some men we interviewed admitted that they had lived as bachelors and enjoyed themselves as though they were single. Many others lived a life of unremitting toil in order to provide for absent families and to save enough money to bring them to Canada.

46

Some, in order to save every cent and to get sufficient postage money to send a letter home, used to comb the borders of highways looking for returnable bottles.

When wives did come, frequently they did not speak English or French. They were grateful to have access to food markets and variety stores where they could speak their own language; consequently, many stores flourished from the outset. But some failed. One man related that he had failed twice and accumulated $11,000 worth of debts in the process. Finally, by holding a full-time job and running the store in the evenings and on weekends, with the assistance of his wife, he was able to save enough to repay what he owed. By 1974, he owned three houses, two stores, and two cars, and owed no money.

As success was achieved in the 1960s, many encouraged their friends, more distant relatives, and hometown acquaintances to come to Canada. They forgot to mention the initial struggles. They never told of the times when they had no money. It is small wonder that newly arrived immigrants expected to find jobs immediately. A decade earlier, the men has been thankful for any job that gave then something to eat; but now new arrivals were asking, "How much will I be paid?" before they considered accepting employment. One pioneer remarked "We got ahead by working more than twelve hours each day. If a man works only eight hours a day in Canada he will always be poor, but if he works twelve hours a day he will be rich. Men could be rich back home in Portugal too, if they worked like that."

Since the late 1950s, the travel agencies of the major urban centres have played a considerable part in assisting the recently arrived. Initially, they acted as translation bureaux and made the necessary arrangements to bring relatives from the homeland to join their kin in Canada. They also filled out forms, especially government documents such as income tax returns. In their capacity as informal immigrant aid units, they often sought to unite the community in more formal organizations. Frequently, though, they were resented by the community for charging fees for services that the immigrants later discovered were offered freely by government and community social service agencies.

Information about jobs in the community was disseminated through informal conversation after mass on Sunday and through chance meetings in the Portuguese pool halls. Some of these halls became known as key locations for finding out about vacancies "up north." The Portuguese food markets and fish stores also became centres where information and gossip were traded.

As the newly found affluence permeated the communities, the men wanted to own cars like their Canadian peers. As a result, Portuguese driving schools were established. Initially, these were run on a part-time basis in conjunction with a full-time job or with other businesses, but eventually the demand was so great that they became full-time enterprises.

47

THE VISITOR PHASE

The years 1967 to 1973 have been referred to as the visitor phase. The Canadian government had become increasingly worried by persistent reports of large numbers of alien workers who had entered Canada as tourists or visitors and then immediately accepted jobs. They were employed without work permits and consequently were subject to all types of abuse, frequently from unscrupulous members of their own community. The Green Paper on Immigration notes that

> by 1964 the problem of visitors-turned-immigrant had got badly out of hand. Frustrated by the criteria for unsponsored immigrants, thousands of people (especially Italians, Greeks and Portuguese) were entering Canada as visitors, making contact with influential individuals or bodies, and then applying to stay permanently. The rapidly expanding use of air transportation contributed to this phenomenon.[15]

Visitor applicants were admitted in Canada on a selective basis in 1966. "This policy . . . was expected to clear away the existing backlog without serious hardship, and discourage the future flow of unskilled, undereducated workers."[16]

In the new regulations governing the act in 1967, "specific provision was made for visitors to apply for landing, while in Canada,"[17] and an elaborate appeal system was also inaugurated.

The new regulations had a boomerang effect. Resident immigrants immediately wrote home and said, "Why don't you come over immediately? The doors are wide open." Subsequently, the travel agents had some exceptionally fat years arranging passages. The metropolitan areas suddenly found large numbers of Portuguese immigrants in their midst. "Policy-makers and legislators had anticipated use of this power in perhaps 5 per cent of all cases, whereas it soon approximated 40 per cent and never dropped below 20 per cent."[18]

Finally in 1972 the immigration program had become chaotic:

> The end result was loss of control of immigration policy and the immigration program. Each year the problem grew: in 1972 more than one-third of those admitted as immigrants had not undergone examination and selection before coming to Canada, and many had initially been refused landing . . . .
>
> By October, 1972, the situation was such that the government saw no option but to revoke the visitor's right to apply for landing.[19]

The appeal system was revised in a bill which became law on August 15, 1973.

Illegal immigration is a major problem within the Portuguese community. The dimensions of this flow may be guessed by comparing the statistics quoted in this book of residents with those published in government documents, and especially the census statistics. The problems associated with illegal immigration as it applies to the Portuguese have been extensively documented in *Networks of Contact*.[20]

The well established men recommended their relatives and friends for employment at their workplaces, and often the newcomer found that he had a job the day that he stepped from the plane. Usually, the newcomers received jobs at the same level as their recommenders; thus, men with highly remunerative jobs were able to obtain similar jobs for those that they recommended. Those who assisted the new immigrant sometimes inadvertently guided him into a dead-end job. Some jobs, on the other hand, were stepping stones to more highly skilled and hence more highly paid jobs.[21]

During the research for this study, some evidence was found of the purchasing of jobs. One man we interviewed stated:

> I went to a man through whom it was possible to get a job – his wife worked at the Immigration Office and had connections. He said I would get a job but had to pay him about $80. He was a member of a profession but had been disqualified from practising his profession and therefore could not work. He phoned the Employment Office and three days later I had a job at ____ where I still work.[22]

Visitors as a whole were as successful in obtaining satisfactory employment as those men who came through regular channels,[23] but possibly some had "had connections."

The visitor phase was terminated on November 1, 1973, when the Canadian government declared that no more immigrants would be allowed to apply from within the country for landed immigrant status. Warning of the termination of amnesty had been given for several months prior to this date. Future levels of Portuguese immigration flow will depend on the proposed new act and the regulations governing it which are under discussion in 1975.

THE SECOND GENERATION PHASE

Towards the end of the 1960s, Portuguese immigration entered the fourth phase – the stage in which the second generation has reached maturity. These young people have received almost all of their formal education in Canada. Many of the young men have entered skilled trades after graduating from vocational schools or technical colleges. A number of the young women have received secretarial training and are employed as secretaries in commerce and industry; others are bank clerks or hairdressers. Some high school graduates are assisting their parents in the family business, in construction contracting, travel, or the restaurant or grocery business.

Another, much smaller group have received or are in the process of obtaining a university education. Some have entered the teaching profession; others are social workers. Frequently, their parents are counted among the pioneers in their home communities. Most of them have grown up in the large Canadian cities, and usually they are bilingual.

Between 1968 and 1970, in most of the larger communities of Portuguese settlement the movement to the suburbs began. Some of the earliest settlers moved because they wanted their children to be in a "good" high school, where students would be well-behaved, in preference to a core area school. In addition, men in the construction industry who were building suburban houses developed a desire to move into these areas.

The middle class Portuguese immigrants who received their professional or business training in Portugal moved to the suburbs immediately upon arrival, as the only appropriate place for them to live. Often, they have completely dissociated themselves from their working class compatriots; indeed, they possess little knowledge or understanding of them. They are frequently annoyed by the financial success that some of the almost illiterate immigrants have achieved. Some are embarrassed by the image of Portuguese communities in Canadian society generally and therefore will have nothing to do with Portuguese associations or community activities. The few people who hold professional positions and make their money in the Portuguese community but live in the suburbs are often condemned by the core dwellers, in the words, "He thinks he's better than we are."

As members of the younger generation reach maturity in the suburbs, they sometimes remark, "I'm not going to spend all my time working and saving like my parents. There's no way I'll do it." The saving habits of the first generation change to consumerism in the second as the young members of the community marry and set up their own households. Thus, as the second generation reaches maturity, there are signs that the values of the Portuguese are being modified again, as they were between the first and second phases of immigration. As "dollar fever" gave way to saving and investment in real estate, saving is giving way to spending in Canadian consumer patterns.

Potential leaders are currently entering the universities and colleges. Some of these are planning to enter the professions, others anticipate careers in the civil services of Canada or in social work within their own ethnic community. Others, but still a very small minority, are dissociating themselves from other Portuguese immigrants. It is too early yet to forecast the future of the as yet unborn third generation.

NOTES

1. Romão, Isabel "Le processus de migration"; Grace M. Anderson, "The Channel Facilitators Model of Migration: A Model Tested Using Portuguese Blue-Collar Immigrants in Metropolitan Toronto" (Ph. D. thesis, University of Toronto, Sociology, 1971); and *Networks of Contact: The Portuguese and Toronto* (Waterloo: Wilfrid Laurier University Press, 1974). See also Chapter 4 of the present study.

2. M. Custodio Tavares, "Canada: Myth or Reality," *Novo Mundo*, Toronto, Sept. 30, 1971, translated and summarized from Portuguese by the Ethnic Press Analysis Service, Department of the Secretary of State, in Howard Palmer, ed. *Immigration and the Rise of Multiculturalism* (Toronto: Copp-Clark, 1975), pp. 110-111.

3. This attitude is documented in Anderson, *Networks of Contact*.

4. Lisbon, Junta da Emigração, *Instruções* . . . , p. 27.

5. The list included Travellers' Aid, Immigrant Aid, Société Canadien d'établissement rural, the Union Catholique des cultivateurs, the Sisters of Service (an order founded in 1922 to help Catholic immigrants, two of whom met ships at arrival in Halifax, St. John's, Quebec, and Montreal), les soeurs du bon conseil, the Catholic Immigration Centre at Windsor, the Catholic immigration Service in Vancouver, and l'Ecole d'apprentissage in Montreal.

6. This situation is, of course, not new, as reports from Frontier College recount. See E. Bradwin, *The Bunkhouse Man: Life and Labour in the Northern Camps* (Toronto: Univeristy of Toronto Press, 1972).

7. Grace M. Anderson, "The Portuguese and Toronto Study" (unpublished data).

8. *Toronto Star*, March 2, 1970.

9. Marvin H. Lipman, "Relocation and Family Life: A Study of the Social and Psychological Consequences of Urban Renewal" (D.S.W. thesis, University of Toronto, 1968).

10. See Daniel Kubat and David Thorton, *A Statistical Profile of Canadian Society* (Toronto: McGraw-Hill Ryerson, 1974), p. 88, for statistics and discussion of home ownership in Canada.

11. Romão, "Le Processus de migration," p. 162.

12. Anderson, *Networks of Contact*, p. 135.

13. *Toronto Star*, May 25, 1968.

14. Raymond Breton and Howard Roseborough, "Ethnic Differences in Status," in Bernard Blishen et al. (ed.), *Canadian Society: Sociological Perspectives*, 3rd ed. (Toronto: MacMillan, 1968), pp. 683-701.

15. *The Immigration Program* (Green Paper on Immigration, Vol. 2 (Ottawa: Manpower & Immigration, 1974), pp. 30-31.

16. *Ibid.*, p. 31.

17. *Ibid.*, p. 34.

18. *Ibid.*, p. 35.

19. *Ibid.*, p. 36.

20. Anderson, *Networks of Contact*, especially Chapter VII.

51

21. *Ibid.*, Chapter VI, "Channels and Gatekeepers Leading to the Present Job."
22. See also, "Senior Immigration Official Admits Taking Bribes from Greeks," *Toronto Star*, July 9, 1974.
23. Anderson, *Networks of Contact*, pp. 28-29.

PART TWO:

Settlements in Canada

Introduction

In this part of our study, we examine reasons why certain areas of the country attracted large numbers of Portuguese immigrants while other areas that seemed equally suitable did not. Arrival time, economic opportunity and chance all played a part in the eventual location of the first wave of immigrants after 1952. Portuguese settlements frequently grew up around these early arrivals as they assisted the newcomers with housing and employment.[1]

In searching for evolving leadership among the Portuguese in Canada we have tended to concentrate on the "success stories" of prominent persons within the community and of early settlers. We have visited many entrepreneurs within this ethnic group; consequently, a Horatio Alger motif[2] tends to run through this section. It should, however, be remembered that for many the apparently easy pathway to success has been one of unremitting toil.[3]

It should also be recognized that we tend to overlook or forget the unsuccessful immigrants to Canada. There are stories in every community of men having nervous breakdowns and returning to their homeland. For many, the insecurity of the job market and the isolation of their daily life was a severe strain. Some left wives and children and a large number of relatives in order to begin a new life in a strange land. They toiled at heavy labour in unfamiliar jobs; initially, many were given employment in remote areas of the country, far from anyone who could communicate with them in their own language. It took tremendous will and endurance to withstand the loneliness and hardship of those early years, and a substantial number of immigrants eventually abandoned their venture and returned to Portugal. Others became ill or injured and were forced to return to the homeland. The construction industry is full of such stories. Others suffered injuries on farms or in industry, often because of their unfamiliarity with the machinery they were handling. Some men returned for personal – usually family – reasons. A few decided that the life of constant labour was not worthwhile.

Immigrants from mainland Portugal discussed returning to the "old country" much more frequently than the families from the Azores. The latter say, "We are not going back, there is nothing for us to do there – no work. We will stay in Canada." They therefore invest their money in Canada, whereas many from the mainland send money back to be invested in Portugal. The vast majority of those interviewed in 1969 never had intended to remain in Canada when they came initially. They hoped to make enough money to return home and live in comfort, or to buy property in the homeland.[4] The amazing fact is that relatively large numbers remained to make Canada their home.[5]

According to one study less than one per cent of the original migrants returned from Canada to Portugal.[6] Many did extremely well for themselves, despite their lack of advanced formal education. Some of the reasons for these successes and the failures of others will emerge in the pages that follow.

THE ETHNIC GROUP LOCATES ITSELF

The original Portuguese settlers of 1953 and 1954 were scattered far and wide across the farmlands of the nation and were posted to isolated northern regions as section hands on the railways. By 1974, large agglomerations of Portuguese immigrants existed in the downtown cores of Canada's metropolises, in selected smaller cities and towns, and in some rural areas. The majority of the more prosperous and the most highly acculturated have followed the trend of other Canadians in moving to the suburbs of major urban centres. Tables 10 and 11 indicate the distribution of Portuguese immigrants across Canada in 1971.[7]

By tracing the movements of the pioneers in each major area of concentration, we have been able to identify nine factors that have influenced settlement patterns. These are briefly discussed below:

Initial Direction by Government or Private Enterprise: As a condition of entry to Canada, unskilled Portuguese workers or farm hands initially were required to accept employment wherever they were directed. In many cases, the new arrivals were recruited through government initiative to work on farms selected by the Department of Immigration for a period of not less than one year. Other immigrants were brought in under contract with private railway companies. They were expected to work wherever they were posted until they had fulfilled the contract and had repaid to the company the cost of their passage and other expenses incurred on their behalf.[8] Usually these jobs were regarded by the immigrants solely as a passport to residence in North America, and were vacated as soon as possible for more remunerative employment in the cities. While large urban centres such as Toronto, Vancouver, and Montreal have acted as a magnet to draw immigrants from the surrounding countryside, often a small residue of workers is still employed in the original area of settlement.

56

TABLE 10
DISTRIBUTION OF PERSONS OF PORTUGUESE ORIGIN
IN CANADA BY PROVINCE, 1971

Ontario	75,197
Quebec	18,799
British Columbia	9,952
Manitoba	4,423
All other provinces	2,000

Source: Luis Augusto Martins, "Emigracão no Canadá," *Boletim,* Sociedade
Geografia de Lisboa, série 89a, Nos. 7-9, Julho-Setembro, 1971, p.
221.

TABLE 11
DISTRIBUTION OF PORTUGUESE IN CANADA BY
CITIES OF MAJOR CONCENTRATION, 1971

Toronto, Ontario	47,500
Montreal, Quebec	17,000
Vancouver, B.C.	7,000
Brampton, Ontario	4,500
Oakville, Ontario	4,000
Galt, Ontario	4,000
Ottawa, Ontario	4,000
Winnipeg, Manitoba	3,500
Hamilton, Ontario	2,500
Kingston, Ontario	2,000
London, Ontario	1,500
Kitchener, Ontario	1,500
Leamington, Ontario	1,000
Windsor, Ontario	1,000
Quebec, Quebec	1,000
Oliver, B.C.	1,000
Kitimat, B.C.	1,000
Thompson, Manitoba	800

Source: Martins, "Emigraçao no Canada," p. 221.

Statistics from the 1971 Canadian census on location of Portuguese immigrants in
specific cities and towns were not released for this study.

57

Crucial "Gatekeepers": Immigrants who have arrived in advance of the main stream of immigrants and can speak both their own language and that of the new country can act as gatekeepers to jobs. The first immigrants make contact with these persons, who direct them to jobs and locations where they themselves have contacts, so that a channelling to particular employment and residential areas occurs.[9] Two such individuals who have played outstanding roles in the settlement of the Portuguese are Manuel Cabral in southern Ontario and Captain Quintal in the Kitimat and Greater Vancouver areas.

Economic Development in the New Country: Economic opportunity often has an important bearing on the location of immigrants after initial work contracts have expired. If many well-paid jobs open up for unskilled and semi-skilled labour at the time when immigrants are ready to relocate, and there are no strongly organized unions to keep them out, certain areas may become foci for the settlement of such groups.[10] An example in the present study is Kitimat.

The Proximate City: Cities adjacent to or in the vicinity of initial employment areas have influenced settlement patterns. Sometimes immigrants became familiar with a particular town because they went there from a farm or from railway section work to do their banking. This was the case, for example, with Winnipeg and Port Credit. The banks assumed great importance for new immigrants because they served as agents for sending money to relatives in the homeland.

Chance Meetings: On the evidence of individuals we interviewed, it appears that chance meetings with compatriots or other persons, particularly at transportation terminals or on planes and trains, have directed new immigrants to job opportunities in certain areas.

Socially Organized Pressure: Sometimes there is social pressure for men to move from isolated northern outposts to areas where they can bring their families and also attend church regularly. This occurred with the Portuguese in the northwestern and northern areas of Canada.

Congruence of Employment with Former Occupation:[11] The nature of the immigrant's previous occupation in the homeland sometimes influenced his choice of job and thereby his selection of an area in which to settle. In this respect, the physical requirements of the job were more significant than the actual skills involved. For example, those who had been farmers in Portugal tended to return to farming or to enter the construction industry, and those who had been store clerks became caretakers or took other jobs involving small physical effort.[12]

Congruence of Climatic Conditions: Although the semi-tropical climates of Portugal, the Azores Islands, and Madeira are not duplicated anywhere in Canada, certain areas have attracted specific immigrant groups because of the climate – notably, Victoria and the Okanagan Valley, especially around Oliver and Osooyos, in British Columbia, and the Leamington and Wheatley district of southwestern Ontario.

Eastward Trend of Relocation: Many new immigrants appreciated the financial advantage of moving to southern Ontario from western towns and cities when they were ready to bring their family from Portugal to join them. The difference in travel costs between eastern and western destinations was and still is substantial, and it was no small consideration to the immigrant who was struggling to establish himself.

While one of the preceding factors may have predominated in influencing Portuguese settlement of a particular city or region, usually several of them combined to attract a nucleus of immigrants to a particular locale.

While in the early days relocation depended on the initiative of the men, nevertheless the role of the women back in the homeland should not be overlooked. Often they provided a stable information network for the highly mobile men abroad by relaying hometown news to their husbands or sons. In addition, many of the mothers of single girls in the village had good reasons for keeping in touch with the mothers of single men overseas and providing them with job information.

Martins has indicated that in 1971 about 60% of the Portuguese immigrants came to Canada from the Azores Islands and only one per cent came from Madeira. The majority of the remainder came from mainland Portugal.[13] In our interviews, we found that the men from the mainland were more frequently found in northern locations and in isolated regions of the country, while those from the Azores were likely to settle with their families in large urban centres. The most logical explanation for this pattern is that the Mainlanders, who generally come from a higher socio-economic background, are more ambitious to obtain the highest possible remuneration, regardless of the sacrifices involved. We also observed that, in order to accumulate the capital to start a small business or purchase a farm, many men chose to work in isolated areas in jobs involving much physical effort, because the pay was high. Men worked in Kitimat, B. C., or Thompson, Manitoba, or Goose Bay, Labrador, in order to be able to relocate eventually in Vancouver, Winnipeg, Toronto, or Montreal.

The trends begun by the decisions of a few are followed by many. The southward, cityward migrations of the early years assumed major proportions in the 1960s. By the middle of that decade, the immigrants were locating in the large urban centres immediately upon arrival from the homeland. They joined relatives and friends in established communities without experiencing, for the most part, the isolation and hardships of the early settlers. As one pioneer expressed it, by comparison to his own initial struggles, "They have it easy now."

NOTES

1. To discover the pattern behind migration activity, we visited every community in which 2,000 or more Portuguese immigrants were known to be living. In each area, we attempted to make contact with six of the earliest settlers. Their geographical mobility and their job histories were gathered in English, French, Portuguese, or occasionally Spanish. Many associational leaders were interviewed, as well as priests of Portuguese congregations, real estate agents, teachers of schools in ethnic areas, Portuguese university students, editors of ethnic newspapers, Portuguese social workers, and various community leaders. The project took three years to complete (1972 to 1974).

2. R. Richard Wohl, "The 'Rags to Riches Story,' An Episode of Secular Idealism." Ed. by Reinhard Bendix and S. M. Lipset, eds., *Class, Status and Power: Social Stratification in Comparative Perspective*, second edition (New York: The Free Press, 1966).

3. See Anderson, *Networks of Contact*, pp. 135, 179.

4. "Portuguese Emigration in 1957," *Industry and Labour*, Vol. 20 (Geneva, Nov. 15, 1958), calculated from statistics on pp. 382 and 383.

5. For a comparison with another ethnic group, see Anthony Richmond, "The Thousand Dollar Cure: A Study of Return Migration from Canada to Britain" (Toronto: York University, 1967, mimeo). Some Portuguese immigrants moved back to the homeland and then returned to Canada.

6. See Anderson, *Networks of Contact*, especially pp. 181-184 for a commentary on the Portuguese immigrants who have returned or who still remain undecided about returning.

7. See *International Migration Review,* Portugal and North American Issue, 1977.

8. *Ibid.*, gives details of contract.

9. See Anderson, "The Channel Facilitators Model of Migration."

10. One member of a trade union in a large Canadian city remarked to one of the authors, "We don't have any 'Portuguese' in our union – we keep it for people like us!" This type of behaviour is, of course, illegal and would be denied in official circles. The particular local for which this opinion was expressed is probably the exception. The majority of executives of trade unions known to the authors express their desire to welcome any qualified person to their ranks, regardless of ethnic background.

11. See congruence and lifestyle regarding the Norwegians and New York, in William Michelson, *Man and His Urban Environment* (Addison-Wesley, 1970), p. 16.

12. See also similar trends documented in Anderson, *Networks of Contact*, pp. 85-119.

13. Martins, "Emigracão no Canadá," p. 221.

FOUR

Settlements in Eastern and Central Canada

ATLANTIC PROVINCES

Portuguese immigrants to Canada have shown slight interest in settling in the Atlantic provinces. The little settlement that has taken place has tended to cluster in places where the availability of jobs and the presence of other Portuguese makes adaptation easier, as in St. John's and Labrador City, Newfoundland, and Halifax, Nova Scotia. In the decade 1960-1970, of the Atlantic provinces Nova Scotia received almost 300 Portuguese immigrants, Newfoundland 152, and New Brunswick 33.[1]

Nova Scotia received some Portuguese immigration in the nineteenth and twentieth centuries by way of the fish and lumber trade to Portugal, the Azores and Brazil.[2] Replacements for Nova Scotian seamen who fell ill in foreign ports included Portuguese seamen who later married and settled in Nova Scotia. In Liverpool, N. S., there were several generations of families bearing the names of Fernandes and Da Silva in the early twentieth century, although the names are not to be found at present. In Shelburne, N. S., several families have names spelled De Mings and Demings, anglicised forms of the name of the first settler at Shelburne, a sailor named Anthony De Mings (Domingos?).[3]

Up to World War II there does not appear to have been any Portuguese settlement in Halifax. The Honorary Consul of Portugal in Halifax informed us in 1974: "When I was a student here just after the Second World War, I am reasonably certain that I was the only person in Halifax of Portuguese descent." By 1955 there was a small number of Portuguese settlers, initially attracted, it appears, by a local demand for fishermen.[4] In Halifax, the Portuguese community is connected mainly with fishing and shipping interests.

In 1973, the Portuguese community in St. John's, Newfoundland, comprised about forty men, women, and children. Many of them arrived after 1962 through sponsorship by relatives. Not all of the Portuguese who came to St. John's remained there. For example, in 1966 a local fishing company hired seventeen Portuguese under contract, but in 1973 only five remained. The others left to find work in Ontario and British Columbia. In 1973, none of the Portuguese in St. John's was self-employed. Employment was quite various. In 1973, it presented the following profile:

Shipping agency and suppliers 4
Fishing industry 5
Mechanics and electricians 6
Restaurants and bars 3

Few Portuguese women were employed.

In 1974, there was a Portuguese community in Labrador City of approximately 80, of whom the majority, as in St. John's, came from the continent. About 10% were from the Azores. In this remote northern community, the main attraction is the employment offered by a local iron ore company; hence, most of the residents are single men. About 10 Portuguese married couples live in Labrador City. Almost half the Portuguese in the community, particularly the older people, intend to retire to Portugal. Younger people with children think of moving to one of the larger Canadian cities where there are concentrations of Portuguese and diverse employment opportunities.

The first Portuguese settler to arrive in Labrador City came in 1957. He now has his own business. Others fill a variety of jobs, ranging from foreman to janitor. As is often the case for Portuguese immigrants to Canada, the men have different occupations from those they had in Portugal.

In both St. John's and Labrador City, because of the smallness of the community, there are no grocery stores specializing in Portuguese foods. Neither St. John's nor Labrador City has a large enough Portuguese-speaking population to establish a Portuguese social club; but in Labrador City, on special occasions during the year, cases of sardines are flown in from Montreal, wine and other food is brought, and a community picnic, barbecue, or party is held.

PROVINCE OF QUEBEC

The Portuguese community in Quebec has grown steadily since 1953, as the men who initially came to Canada to take agricultural work have moved into urban centres. By 1974, there are about 43,000 Portuguese residents in the province. The major communities appear on p. 63. Each of these communities has grown substantially since 1960, largely as a result of sponsored immigration.

The first nucleus of the Montreal community was de Bullion Street. By 1974, it had expanded to encompass an area roughly bounded by Park Avenue, Mount Royal, Saint Denis, and Sherbrooke Street. There is currently a clear movement of Portuguese to the north of Montreal. We would not suggest that the area is exclusively inhabited by Portuguese: the area in which they are concentrated has long been a reception area for

TABLE 12
ESTIMATED POPULATIONS OF QUEBEC CENTES: 1974

Montreal	35,000
Quebec	2,000
Hull	3,000
Sainte Thérèse	2,000
Schefferville	1,000
Trois Rivières	1,000
Sept–Iles	500
Sherbrooke	500

Source: Information provided by community leaders.

immigrants. Thus, they live side by side with Greeks, Spaniards, Latin Americans, and other nationalities, as well as native French Canadians.

The development of the Portuguese community in Montreal was linked to employment opportunities. One of the first Portuguese-speaking arrivals came to the city from Venezuela, a country which has long attracted Portuguese immigrants. He had experience in the construction industry and soon organized a contracting company that subsequently provided work for many new arrivals from Portugal. Another early business was a general grocery on Saint Dominique which gradually was extended to neighbouring houses to provide *comidas* (food) and *dormidas* (sleeping accommodation) to recent immigrants. The owner, an Azorean, was able to advise new arrivals about job opportunities.

From 1955, Portuguese settlers began to arrive in Montreal without prior commitments to agricultural contracts. Many had a higher educational level than their predecessors and were more proficient in the official languages, especially French. Indeed, one of the reasons why some Portuguese have been attracted to Quebec is that they can already speak French, through their formal education in Portugal or through working temporarily in French-speaking Europe.

By 1960 and up to 1970, there was a significant growth in the number of small Portuguese businesses in Montreal: groceries, bakeries, fish shops, various variety and record stores, furniture and repair shops, travel agencies and restaurants. A number of families had members working in labouring, furniture-making, mining, and other jobs. There was also an inflow of professional people, including teachers in the French-language school system.

63

TABLE 13

IMMIGRANTS BY LAST PERMANENT RESIDENCE IN PORTUGAL,
QUEBÉC, 1948–1971

Year	Number	Year	Number
1948	19	1960	1,338
1949	23	1961	629
1950	28	1962	734
1951	44	1963	988
1952	92	1964	1,104
1953	231	1965	1,114
1954	639	1966	1,516
1955	464	1967	1,587
1956	656	1968	1,229
1957	1,687	1969	1,175
1958	512	1970	1,230
1959	1,035	1971	1,478
	Total 1948–1971		19,552

Source: *The Position of French Language in Québec: Vol. 3, The Language Groups.* Report of the Commission of Inquiry on the Position of the French Language and on Language Rights in Québec. Québec City, Government of Québec, December 1972, pp. 477 and 478. These three volumes are popularly known as *The Gendron Report.*

The Portuguese origins of the community in Montreal are diverse, but there is a higher proportion of continentals than in Toronto. In 1974, about 60% came from the Azores, 38% from the continent, 1% from Madeira, and 1% from other regions. It was not possible to carry out an extensive first-hand study in Montreal, but we were fortunate to have access to a study completed in 1972. A Canadian Portuguese committee, in 1968, had undertaken a study of the major problems of Portuguese persons in Montreal and concluded that the most pressing matters revolved around employment: "to find stable, well-remunerated work, at the level of their aspirations and of their competence."[5] Romão subsequently conducted a study of integration "in the world of work and of acculturation,"[6] based on a sample of 30 Portuguese immigrant men in the city of Montreal. She considered various indicators of acculturation, including languages spoken, newspapers and magazines read, affiliation with ethnic associations, sports and leisure activities, and church attendance. The situation is complicated in Montreal by the option of acculturation to French or English linguistic groups. By and large, the majority chose the latter.

The Gendron Report indicates that "the proportion of Montréal's population of other origins whose mother tongue is neither English nor French is the highest in Canada, 65.7% . . . . Montréal's percentage of foreign born residents is the highest in Canada, 56.2%."[7]

The Didier and Bordeleau study indicate that the reason 72% of Portuguese in the sample gave for selecting English-language schools was "a person who knows English can work anywhere in North America."[8] Many respondents in our study also made this point. The Brazeau-Carlos study indicated that 42.2% of Quebeckers of other origins learn French at work and 46.9% learn English. Immigrants are willingly multilingual.[9] Since the large majority of adult Portuguese immigrants were born in Portugal, Portuguese is the mother tongue of nearly all the adults in this community, as it is in other Portuguese settlements across Canada.

Romão's sample was predominantly urban in background. More than half had lived in Lisbon prior to coming to Canada. They included nine administrators, managers, or professional men; four office workers and salesmen; twelve highly skilled workers; four semi-skilled workers, and one unskilled man.[10] More than half the sample had been highly skilled specialists in their own country before coming to Montreal. Frequently, the men had received their early training in the technical or professional schools in mainland Portugal, or had attended academic or commercial high schools. We have no way of knowing how representative this sample is of the wider community in Montreal.

Only two persons in the sample had major misgivings about leaving Portugal to live in Montreal, but more than half missed the Portuguese way of life. One man commented, "It seems to me that there was more joy there,"[11] and he appeared to express the views of many. Others missed the family, the climate, the beaches, the sea, and football (soccer). Most of the sample in Montreal and also in other areas of Canada were more or less satisfied with life in this country, but it was the material aspects of Canadian life that pleased them most.

Some immigrants have also moved to large construction sites in the province. For example,

> the James Bay hydro project was touted by Premier Robert Bourassa for the jobs it would give to the people of Quebec, where unemployment is chronically high. But many Quebeckers – like many Maritimers, Ontarians and Western Canadians – were unwilling to forsake urban comforts for work so far in the bush, even at high pay. Although the jobs were supposed to be reserved for residents of Quebec, it was found necessary to recruit Portuguese and Italian laborers from Toronto and elsewhere to complete the work crews.[12]

65

TABLE 14
KNOWLEDGE OF OFFICIAL LANGUAGES BY PORTUGUESE
IMMIGRANTS IN MONTREAL, 1972

Language		Speaking	Writing	Reading
French	Little and none	4	9	4
	Sufficient and fair	18	18	17
	Good and very good	8	3	9
	Total	30	30	30
English	Little and none	7	8	6
	Sufficient and fair	11	14	12
	Good and very good	12	8	12
	Total	30	30	30

Source: Adapted from Isabel Romão, "Le processus de migration, la mobilité professionelle, la mobilité sociale et l'acculturation chez les ressortissants d'origine portugaise à Montréal," Université de Montréal, Sept. 1972, p. 170.

Studies of Portuguese immigrants in Montreal are currently being undertaken by Roskies at the University of Montreal and by Fernández and Pereira da Rosa at McGill University.[13]

PROVINCE OF ONTARIO

Statistics issued by both Canadian and Portuguese sources indicate that about 65% or 70% of Portuguese immigrants to Canada live in Ontario. By far the largest number of these immigrants is concentrated in Metropolitan Toronto. The Portuguese government has traditionally recognized Montreal as its official centre in this country: the major Portuguese trade mission is established there, as is the senior Portuguese consulate. Among Portuguese Canadians, however, Toronto is considered the hub of activity for commerce, for the importing business and for many kinds of cultural events.

In Ontario, the major centres of Portuguese settlement are Kingston and Ottawa in the east; cities throughout the Golden Horseshoe from Oshawa to Hamilton; cities in the Golden Triangle, centring around Galt-Cambridge; and cities and towns in western Ontario such as London, Windsor, Strathroy, Leamington, and Wheatley. In the urban areas, the men are employed in construction trades and building services (frequently janitorial positions) and in industry. Others work in market gardening or landscaping in cities and towns or in rural areas. A few men are employed in the Lake Erie fishing trade, and some still work on farms or are thinly scattered in relatively isolated locations. Many of the women work in textile mills or garment factories, in hospitals, or in private homes as cleaners or "daily helps." Entrepreneurs of many kinds are found, including importers, storekeepers, construction contractors, and janitorial service agents. Travel agencies abound in the largest centres, and some cities have a number of Portuguese restaurants.

Now a new generation is coming to maturity. Many of the young people have had much greater educational opportunities than their parents. Consequently, some are entering the professions, many are engaged in providing services for their communities, as well as establishing a link between the Portuguese-speaking community and the wider Canadian society. Many Portuguese Canadians now settled in other parts of Canada have at one time lived and worked in an Ontario community. Conversely, a large proportion of those now living in Ontario obtained their start in other provinces.

Ottawa: By the mid-1950s there were about 500 Portuguese living in the Ottawa-Hull region. By 1974 there were approximately 3,000 Portuguese Canadians in Hull and a further 2,000 in Ottawa. The main concentration of homes on the Ottawa side of the river was in the Sandy Hill area and the Lower Town; in Hull most lived in the centre. There is also a small group of Portuguese families in Vanier. Hull Portuguese are mainly Azoreans (90% in one recent estimate) whereas in Ottawa there are far more from continental Portugal. In Hull there is a strong tendency to enter the social milieu of French-speaking Canadians while in Ottawa English seems to predominate.

Portuguese in the Ottawa-Hull region had first been attracted by the variety of service positions available, particularly janitorial work in government buildings. As the community increased in size a number of shops opened to serve the needs of the Portuguese: bakeries, groceries and fish shops. One of the wealthiest individuals in Ottawa first became prosperous by organizing the collection of bait worms. An unpublished 1974 study (Kemp and Morriset) showed that in Hull 54% of working Portuguese men were employed in English-speaking concerns, 27% in French and 12% in Italian. By contrast, 71% of the women worked in French-speaking enterprises.

The first community activities in Ottawa derived from the church until in the early 1960s the Lusitania Portuguese Club was founded on Bronson Avenue. This served as a social club for the Ottawa-Hull area until a new Portuguese community centre with adjoining church was established in Hull on December 15, 1974.

Kingston: In 1973, approximately 3,000 Portuguese persons lived in the city of Kingston. About 85% of these were from the Azores Islands and the

67

remainder from the mainland. The community is a thriving one. The majority are manual workers, and about half of the men work in the construction industry. Many joke about the fact that they are more proficient in Italian than in English because of the close association with Italians in their work. Other men and women work in hospitals in the housekeeping staff section. In one large hospital, more than 20% of the nonmedical staff are of Portuguese background. Others are employed as janitors, particularly in the schools. In Kingston, as in other areas of Canada, janitorial work has become an occupational specialization.

There are about 20 independent businessmen in the community, most of them in some area of the construction industry. There are two general building contractors and several masons, plasterers, bricklayers, and cement finishers. Real estate salesmen do a thriving trade, in large measure serving their fellow countrymen. One was salesman of the month for a major agency for every month between January and June, 1972.[14] One highly successful man owns a large restaurant and a motel. Several own grocery stores specializing in imported foods from the homeland. A baker distributes *pão português* (Portuguese bread). Very few Portuguese professionals live in this community. There are, however, two medical doctors and a librarian, who is also well known as a musician and television performer. The wives of immigrants usually work in the hospitals or in private homes as cleaners. Those married to businessmen may assist with the office work. Storekeepers' spouses normally help in the store.

The first Portuguese settlers in Kingston were three single men who arrived together from Montreal. Eventually they left the city, and their current whereabouts are not known. The first family arrived in 1955, and their home subsequently became the gathering place for all the single Portuguese men of the city. The family had worked for nearly 15 months on a farm near Halifax, but on the urging of relatives they decided to move to Kingston. Since they had several children, the higher wages they could earn in the city's construction industry were a strong attraction. Once they became established in Kingston, many of the single men returned to the homeland to marry and bring their brides back to Canada. Others married by proxy the fiancées they had left behind, and these women subsequently joined their husbands in Canada.

A large wave of immigrants arrived in Kingston in 1957. By 1962, there were about 1,500 Portuguese persons in the city. Many of the original settlers had brought over their relatives, and many encouraged former neighbours to join them in Canada through independent application. One of the early arrivals, who is a professional man, was directed by an immigration consultant in the mainland to come to Kingston. Through the dynamism and initiative of one or two families, the city has a highly organized Portuguese community.

In mid-1972, one local Portuguese man was transferred from Kingston to Peterborough by the company for which he works. As he was the only person of that ethnic origin in the city, he felt isolated and began to encourage others to join him. And so the process of relocation and growth has commenced in yet another area.

SOUTHERN ONTARIO

The Golden Horseshoe

Toronto: The largest settlement of Portuguese immigrants in Canada is located in Metropolitan Toronto. It numbers 92,000.[15] This cosmopolitan city was one of the earliest areas of residence during the immigration period following World War II. The community dates its official inception from June, 1953. Some immigrants came directly to Toronto from Portugal, but the majority who arrived in the city before 1957 were from rural farming areas of Canada or from isolated regions where they were employed in railroad gangs or as maintenance workers.

The immigrants were drawn to the centre of the metropolis, where older housing was available at reasonable prices. Rumours of highly paid jobs spread rapidly to clusters of Portuguese immigrants scattered throughout the country. As the word spread, the men dropped their jobs and set off for the "big city." It was a newer version of the gold rush, but this time the trend was southward.

Many of the immigrants did, in fact, find more highly paid jobs in Toronto, but they also found a higher cost of living. Being resourceful, they sought ways to pare the cost of living to a minimum. In the early days, for example, some of them would rent a bed in a rooming house for eight hours, so that the same bed might be used three times in twenty-four hours. After a few months of hard saving, small groups of men were able to pool their resources and make a small down payment (often $500) on a house in the Alexandra Park or Kensington Market area of Toronto. Frequently relatives lent money towards the down payment and were promised an inexpensive bed in the new home. The new owner also provided rooms for other relatives, friends, and acquaintances.

Reuniting of couples often awaited the purchase of a home. Ferguson's research shows an average time lapse of 3.6 years between the arrival in Canada of the husband and the wife.[16] Some men, by extreme thrift, acquired an interest in a grocery, vegetable, or fish store on Augusta Avenue in the Kensington Market district. Previously, most of their food had been purchased in Italian stores. Now the immigrants were able to get their accustomed food through people speaking their own language.

The men worked hard to upgrade and renovate their recently acquired houses. In the early 1960s, however, the Alexandra Park district was slated for demolition and urban renewal. The area had had a long history of immigrant reception: Jewish people, Ukrainians, Poles, Italians, and Hungarians arrived in a series of migrations; and between 1953 and the mid-1960s, the Portuguese poured into the district and the adjacent Kensington Market area. When the work of demolition on Alexandra Park

TABLE 15
POPULATION OF METROPOLITAN TORONTO BY
MOTHER TONGUE, 1971

Total Population	2,086,020
English	1,471,485
Italian	207,745
German	52,350
Greek	43,880
Portuguese	39,560
French	37,250
Ukrainian	31,424
Polish	28,985
Chinese	21,520
Dutch	9,405
Other	142,410

Source: Statistics Canada, Advance Bulletin, 1971 Census of Canada.

TABLE 16
BIRTHPLACE OF HOUSEHOLDERS BY BOROUGH OF RESIDENCE,
METROPOLITAN TORONTO

	Canada	Portugal
City	34	78
York	6	6
East York	6	–
Etobicoke	15	4
Scarborough	14	4
North York	25	12
Total	100	100
Per Cent of all Householders	49.6	0.7

Source: Anthony Richmond, *Ethnic Segregation in Metropolitan Toronto, February 1972, p. 306.*

finally commenced, the residents were forced to seek accommodation elsewhere. Marvin Lipman's study shows that this process induced a higher degree of overcrowding than previously existed among the Portuguese families in the adjacent areas.[17] Relatives and friends tried to accommodate the displaced in their own homes. This is in contrast to native-born Canadian residents, who frequently moved to the suburbs over five miles away: "82% of the Portuguese group moved within a mile and fully 92% within a two mile radius .... Fully two-thirds of the fifteen Portuguese tenants [in Lipman's sample] before relocation became owners afterwards."[18]

> The continuing overcrowding of the Portuguese group is apparently explained by the fact that many of this group moved from the second floor of someone else's house to the main floor of their own home, and then rented the second floor to someone else.[19]

Edith Ferguson comments on the importance of home ownership:

> Owning a home is tremendously important to the rural immigrant as, indeed, it is to a rural Canadian who migrates to the city. In the villages of Italy and Portugal each family had its own home, even though it may have been small, poorly furnished and overcrowded. New immigrants find themselves here with no possessions, nothing but their hands. They bend every effort toward saving for a home, which gives them security, some roots and some status in the community. *Without it, they are nobodies.*[20]

Ferguson also found in research done from 1962 to 1964 that the average length of formal education for Portuguese immigrants in Toronto was 3.7 years for men and 2.8 years for women. Many of the immigrants came from the Azores Islands where education beyond Grade 4 level was not usually available at the time when the immigrants in her sample were of school age.[21] Several years later, Anderson's study of working class Portuguese men did not shown much elevation in the educational level of a sample of over 200 working class males.[22] Lipman's study showed that in 1968 the average size of a Portuguese extended family was 5.4 persons per household.[23]

Data from the period 1962-1964 show a diversity of blue collar occupations among Toronto Portuguese similar to that found among Portuguese in other large urban centres across the country (see Table 17). Half of the men in the sample were farmers before emigration (Table 18). The large majority of the immigrants are manual workers. A few Portuguese professionals have come to Toronto, but these are exceptions:

> There are three Portuguese doctors, two Portuguese lawyers, and a sprinkling of other professional people. And there are importers, real estate agents and other businessmen whose lives brim over with success.[24]

71

TABLE 17
PRESENT OCCUPATON OF PORTUGUESE MEN (N = 100)

Construction		23
Labourer	16	
Carpenter	5	
Roofer	2	
General labour		11
Factory work		12
Restaurant and hotel work		12
Cook and cook's helper	6	
Kitchen help	4	
Waiter	1	
Bartender	1	
Cleaner		7
Railway labourer		6
Gardener		3
Garage helper		2
Other		10
Unemployed		8
Not available		6

Note: Men working at other occupations include a precision tool grinder, a welder, a repairman, a driver, an animal tender, a boat painter, a house painter, a fisherman, a worker on a mushroom farm, and a worm picker.

Source: Edith Ferguson, *Newcomers in Transition* (Toronto: International Institute of Metropolitan Toronto, 1964), pp. 45-46.

TABLE 18
FORMER OCCUPATIONS OF PORTUGUESE MEN (N = 100)

Farming		50
Construction		13
Carpenter	6	
Electrician	5	
Stonemason	1	
Plasterer	1	
Baker		4
Driver		4
Auto mechanic		2
Bookkeeper		2
Cook		2
Other		16
Not available		7

Note: Former other occupations were dental technician, donkey trucker, postal clerk, tool and die maker, waiter, railway labourer, restaurant owner, owner of dry goods shop, blacksmith, electronic technician, factory workers, fisherman, house painter, boat painter, basket weaver, and cabinet maker.

Source: Ferguson, *Newcomers in Transition* , p. 46.

TABLE 19

EMPLOYMENT VISAS ISSUED, BY DURATION OF
VISAS AND PRINCIPAL COUNTRY OF
ORIGIN (PORTUGAL), 1973

1–3 months	194
4–6 months	267
7–9 months	172
10–12 months	990
Total	1,623

Source: *Immigration and Population Statistics* (Green Paper on Immigration, Vol. 3) Ottawa: Manpower and Immigration, 1974, p. 75.

Kensington Market is considered to be the heart of the Portuguese district, even though many successful immigrants have now moved to the suburbs. The area is still the commercial centre of the community. The following description gives a vivid picture of its character:

> The Portuguese, like the equally charming Newfoundlanders, like to paint their houses bright colors, scarlet being the favorite. They will even occasionally paint the mortar between the bricks white.
>
> They often grow cabbages and other vegetables in their front yards unless the yard contains a shrine to Our Lady of Fatima, in which case flowers are preferred.
>
> They are more old-style religious than most Canadians. One of the hottest items in the market drygoods stores recently has been a color print of The Last Supper with a frame that doubles as a mirror ($4.99).[25]

The Toronto community makes available a wide range of goods and services to its Portuguese residents in their own language.

The Portuguese in Toronto have been the subject of several detailed studies,[26] and they will not be discussed at great length here. Suffice it to

73

say that they comprise the most diversified community of Portuguese-speaking people in Canada. They come from backgrounds as varied as the Azores Islands, Madeira, the former Portuguese territory of Goa in India, and Macao, and a few immigrants are from the Cape Verde Islands off the African coast. Many are from continental Portugal, from towns and villages in the north of the country, from Lisbon and its surrounding area, from the Alentejo and from the far south, the Algarve. The immigrants are from a variety of racial backgrounds, predominantly white, with some Asians and a very small proportion of "black Portuguese." Although so different in background they view themselves as united by their language and a sense of a Portuguese tradition, although simultaneously they may question the Portuguese ties of other subgroups. There is also a settlement of Brazilians in the city which forms a distinctive national group although they are Portuguese-speaking. In 1975 there were almost one thousand Brazilians living in Toronto and about 750 elsewhere in Canada.

Although outsiders often refer to the Portuguese community in Toronto as an entity, it is really a conglomerate of many smaller communities linked by *Portuguesismo*. They draw together on occasions of special celebration such as Portuguese feast days. Afterwards, they go their separate ways until the next public occasion.

Oshawa: The first Portuguese immigrant to Oshawa came from a small town north of Lisbon. He was sent by the Immigration Department on a contract to work as a gardener. In Portugal, he[27] had been considering emigration for some time. When he heard that immigrants could come to Canada, he tried to apply in 1954 but was told that they were only taking people from the Azores. If he wanted to move to these islands and apply, he could do so and would probably be accepted. He then went to see a lawyer, a member of the Portuguese legislature, who spoke to the Minister of the Interior. He received a call shortly thereafter instructing him to begin immigration proceedings by filling out the necessary forms.

He arrived by ship in Halifax on May 8, 1955, and left by train for Montreal. There, farmers were picking up immigrants as they arrived on the boat trains. He was taken to a farm in the Ottawa Valley and began working to fulfill his employment contract. One day he decided to go into the city to find other work; but when he arrived at the local railway station, he accidentally caught a train going to Toronto. There he happened to meet other Portuguese immigrants and great was his delight at finding someone who could speak his own language. These men told him that they were headed for jobs in North Bay and invited him to join them. He did so, but at the end of the summer, the work ran out and he returned to Toronto. He contacted the Immigration Department to find winter employment, and they gave him a choice of working in Kitimat, B. C., or in Oshawa. He chose the latter and was given a job as a gardener.

74

For several years he worked in the city. Shortly after obtaining employment in Oshawa, he invited a friend to join him, and then he made arrangements for his wife to come to Canada. Together, the two men purchased a house. He had heard that good jobs were available in an automobile assembly plant in Oshawa, so he applied, was accepted, and began work on the assembly line. His friend also became interested in working at the plant, for the wages were high and the work steady. He filled out the necessary employment questionnaire but was told that he was too short for the job. He reapplied several times, always with the same results. He then had the idea that perhaps he could remedy his handicap by placing two-inch-thick rubber strips under his shoes. This ruse succeeded, and he too became employed by the company.

The first man left the assembly plant briefly to return to gardening but later went back to his old job. In 1969, he bought more property and opened a Portuguese general store. This is run with the assistance of his family, but during the evenings and on weekends he works in the store. This arrangement does not, of course, give him much free time.

Early in 1957, there were only four Portuguese men in Oshawa, but by 1974 the community had grown to approximately 1,000.

Brampton: The Portuguese community in Brampton, Ontario, is reputed to have been started by a man who jumped ship from a whaling boat. He opened a store in the town many years ago, but he has since died. One of the first recent immigrants arrived in Canada from São Miguel in the Azores on March 28, 1956, and took the train directly to Vancouver. From there, he was assigned to work on the railway as a section hand in British Columbia, where he completed one year's service. Then he journeyed to Toronto and was employed for nine months in construction. He later worked on a series of farms in southern Ontario, before settling in Brampton in 1958.

According to Martins, there were 4,500 Portuguese persons in Brampton in 1971,[28] and the numbers have increased steadily since that time. Many have been attracted to the area by the job opportunities in the steadily expanding construction industry in Brampton and in nearby communities. The members of the Portuguese community attend St. Mary's Church in Brampton, where Father Eduardo Couto officiates.

Mississauga and Streetsville: The extension of Portuguese immigrants into Mississauga is part of the general expansion from the Toronto community. Also, a mushroom farm in the area has attracted Portuguese workers. There were 500 families in Mississauga in 1974, 50% from mainland Portugal and the remainder from the Azores Islands.

One of the earliest pioneers to arrive in this area came to Canada in 1954. He arrived by ship in Halifax and then was sent by train to Niagara Falls. After two weeks of waiting, he was sent to Winona to tend the vineyards. He had heard of Manuel Cabral in Galt and after the harvest went to that town to seek employment. The following spring (1955), through Cabral, he obtained a job on a mushroom farm in Mississauga.

He has remained there ever since, and many compatriots have joined him. Another man who arrived in Canada in 1954 works at the same farm (1973) although his first job was on a farm near Cornwall. He had then moved to a farm near Ruthven and that winter made his way to Galt, where he met Cabral and his compatriot. It was not until 1966 that he brought his wife to Canada, but he had two extended visits in Portugal during the intervening years.

A third man came to Mississauga from the island of São Miguel. He arrived in Halifax in March, 1954. He was first sent to work on the railway between Fort William and the Manitoba border. He was a section hand and retained that job until 1959, when he decided to move to Toronto. He wanted to educate his children, for up to that time they had been living in a very isolated area of Ontario distant from schools. On arrival in Toronto, he contacted the Canada manpower office and soon found work with a printing company. One day his employer heard that he was thinking of buying a house and advised him to locate in Cooksville as the company would be moving there the following year. He took his employer's advice, but the market situation changed, and the following year prices had risen so considerably that it did not seem feasible to relocate the plant. Commuting to Toronto became frustrating for him, and he reluctantly decided to find new employment near his home. He is now working in another printing plant in the area.

White collar employees also are relocating in Mississauga. One came from the Azores in 1957 and was sent to work on the sugar beet harvest near Lethbridge, Alberta. At the end of the season, he was faced with the problem of finding a new job. A group of Portuguese men learned from some German immigrants they had met that Vancouver offered better prospects for employment. The Portuguese worked in a series of jobs in Vancouver and then in 1963 came east to Ontario. He soon found employment in Toronto and eventually was made supervisor of a warehouse. In 1969, he became an insurance agent. Many of the new arrivals in this growing suburb of Toronto have recommended the location to friends and relatives, and the area is a flourishing district of settlement for recent immigrants and for young adults of the second generation.

In 1974, the town of Streetsville was incorporated into Mississauga. It is a small community with a thriving Portuguese population of 200 families, or about 800 persons. Roughly 95% of the Portuguese in the town are from the Azores Islands, and 30% of these come from the village of Aguadato. The majority of the residents are employed in small factories or in maintenance services. Only three men own their own businesses, a real estate agency, a fish market, and a restaurant. A Portuguese Canadian Integration Centre and Chaplaincy, opened in 1971 and organized by Father Enrico Kea Capelão, serves to focus Portuguese activities in the area, and through its initiative a festival is held in early June each year.

Oakville: The Portuguese community in Oakville, situated midway between Toronto and Hamilton, is prosperous. This is scarcely surprising since Oakville, with a total population of 61,490 (1971 census) has one of the highest per capita incomes in Canada.[30] Oakville's earliest Portuguese settlers were directed there in the spring of 1954 through the Department of Immigration to work in nurseries, which had been experiencing an extreme shortage of skilled labour.

One immigrant drawn by that demand arrived by ship in Halifax in March 1954. He took the train to Montreal, and was then directed to Hamilton by immigration officials, who found him work in a nursery in Oakville. He lived in a bunkhouse nearby with one other Portuguese man, five Germans, and five Danes. He remained in the nursery business until 1963, when he switched to automobile assembly work. After some time, however, he found this type of employment "nerve shattering" and is now a janitor in a school in Oakville.

Another pioneer also arrived in March, 1954. He was first employed on farms in the area surrounding Oakville, then in a nursery in Oakville. Eventually, he wanted to take an extended holiday in "the islands" and left his job. On his return, he obtained employment as a caretaker in a school.

Another immigrant came to Halifax at the same time as the first man, from the island of Fayal in the Azores. He was directed to work first in London and then in Woodstock. At the end of the agricultural season, he found a job in a lumber camp near Thunder Bay, where he remained for nine years. Initially, he came to Oakville to work in a factory. There he heard that there were better jobs to be had in the United States. He decided to try his luck for a year in San Francisco, but he did not enjoy life there and returned to Oakville, where he obtained employment in another factory. Very few immigrants move permanently to the United States, for there they are regarded as "greenies" (greenhorns) by an older generation of Portuguese whereas here they are all first generation. Another immigrant from São Miguel arrived in April, 1954, and was sent to work on a farm in Quebec. After some months, he left for Ontario: "A friend in Winona, who had come to Winona one month before me, told me about a job, through my wife in Portugal, who then sent me his address. The friend then picked me up at the Winona post office." That fall the two men worked in the tobacco harvest and afterwards on a farm in the Grimsby area. In April, 1955, he went to Galt (now Cambridge); and the following fall, when jobs for the unskilled appeared scarce, he contacted Manuel Cabral, who helped him through the winter by providing accommodation and board. In the spring, he went to Hamilton, and the Immigration Department located a nursery in Oakville which needed experienced help. He is still employed there. As soon as he was able, he started to bring over his relatives and continued until most of his family was in Canada. Most of these relatives in turn called other kinfolk to Oakville, so that the numbers of Portuguese immigrants in Oakville were augmented year by year.

Another man from São Miguel arrived in Canada in the mid-1950s and

77

was sent to a tobacco farm in southern Ontario for four months during which time he had no contact whatsoever with Portuguese-speaking people. At the end of the harvest, he went to Galt to see Manuel Cabral. He was directed to a job in a steel products company in Hamilton but left after a few months for a job in a nursery in Oakville, which he has found to be much more congenial.

One of the early entrepreneurs in the area and his brother worked at arrival on a farm in Port Credit and later entered the construction industry. When he received a letter from a friend in Kitimat, B. C., about job possibilities there, he went and remained for ten years. In all these years, he dreamed of setting up his own business. When he had saved enough he returned to Ontario and looked around for a suitable location. He settled on Oakville and opened a grocery and meat market there. He also qualified as a real estate salesman and has a full-time job with a local agency.

Hamilton and Burlington: There is a thriving settlement of Portuguese immigrants and their families in Hamilton. The heart of the Portuguese district is in an area bounded by York, Barton, Bay and Locke Streets. More recently, some of the well established couples have moved out to Burlington.

From the beginnings of Portuguese immigration in 1954, when there was only a handful of men in Hamilton, until 1968, when there were estimated to be more than 3,000 Portuguese Canadians living in Hamilton and another 2,000 in the immediate area,[31] there has been a steady stream of immigrants coming to the city and finding employment in a variety of industries and services. In 1974, there were estimated to be 6,000 Portuguese immigrants and their families in the area. The size of the groups from the Azores Islands and continental Portugal is approximately equal in Hamilton. There are several real estate agencies, a driving school, grocery and fish stores, a bakery, and a building maintenance company, all serving the Portuguese-speaking people.[32]

The first Portuguese immigrant to come to Hamilton arrived in March 1954 from São Miguel in the Azores:

> Melo's first job was as a laborer for Fitzsimmons nurseries on Highway 6, just south of Clappison's Corners. He couldn't speak a word of English, his pay was only $120 a month, and his formal education had ended when he was 12 and went to work as a labourer on his father's farm.
>
> Today, Melo, now a Canadian citizen, fluent in English, and landscape manager and chief designer for Fitzsimmons Nurseries, was to present Mayor Victor Copps with a Portuguese flag in ceremonies marking the beginning of Portuguese week in Hamilton . . . .
>
> Melo decided to come [to Canada] in response to newspaper advertisements.
>
> "It was a Saturday morning when Tony was driven in here with another Portuguese immigrant and a man from the immigration people asked me if I wanted any help.

The Canadian boys who were working for me had decided it was too cold and wet to work and had refused to go out. Tony and the other Portuguese went out.''

Fitzsimmons' wife, Mary, a teacher at Holy Rosary Separate School in Burlington, took an interest in Tony and began giving him hourly English lessons each night. Tony supplemented them with evening classes at Westdale Secondary School.

A year later he was operating the cash register in the showroom, had a chauffeur's permit and was learning landscape design.

Tonight Tony Melo will be guest of honor during Portuguese folk dancing displays in Gore Park and at a Portuguese wine tasting reception at the Hamilton Press Club.[33]

Another Azorean came to Hamilton via Halifax in the spring of 1954. At first, the Immigration Department found him work on nearby farms, but this type of employment lasted only for the summer months. He was feeling very isolated initially and wanted to return to his homeland, but it was suggested that he talk with Manuel Cabral in Galt, who persuaded him to stay. In the fall of 1955, he obtained work in a yard in Hamilton cutting up scrap iron. He is now employed by the local gas company.

By 1974, the early settlers in Hamilton had entered a number of different occupations. For many of the men who arrived with only elementary school education, the ways of advancement were through jobs which required a strong physique, such as work in the steel mill. For others, it was a case of being able to work extremely long hours initially. There are, of course, a few Portuguese immigrants who, because of their education or aptitude, were able to enter white-collar jobs. Others opened small businesses, especially retail stores.

The Golden Triangle

Cambridge (Galt, Hespeler, Preston): The city of Cambridge was formed in 1973 through the amalgamation of the three municipalities of Galt, Hespeler, and Preston. Galt-Cambridge has been a centre of Portuguese immigration since 1953. This came about largely through the efforts of one man, Manuel Cabral, a Portuguese American who had been previously established in the area.

Manuel Cabral was born of Portuguese parents in Somerset, Massachusetts, in 1894. As a young man in New England, he learned the trade of metal tack-making, which was much in demand then. He travelled widely in the United States, gaining considerable experience. In 1919, a manufacturing plant in Morrisburg, Ontario, had severe problems in locating a tack-maker. They wrote first to England, but no one responded to his requests. Then the manufacturer sent a letter to the superintendent of the Tack-Makers Association in Massachusetts. The superintendent, upon receiving the latter, commented, "I'll ask young Cabral, he's a vagabond, he's the only one I know who would be interested." And in 1919 Manuel Cabral came to Morrisburg, Ontario. He stayed one year and then re-

79

turned to the United States. In 1928 he returned to Canada and the tack-making industry.

After some time, he started his own plant at Ayr under the name of The Maple Leaf Tack Factory. Some years later, when chatting with a nephew who was selling frozen fish to mink ranches in the United States, Cabral became interested in opening a similar business in Ontario. He sold the tack factory and opened a mink-feed business. He made Galt his base in 1946. It was necessary to obtain large quantities of frozen sea food, since freshwater fish were believed to contain an enzyme that destroyed the vitamin B complex in mink.

Cabral travelled widely in Ontario selling his supplies to mink farmers. He remarked, "I was in business for thirty years and used to cover all of Ontario from Fort Erie to North Bay to Ottawa. Everywhere I went I asked if they knew of any Portuguese-speaking persons, but I couldn't find one, not one, in my travels – that is, until 1953, when I started bringing them to Galt."

He frequently travelled to Rhode Island to see exporters of sea food and to make arrangements for a summer supply. In 1953, a Portuguese acquaintance asked him if he would be willing to pick up his nephew, who was stranded in Montreal, and bring him to Galt. By the following spring, this young man had encouraged his brother and his brother-in-law to emigrate to Canada from the Azores. Originally, these two men were sent to Leamington, but Cabral telephoned to the Department of Immigration and requested that they be allowed to come to Galt to work for him. The Immigration officials agreed.

Cabral provided living quarters on his own property, and in his spare time taught the men English. In the fall of 1954, when the tobacco season was over, seven men arrived at his home. They had been given his name. An apartment owned by Cabral was empty, so he lodged all the men there. Soon the word spread, and others arrived, making fourteen men altogether. He found work for eight of the men through his own contacts locally, and the Department of Immigration located work for another six.

By 1955, about twenty-five Portuguese men were employed on the railway in Galt. There were over seventy men in the area then, and it was decided to form a club. A group of them built a clubhouse on the property of Manuel Cabral, the first clubhouse of a Portuguese association to be built in Canada. The association itself did not last long in its original form, for squabbles soon broke out and the club disintegrated. It was, however, reconstituted some time later and became one of the large associations of Portuguese Canadians.

By 1957, Portuguese men who had initially come to Canada as farm labourers or as railway workers were flooding into the area. Usually they went to Manuel Cabral to ask where there were job vacancies. He accompanied them to textile mills in Hespeler, to the foundries, and to manufacturing plants in Galt. Many obtained work in construction, and some in automobile body shops. Once they were established, they brought their

Portuguese arrivals from the Azores, c. April, 1956. (Courtesy Mr. N. Oliveria, Hamilton)

Working in the tobacco fields, Southern Ontario, 1954. (Courtesy Constantine Dutra, Oakville)

A Portuguese labouring in Kitimat, B.C., as early as 1955. (Courtesy Portuguese Consulate, Toronto)

Portuguese immigrants working on railway construction, 1957. (Courtesy Alberto Cabral, Sr., Edmonton)

The first organized Portuguese soccer club in Canada, Kitimat, B.C., September, 1956. (Courtesy Portuguese Consulate)

Music and song at a Portuguese recreational festival featuring Portuguese-Canadian artists. (Courtesy Portuguese Consulate)

The Portuguese community in Kensington Market, Toronto. (Courtesy William E. Nassau)

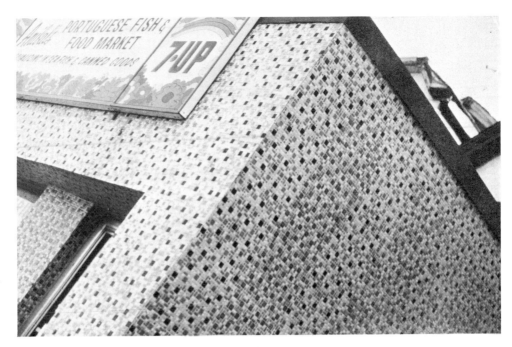

A Portuguese storefront mosaic. (Courtesy Grace M. Anderson)

*The Portuguese communities join in Centennial Year celebrations, 1967.
The Portuguese float, Kingston, Ontario. (Courtesy Maria Ramos)*

One of the many Portuguese artists who regularly visit Toronto and other areas of Canada and sing the most typical of the Portuguese songs – FADO. (Courtesy Portuguese Consulate)

Canadian and Portuguese flags flying side-by-side at Toronto City Hall to mark a Portuguese national holiday. (Courtesy Portuguese Consulate)

A well-known Portuguese writer, Fernando Namora, during one of his visits to the Portuguese community in Ontario. (Courtesy Portuguese Consulate)

kin and often also encouraged their friends and neighbours from the homeland to join them. Some of the immigrants remained in several of the poultry-breeding establishments near Galt. As wives joined them, they found work in the local industrial plants or in private homes or institutions.

In the spring of 1976, there were an estimated 12,000 Portuguese persons in the city of Cambridge, at least 9,000 of whom lived in Galt. Usually members of the community are referred to by other Portuguese persons as the "Galt Portuguese" and by Anglo-Saxon members of the area as "the New Galtonians."

Galt claims to have the highest percentage of Portuguese among its population in Canada.[34] It is sometimes joked that Galt is a bilingual city, but it is English-Portuguese bilingualism rather than English-French:

> Immigrants arriving here today from Portugal will find they can buy groceries, furniture, do their banking, hear a sermon in church and even take driving lessons – all without knowing a word of English.
>
> The Portuguese Club on the Puslinch Townline Road is one of the largest ethnic clubs in the area and the Portuguese Oriental Soccer team is one of the area's best. Last year the team represented the former city of Galt at the Can-Amera Games in Saginaw Township, Mich.[35]

The immigrants came to Cambridge predominantly from the Azores islands of São Miguel, Terceira, and Santa Maria, with a few from Fayal and Pico. There is a Portuguese Club of Fayal in Galt-Cambridge. A considerable number of continental Portuguese are resident in the area, as well as a few from Madeira and Brazil.

A survey of one of the separate schools in Galt in September 1970 indicated that 44.8% of the pupils were of Portuguese extraction:

> Fearful that their offspring may lose cultural ties many parents now send their children to special classes on Saturday morning(s) where the native language is taught and important cultural values are reinforced .... English classes for adult immigrants started in March, 1970 under the direction of Conestoga College – Adult Education Branch. There are six levels of progression with the average adult spending about sixty hours in each level. Enrolment has been steadily increasing with a predominance of men. The projection for September, 1971, involves a day-care centre with afternoon classes for the women.[36]

Kitchener: The earliest arrivals from Portugal came to Kitchener through Manuel Cabral. They, in turn, brought relatives, who encouraged others to locate in the area. In May, 1974, there were an estimated 3,000 Portuguese immigrants in the city, the majority of whom lived in the area bounded by Joseph Street and Courtland Avenue. Recently, families have moved to the suburbs, especially the Forest Heights area. Although many boats, and a large number work on the boats as crew members. Some of the men and women gain their livelihood in the fish processing plant. Others are employed in the wood products factory in Wheatley. Some own farms, and a few operate them on a full-time basis. The majority, however, hold jobs in one of the small towns or in the city of Leamington and run the farms as a sideline, assisted by other members of the family.

A feature of the distribution of Portuguese families in this region is that they have organized themselves occupationally according to their region of origin. The majority of men who work on the fishing boats come from Nazaré, a fishing town situated north of Lisbon. They keep in close touch with fellow townsmen who live in Toronto and together they have formed a club with a membership that includes 300 families in southern Ontario. When there is a Portuguese festival in Wheatley or Leamington, the folk dancers of Nazaré send a group from Toronto to perform locally. The men from Nazaré who work on the fishing boats earn an excellent livelihood, and the owners' incomes are even more substantial, equal to that of proprietors of other small but flourishing businesses. The fishermen work for only eight months of the year, because fishing in Lake Erie ceases between the months of December and April. Many of the men are in Canada without their families; they are not landed immigrants but come over on a work permit, on a "three-month-renewable" basis. Others are settled with their families and own their homes in this region of Ontario.

For centuries, the hometown of Nazaré has been accustomed to long absences of the able-bodied men. Many have served with the White Fleet that fishes the Grand Banks. One pioneer in Leamington said:

> Almost all the men here were fishermen on the Grand Banks .... I have been fishing for 27 years. I was trained in the Lisbon Escola de Pesca [School of Fisheries] in a six months' course. I had worked 16 years in the codfish industry off Newfoundland before coming here. We leave early in the morning, sometimes 5 a.m. and come back around 5 or 6 in the evening.

"At times," reported one of the seasonal fishermen from Leamington, "the men rise at 3 a.m. and are not through work until 10 p.m. They are often eager to work as much as possible to have money to take back to Portugal." Bunks on the fishing tugs enable the men to catch a little sleep on the way to the fishing area and on the return trip. The fishing groups are frequently situated an hour or two distant from the home port.[38]

When a boat is taken over by a new owner, he repaints the vessel. Then the priest is called and the boat is officially given a "baptism" and blessed. Champagne flows freely, and many members of the Portuguese community go out for a Sunday afternoon boat ride. Then the boat is used for its regular work commencing on Monday morning. The fish packing plant owns the largest number of boats. Many of these are mastered by Portuguese fishermen and manned by a Portuguese crew. Some boats are Italian-owned, but frequently the majority of their men are Portuguese. In their spare time, the men who are in the area without their families congregate at a local hotel to chat over a glass of beer, or in a Portuguese pool hall, or at a Portuguese-Canadian grocery and fish store.

In contrast to the fishermen of Nazaré, the Portuguese who are employed in the wood products mills usually come from the Azores. An Azorean is reputed to have been the first Portuguese Canadian in the area. Born in São Miguel, he arrived in Halifax in October, 1953, and worked on farms in various locations in southern Ontario during the next eighteen months. Hometown friends who were at that time living in Hamilton advised him by letter that there was employment on a farm at Ruthven. After a few months there, he came to Wheatley in 1955 and obtained a job in the wood products mill. When he had gained some years of experience in the company, he was promoted to the position of foreman, in which capacity he has served for several years. Nearly three-quarters of the people who work with him are also of Portuguese background.

At one time or another, nearly all of the 67 families in the town have called upon this first arrival for advice or assistance. In an interview, he related the early problems of communication that he encountered. Initially, he was working on a farm for Polish people and he began to learn Polish. Later, he was working with Italians, so he started to try to speak Italian. By the time he came to learn English, he said that he was "all mixed up." He now speaks excellent English.

Wives of men employed in Leamington, Wheatley and neighbouring towns often are themselves employed in either fish processing or food processing plants, usually on a seasonal basis. The men working in construction are mostly from mainland Portugal. One owner of a small construction company comes from Aveiro. He has nine Portuguese men working for him on a regular basis.

Some of the men from the continent work in Windsor and leave their families to look after the farm in the Leamington area during the week. They themselves tend the farm on the weekends. In the early years, when a couple first purchased a farm on a full-time basis, they sometimes supplemented their earnings by leaving adolescent children to run the farm during the tobacco season and themselves going to the tobacco-growing region surrounding Delhi to obtain cash employment for several weeks in the fall. Now they more frequently share crop a rented farm during their early years in Canada. They usually find, however, that they can build up capital more quickly by working in industry or in construction.

NOTES

1. Canada, Department of Manpower and Immigration, *Annual Statistics on Immigration by Country of Origin, 1960-1970.*

2. T. Raddall, *Halifax, Warden of the North*, 2nd ed., p. 38, corrects a passage in the first edition, referring to a cluster of Azorean immigrants, who were in fact English, long delayed in the Azores, who arrived accompanied by a Sicilian soldier.
3. We are greatly indebted to Mr. Thomas Raddall for this and other information. Anthony De Mings is mentioned in *Collections of the Nova Scotia Historical Society*, Vol. 6, p. 63. Mr. Raddall points out that Portuguese Cove was not so named on the earliest maps, but only after the foundation of Halifax in 1759. He writes: "I was stationed at Portuguese Cove as wireless operator in the summer of 1922. It was then a small fishing village and I knew the people well. None had a Portuguese name. It was supposed that a 'Portuguese man' had fished there long ago."
4. Arthur R. Moreira, Q.C., letter of December 20, 1974.
5. Romão, "Le processus de migration," p. 1.
6. *Ibid.*, p. 5.
7. *The Position of the French Language in Quebec, Book 3, The Ethnic Groups* (popularly known as The Gendron Report, Vol. 3). Quebec: Government of Quebec, Dec. 1972, p. 57.
8. *Ibid.*, p. 101.
9. Brazeau-Carlos study quoted in *ibid.*, pp. 95-96.
10. Romão, p. 86.
11. *Ibid.*, pp. 191ff.
12. "Need for immigrant workers," *The Toronto Star*, July 26, 1974.
13. Ethel Roskies, "Life Change and Illness in Immigrants," Dépt. de Psychologie, Section Clinique, Université de Montréal; Ronald Louis Fernández, "The Logic of Ethnicity: A Study of the Montreal Portuguese," Ph.D. dissertation in progress, McGill Univ. Anthropology; Victor M. Pereira de Rosa, "Emigration et Dépendance: Les Portugais de Montréal et le Portugal," Ph.D. dissertation in progress, McGill Univ. Anthropology. See also *Portugal Em Montréal, 1975*, IPP, Hurtean St., Montreal, 1975.
14. For further information on real estate agents, see J. Douglas House, "Entrepreneurial Career Patterns of Residential Real Estate Agents in Montreal," *The Canadian Review of Sociology and Anthropology* (May 1974); and for real estate as a means of upward mobility, see Merrijoy Kelner, "Ethnic Penetration into Toronto's Elite Structure," in *Critical Issues in Canadian Society*, Craig L. Boydell, Carl F. Grindstaff, and Paul C. Whitehead, eds., Toronto: Holt, Rinehart and Winston, 1971), pp. 329-337.
15. "British Outnumbered, Radio Survey Shows," *Toronto Star*, July 6, 1974. (The description of a survey conducted by Toronto's multicultural station CHIN-AM-FM.)
16. Edith Ferguson, *Newcomers in Transition: A Project of the International Institute of Metropolitan Toronto, 1962-1964* (Toronto: International Institute of Metropolitan Toronto [c. 1965]), p. 33.
17. Marvin H. Lipman, "Relocation and Family Life: A Study of the Social

and Psychological Consequences of Urban Renewal" (D.S.W. thesis, University of Toronto, 1968).

18. *Ibid.*, pp. 79-80.

19. *Ibid.*, p. 84.

20. Ferguson, *Newcomers in Transition*, p. 35 (our italics).

21. *Ibid.*, p. 42.

22. Anderson, *Networks of Contact*, p. 56.

23. Lipman, "Relocation and Family Life," p. 66.

24. Dan Turner, "The Portuguese Find 'Making It' Has a New Twist," *Toronto Star*, December 8, 1973.

25. *Ibid.*

26. M.L. Bear, "A Study of the Program for New Canadians at St. Christopher House" (M.S.W. thesis, University of Toronto, 1955); Edith Ferguson, *Newcomers and New Learning: A Project of the International Institute of Metropolitan Toronto, 1962-1964* (Toronto: International Institute of Metropolitan Toronto [c. 1964 or 1965]); Ferguson, *Newcomers in Transition*; Lipman, "Relocation and Family Life". Anderson, "The Channel Facilitators Model of Migration;" Grace M. Anderson, "The Education Ladder and Success," *The Journal of the American Portuguese Cultural Society* (New York, Fall 1971); John Hamilton, *Portuguese in Transition* (Toronto: Toronto Board of Education, Research Dept., December 1970); M. Streeruwitz, *Portuguese Directory for the Metropolitan Area of Toronto* (Toronto: International Institute of Metropolitan Toronto, 1972); Caroline Bieler, "The Institutions of Portuguese-Canadian Integration in Toronto" and "Ethnicity and the Entrepreneur" (Brown University, Anthropology, Spring 1973); Estellie M. Smith, "Portuguese Enclaves: The Invisible Minority" (State University of New York at Brockport, 1973); Anderson, *Networks of Contact*.

27. Names of living persons have been omitted, except where the pioneer founded an association or a newspaper, or was crucial to the settling of an entire region.

28. Martins, "Emigração Portuguesa no Canadá," p. 221.

29. See p.

30. *Taxation Statistics 1974 edition: Analyzing the Returns of Individuals for the 1972 Taxation Year and Miscellaneous Statistics* (Ottawa: Revenue Canada, Taxation; Information Canada, 1974).

31. "From Laborer to Manager, No. 1 Launches Portuguese Week," *Hamilton Spectator*, June 7, 1968. See also "Portugal" in *Celebrating "Canadians All" 1867-1967* (Hamilton, Kiwanis Club of Hamilton Inc., 1967).

32. See also Serviço Central de Informação, Direção de Cidadania, *Serviços Principais para o Recém-Chegado a Hamilton* (Hamilton: Direção de Cidadania, Secretariado da Provinciae Ministerio da Cidadania, n.d.).

33. "From Laborer to Manager."

34. "There's one Portuguese-speaking person among every seven residents of Cambridge and almost one in four in the former city of Galt," in

87

"10,000 Portuguese Repainting Cultural Image of Cambridge," *Kitchener-Waterloo Record*, April 18, 1975.

35. Gerald Wright, "7,000 Portuguese Give Cambridge Bilingual Flavour," *Kitchener-Waterloo Record*, January 22, 1973.

36. Donald J. Thomas, "Problems of Acculturation of the Portuguese Immigrants in the City of Galt" (unpublished essay, Waterloo Lutheran University, 1971), pp. 4-5. See also Alison Adair, Paul Zarnke, Edcil Wickham, "Self Determination in Ethnic Communities: A Practical Example," Wilfrid Laurier University, Graduate School of Social Work. A paper presented to the annual meeting of the Canadian Association of Schools of Social Work, Quebec, May 27, 1976, for an account of the establishment of the Cambridge Portuguese Information Centre.

37. See Mark Ronayne, "Companhia Baccalhoeira," in *"Trade News" of the Department of Fisheries of Canada* (July, 1954); also "Dory on the Banks: A Day in the Life of a Portuguese Fisherman," *National Geographic*, April 1968.

38. For further details of the social organization of the fishing industry, see Raoul Anderson and Cato Wadel, eds., *North Atlantic Fishermen: Anthropological Essays on Modern Fishing* (St. Johns: Memorial University of Newfoundland, Institute of Social and Economic Research, Newfoundland Social and Economic Papers No. 5, 1972).

FIVE

Settlements in Western Canada

INTRODUCTION

The Portuguese settlements in the Western provinces tended to grow less rapidly than those in Central and Eastern Canada for reasons indicated in the previous chapter. Nevertheless, many of them show similar characteristics in that the majority are situated in the most highly urbanized areas such as Vancouver, Calgary, Edmonton and Winnipeg. However, communities have also grown up around former construction sites, such as Kitimat in northern British Columbia. Portuguese families are also settled on fruit farms in the southernmost part of the Okanagan Valley.

PRAIRIE PROVINCES[1]

Manitoba

The Portuguese population in Manitoba in 1973 was estimated at 8,000 to 8,500, with concentrations in two main centres, Winnipeg and Thompson. Winnipeg contained about 5,000 Portuguese (single men, married men without families in Canada, and 1,800 families) and Thompson had about 1,500. The remainder of the Portuguese population was scattered in northern areas. Many work in the construction and lumber industries in The Pas and Lynn Lake; in Gillam, they are employed in the building of a dam.

Winnipeg: Approximately 65% of Manitoba's Portuguese community is from the Azores Islands, mostly from São Miguel. The vice-consul has estimated that 99% are labourers. In Winnipeg itself, there are a few professionals. One woman is a medical doctor. The vice-consul, a distinguished architect, has designed many important public buildings throughout Canada; he also lectures on architecture at the University of Manitoba. There are, of course, real estate agents, food importers, and others who serve the Portuguese community in Winnipeg and elsewhere.

89

But the professionals and entrepreneurs are a small minority among the Portuguese-Canadian population of Winnipeg.

The first to come to the province were the farm labourers. Later, tradesmen came. The first immigrants arrived alone, either as bachelors or as married men who had left a wife and family in the homeland. Only in the past seven years (1967 to 1974) have the men started to bring in their wives and families to any noticeable extent.

Most of the men from the Azores tend to stay in Winnipeg, while the men from the mainland are more likely to go to the northern areas for higher wages. This can be explained in terms of differential satisfaction with the level of remuneration and relative deprivation, or in this case relative affluence.[2] Most of the men from the Azores Islands were poorer than those who came from the mainland. Therefore they were more content with urban wages. It was the very ambitious mainlanders who were usually attracted to the more highly remunerated jobs in isolated locations in the north. Educational achievement also contributes to differentiations in the community. The low educational attainment of the majority of the first generation immigrants contrasts with the high educational achievements of a handful of leaders. There are now several second generation students completing high school and entering university who also should be able to provide leadership in the coming years.

The area of Portuguese concentration in Winnipeg is bounded by Logan Avenue, Ellen Street, Ellice Avenue, and Arlington Street. It is on the fringes of French and Italian districts and can be easily recognized by its brightly painted homes, with occasionally an old dilapidated house among the freshly painted structures. As in Toronto and Montreal, the owners of older houses work with their relatives and friends to bring them up to the same standards of gaiety and cleanliness that characterize other Portuguese homes on the street. This area of Winnipeg was degenerating into a slum but is now becoming a colourful part of the city, through the efforts, initiative, and hard work of the immigrants.

Frequently, the Portuguese community in Winnipeg feels that it is being ignored by the populace at large and by the press in particular. On August 1, 1970, the following letter was printed in the *Winnipeg Free Press*:

> Sir:
>
> Congratulations on your centennial souvenir supplement, July 13. However, I wish to make a strong complaint about the fact that you didn't mention the Portuguese immigrants.
>
> Perhaps you are not aware that there are about 6,000 Portuguese people in Winnipeg; Thompson and Whitemouth have quite a few also. We have our own priest, vice-consul, radio station, four grocery stores, a real estate firm, a Portuguese association and we have all been very much involved in the growth and development of this Province.
>
> A. P. T.

Members of the Portuguese community also complain that their language is ignored. They point out that many institutions offering language instruction in evening classes will give courses in Spanish but none in Portuguese, although there are relatively few Spanish-speaking persons in Winnipeg in comparison to the large Portuguese population. They also object that they are frequently mistaken for Spanish or Latin American persons. In Europe there has been a long history of Portuguese and Spanish antagonism and rivalry.

One of the earliest arrivals in Winnipeg now owns a small residential construction company. He arrived, via Halifax, on May 18, 1955, and recently gave this account of his decision to settle in Winnipeg:

> I was in [a] fruit warehouse a week in Winnipeg. Then I see [an] Italian who told me C.P. was hiring here in Winnipeg. (I speak some Italian.) So I went with him and got hired. The work was on the tracks close to Kenora for the first four months. [I worked in] other places nearer Winnipeg later on. Then I used to come to Winnipeg every two weeks. I opened a bank account and came on a Monday to deposit money and send it back to Portugal. I was single then – I just married ten years ago. I met my wife over there in 1961 when I went back over. It was the second time I went back.

He now has a small construction company employing eight or nine men in the summer. If he has to lay off capable men for lack of work, he finds jobs for them elsewhere.

Two Azoreans whose careers in Winnipeg are of interest arrived on June 19, 1957, with four other men from the homeland. The first, who comes from a family of emigrants and entrepreneurs, is now a prosperous realtor. Since his arrival he has assisted about 100 other people from the homeland to become established in Canada. His family are cattle dealers in a small village in São Miguel. At the age of fourteen, he was already helping his father and being instructed in the ways of business. By the time he emigrated to Canada ten years later, he had considerable business experience behind him. First, he was employed by the Canadian National Railway in various locations in northern Ontario. Then he decided to come to Winnipeg to obtain employment so that he could attend night school to learn English:

> One day I decided to be a Canadian and it was then that I decided to learn the language and after I will make money. The first pay cheque we received I cashed for the other men. I had brought dollars with me. My father taught me when I was 18 about banking and serving the public.

In Winnipeg, he obtained a job in structural steel construction. He asked to be given work with English-speaking men so that he could learn the language. Then he began assisting other Portuguese men to come to Canada from the homeland. He filled out government forms for them, as well as initial applications. When new immigrants arrived, he told them, "If there is anything I can do, call me any time of the day or night." The first winter when the men returned to the city from remote northern and rural communities, he offered them accommodation in the rooming house he ran. The next spring, the men scattered again to various jobs in different parts of Canada. Now, he claims to be known all over the country. He also started to bring his teenage brothers to Canada and encouraged them to take advantage of the opportunities that the country offers.

Eventually, he decided to go into the real estate business and applied for a position as a salesman. After he had begged for work for one-and-a-half months, the real estate owner told him, "We have twenty salesmen and they are barely making a living, and you do not even have the language." He replied, "Give me a chance – I will even deposit the money for the first month's salary with you." After much persuasion, he was given a chance. The first week he sold a house, and the second week another. A girl in the office was then assigned to him to coach him on how to pass the realtor's examinations for accreditation.

When his employer gave up the real estate business, the man decided to go into business for himself. He started a realty company and also offered a variety of services to other Portuguese immigrants, including driving lessons through his own driving school. "We don't do much advertising: we give service and the service talks." His business provides mortgage loans, fire insurance, and offers to trade homes as well as buy and sell them.

The second man came to Canada through the auspices of the Welch Company of Montreal, who were recruiting immigrant labourers to work for the railway companies. He first heard of people coming to Canada in 1956. "Next year everyone visited [São Miguel] like big shots, so I applied." He came alone, although he had been married for three years, and travelled wherever there were good employment prospects. His first job was at Dougall, Manitoba, on the railway. Later, he went to Thompson as a carpenter (the trade he had brought with him from the homeland). Then he went on to Square Rapids, Saskatchewan, working shifts on the construction of the dam. For a time he worked for a cousin in California, before returning to Canada and going to work in Edmonton. Subsequently, he spent brief periods in Toronto and Montreal.

Altogether, he was without his wife and family for twelve years. He returned to Portugal on three separate occasions. Finally, when her mother died, his wife demanded that she come to Canada to join him. She also insisted that he live in a city. He agreed but said, "If you come to the city, you go to work too." She is currently working in a factory as a seamstress.

When he recalls the struggles of the first few years, his most vivid memories are of the overwhelming sense of loneliness and the initial hardships. At times, while working on isolated railway lines, the men were short of water for washing themselves or their clothing. He comments, "I was alone, a man who is alone in this country was like a bum. I could not sleep nights . . . . I should have brought my family here ten years before . . . . I want to give [a] good education to my kids."

Another early settler in Winnipeg is now (1973) a prominent member of the Portuguese community, owning a flourishing supermarket. He had a friend who had arrived in Canada in 1955 who wrote and suggested that he join him in Winnipeg. "I had always had ambition to come to America," he recollects. Initially, he was employed in Red Lake, Ontario, in a gold mine but he was a machinist by trade and he became a mechanic in Thompson while working for The Foundation Company there.

In 1961, he decided to go back to Portugal, and while there he married. On his return, he obtained a job as a machinist with the Canadian National Railways. Meanwhile, he was in touch with a friend who was the local manager of a branch of a Toronto-based Portuguese importing firm. The manager wanted to marry a Toronto girl, but she did not wish to relocate in Winnipeg, so the friend decided to move to Toronto. He talked the situation over with his wife, and it was decided that they would jointly take over the store. She would work in the store during the daytime, and he would continue with the railway. Before long business expanded to such an extent that they needed extra help in the store, and the husband's foreman encouraged him to go into his own business on a full-time basis and assured him that there would be a place for him in the railway shop if things did not work out well. Originally, the store was owned in partnership, but later he bought out the partner and since then has operated the store with assistance from his family.

He also sponsored his younger brother for immigration to Canada. When he first arrived in Canada, the young man was seventeen years old. He found a job as a sandwich-maker in a lunchroom in Thompson, Manitoba, but he wanted to go to Winnipeg: "I was tired of being in the bush, I was too young, I wanted to have some fun." In the city, he attended technical high school. His English was good when he arrived, and he had had the equivalent of grade ten education in Portugal. "I applied to ____ Lumber for a job. The foreman was from Newfoundland and had seen Portuguese fishermen. I asked for a job thinking that I might get something in the yard." He was given a job in the office, since he had already had some office experience in Lisbon.

During the nine months that he stayed there, he improved his English. He then returned to Thompson, thinking that he would get back his former job. But he was given work in the yard at 40° below zero, shovelling snow. He started thinking that if he wanted to get ahead in Canada he would have to learn a licensed trade. He later enrolled at the Manitoba Institute of Technology in Winnipeg. There, he received training as a pipe welder. He was an apt pupil and eventually became a fully qualified welder. Subsequently, he obtained jobs in various parts of Canada, from Prince Rupert, B.C., to Timmins, Ontario, working out of Winnipeg, Calgary, or Edmonton. In June 1969, he was married; and in that same month, he became a partner with his brother and two other men in operating two supermarkets. Finally, on April 1, 1970, the elder brother bought the larger supermarket and his younger brother purchased the smaller store. These are managed independently but with frequent co-operation.

The younger man often reminisces about his experience with other Portuguese workers on various projects. He recalls that Grand Rapids Dam in Manitoba was built almost entirely by Portuguese labour; in fact, all the bunkhouse notices were in Portuguese. In the Kettle Rapids project, 50% of the labourers were at one time Portuguese. There were many from the homeland employed at Great Dam in northern British Columbia and on the Nelson River project. Since he attended the technical institute, a number of other Portuguese immigrants have followed his example and become unionized welders.

There are several Portuguese general stores in the city of Winnipeg. Jack Lopes Restaurant and Billiards Hall is reputed to be an informal labour exchange. Men are known to wait around all day in the hope of being called "up north" where "even unskilled labourers make $1,000 a month." There is also a Portuguese barber shop nearby where news is exchanged.

The career outlines described thus far refer to the first generation immigrants. The Portuguese community in Winnipeg is now coming of age, however, and there is a new generation reaching maturity. One among these, for example, in the summer of 1973 helped to organize a summer school to teach the Portuguese children of the community. The younger and more recent arrivals are being taught English; the older children are learning Portuguese and the history and traditions of the country. The curriculum also includes soccer and other sports and games. The school is government-sponsored, under the Opportunities for Youth Program, and eight Portuguese high school and two university students are employed as teachers.

Much of the co-operative spirit and coordination of activities in the city of Winnipeg is due to the dedicated efforts of Father Peter Fernandes, a priest from one of Portugal's former overseas provinces. He has lived in Brazil and in England, where he studied at Cambridge University. He is dedicated to the people of his parish and is widely respected in the community. When he speaks, the immigrants listen; if he announces a programme or an event in church on a Sunday, the people usually support it. He has been very influential in reuniting families. He has a reputation for telling the men who are working in Canada without their families, "Bring your family here now." Generally, they respond positively.

While the church emphasizes the religious and moral aspects of life, the

Portuguese association sponsors social events, folkloric dancing and soccer teams. The community is served by a Portuguese newspaper *O Mundial*. The Portuguese in Winnipeg are a well-articulated community and have been fortunate in obtaining several very capable leaders who can coordinate and give direction and momentum to their activities.[3]

The majority of Portuguese immigrants in Thompson, Manitoba, work for the International Nickel Company. In the early years, many were employed by The Foundation Construction Company, which built the facilities and opened up the mine.

Alberta

In Alberta, the major Portuguese settlements are located in Calgary and in Edmonton. In June, 1973, the estimated populations were 1,500 in Calgary and 5,600 in Edmonton. Perhaps it is misleading to speak of a community in either of these cities. While the Portuguese readily recognize their shared political background and language and some cultural affinity with each other, they interrelate as a number of discrete and distinctive groups. Their lack of unity is manifested in conflicts and disagreements over local issues. Church-oriented are against secular-oriented persons; mainlanders oppose those from the islands; the highly educated attempt to exert their superiority over the less well-educated.

The most hotly contested issue is the relationship of the ethnic organizations (and the social events they sponsor) with the ethnic church. Some of the immigrants who rally around the church deplore the attitudes of others who use it as a social and cultural centre, ignoring its spiritual claims and neglecting to support it financially. Others wish to have nothing to do with the church, its social activities, and its subsidiary organizations. They resent the religious aspects of Portuguese cultural activities, and the parades and processions which commence and end at the church. Occasionally, the various Portuguese groups combine to present an appearance of unity to outsiders, but such union is sporadic. In recent years, for example, there has been so much bickering within and between religious and secular groups about which organization should decorate the Portuguese float for the Calgary Stampede parade that one family has volunteered to take full charge of it to ensure that the float will be completed. This has solved the particular problem of preparing the float, but it has created more conflict, for publicly volunteering one's services leads to open jealously and gossiping within the subgroups of Portuguese residents.

The rifts within the community appear to be the outward manifestations of deep-seated social and cultural cleavages that originate in the homeland.[4] In the small village communities of Portugal's island provinces, for example, gossip may well have served to sanction striving for competitive advantage over one's neighbours. Norms of sharing also minimized economic ambition in the islands. Many were living at subsistence level, and kin and friends lived nearby. The tradition of the well-to-do giving to the poor is old and well-established, even in the mainland villages; and this emphasis on sharing is reflected in a Portuguese proverb: "He who gives to the poor lends to God."[5] The norms of a rural village may not, however, be readily adaptable to the modern North American industrial-urban environment. Individualism and personal attainment are highly valued in the wider Canadian metropolitan society; and while many Portuguese immigrants have adopted these goals, their leadership potential is often destroyed by petty rivalries. The communities in Calgary and Edmonton are large enough to be able to split into factions and not big enough to be able to form mutually exclusive clubs and associations that can operate independently of each other. The fact that these communities are much more recent than their eastern counterparts probably has to some extent accentuated the conflicts as aspiring leaders jockey for positions of eminence.

The Portuguese first came to Alberta in 1957, when about twenty manual workers arrived by train from the East. Some were sent to assist with the sugar beet harvest on the farms around Lethbridge. At first, the farm owners were reported to be wary of employing Portuguese workers in their fields. Gradually, however, the word spread that the Portuguese were excellent, reliable workers, and subsequently the local farmers welcomed them.

Trainloads of track workers were also recruited for work on the railway lines. Again the Portuguese quickly earned a reputation for hard work. Indeed, it was said that the railway companies adopted a new slogan: "We have no job openings. But if you have a Portuguese worker, we will find him a job." Most of the Portuguese railway workers who came to this part of Canada probably were brought from the Azores under contract with the R. F. Welch Company.

Calgary: In Calgary, Portuguese Canadians have traditionally been concentrated in the southwestern and southeastern sections of the city. Recently many have moved farther out to the suburbs, but in the same sector of the city. Frequently, Forest Lawn is the reception area for new immigrants arriving in Calgary. It has been described by a local school teacher as "an area where many people are struggling to get ahead. Rents are low, and Forest Lawn is a solid working class area."

The story of the settlement of Calgary by the first group of Portuguese Canadians focuses on the entrepreneurship of an Azorean. In the homeland, he was a waiter in one of the leading hotels in the Azores and had learned some English there through contact with English-speaking airmen.[6] He was married and lived in a house he had built in Santa María.

In 1957, there was an advertisement in the islands for emigration to Canada. He responded immediately. He borrowed a thousand dollars from his mother and an aunt to make the trip, and unlike most of the men who came over at that time he insisted on bringing his family with him. He also demanded that he be given urban work instead of being sent to work on an isolated farm or on the railway.

The loneliness of life in the unfamiliar city was almost unbearable in the early days, although he had his wife and daughter with him. He determined to bring members of his own family and his wife's relatives over to join him; and to date he claims to have sponsored the immigration to Calgary of forty-three of their relatives. They, in turn, have brought others. He has a sense of mission in his sponsorship efforts and feels that "This is my victory." In 1973, he was asked to address a gathering in The International Centre on the founding of the Portuguese community in Calgary. The speech he gave on that occasion is as follows:

. . . Sixteen years ago when I arrived in Calgary with my wife and a child and others, 23 Portuguese all together, I could hardly speak English but I was the interpreter for all others to help them out to get jobs. Some went to the farms and others went to the Railroad, and I was left with my family all by ourselves in this City of ours. My first job was a busboy at the York Hotel at seventy-five cents an hour because I could not speak or write good English. In Portugal I was a good waiter in a first class hotel. My economic situation was poor and I had to write to two families relatives of mine in one envelope to Portugal. We were making a living with four or five dollars [sic] a day which I use to take home from tips. Three weeks later I was walking home from work with my head toward the sidewalk thinking [about] my home in Portugal, my relatives and everything that was dear to me, when I heard a voice calling somebody but I paid no attention and continued to walk. Then, for a second time I heard again the same voice, and this time calling my name. I look all the way around me, then I saw a man with his arms in the air calling for me and saying, "Manuel don't you know me? I'm Joe." This man was going to cross the street full of traffic. I warned him not to cross but to go into the intersection and cross with green lights. He paid no attention. This man ran towards me and hugged me crying like a child and his tears were running down on his face. This man was alone, full of love for everything that he left behind. I brought him to my home and he had supper with us. Next day I took him to the railway station and helped him to buy a ticket to Toronto. I came home with tears in my eyes because I wanted him to stay with me, I didn't want to stay alone. A few days later I started receiving letters from friends who wanted to come to Calgary and if I could help them to find jobs and send for their families. Certainly this was my hope, because I wanted to bring to Calgary as many [people from the homeland] as I could, and our Portuguese community started that way. Today we have about 1,500 people and I'm still working for my community. The reason I'm joining the Calgary Citizenship Council, ladies and gentlemen, is because I want to ask you, give me your hand and help me to guide my community on the right direction.

He has assisted members of the community in many ways. He has frequently acted as an interpreter for teachers and parents; he has also interpreted in occasional court cases. In 1958, he tried to start an evening school for teaching English to his fellow countrymen, arranging for five university students to teach English, but they had difficulty conveying the meaning of certain words without a knowledge of Portuguese. In the past, he was an active member of the Luso Canadian Club, but he has since dissociated himself from it and is now representing some of his people in various multi-ethnic activities. He is active in the Portuguese parish.

A Portuguese grocery and a new and used furniture store in the Forest Lawn district serve the needs of Calgary's Portuguese community. In these stores, little English is spoken. There is also a Portuguese grocery store in another part of the city which is owned by an immigrant who came to Canada in 1960 from a town near Lisbon. He first worked for the Canadian Pacific Railway. After several years, he left to open the store. He stated that in Calgary 95% of the Portuguese people own their own homes, and that after a year or a year and a half of living in the city "everyone" buys his own home.

No statistical data are available pertaining to ethnic groups to confirm or deny this speculation, but it is known that the incidence of home ownership among Portuguese immigrants is high and well above the average for Canadians as a whole. In part, this may be accounted for by the fact that many of the immigrants have a rural background and place a high value on ownership of land. The purchase of real estate in an inflationary situation is known to be a "hedge" against disappearing savings. Perhaps there is also a psychological factor, insofar as immigrants faced with drastic social change may gain a sense of security from ownership of property.

A notable characteristic of the immigrants in Calgary is that many of them have a history of migration in their family. Some of their relatives migrated to Portuguese communities in California a generation ago, and uncles and aunts now visit them, sometimes annually, from the United States. The Canadian immigrants are much less inclined to visit in the States, but are more likely to spend their money on a visit to the homeland. In some cases, grandparents lived for a time in California and then returned to the Azores; one or both parents then migrated to a New England community for a few years and returned. Some of the younger men had previously been in Brazil or Venezuela before coming to Canada. Thus, among this relatively small population of Portuguese Canadians, there is a considerable history of trans-oceanic migration.

Edmonton: The Portuguese population of Edmonton was estimated to be 6,000 in 1974. The heart of the Portuguese district is an area bounded by 95th Street, the Exhibition grounds, and 111th and 118th avenues. It contains many of the city's older houses, some of them very dilapidated, but the entry of immigrants is upgrading the district. Often the homes of recent arrivals are painted in bright colours. Vegetables grow in neat rows in the back and side gardens of the houses; in front, flowers bloom during the summer months. Initially, the immigrants purchase homes at very low prices because the surrounding district is poor and rundown. But as more of their relatives and friends move into the area, the property improves and its value is greatly increased. Many immigrants are able to purchase a second or even a third house.

The adjacent Norward district is becoming increasingly an area of Portuguese settlement, although it is currently known as "Little Italy." Portuguese Canadians are also spreading out into the Wellington district in the northwest and in the Calder area. From there, they are scattering outwards to the suburbs, with only a few locating in the southern section of the city. Some of the earliest immigrants to Edmonton have already moved to the suburbs. This is especially true of the more financially successful, who like those in other parts of Canada sometimes attempt to cut their ties with the rest of the Portuguese community. The few professionals in the city settled in the suburbs when they first moved to Edmonton.

Many of the early Portuguese immigrants who came to this part of Alberta have since moved on. As elsewhere, the men came alone; and when they could almost afford to bring their families to Canada, the cost of bringing them to Edmonton often appeared to be prohibitive. Thus, as noted earlier, many moved to the East, usually to Toronto and Montreal, and occasionally to New England.

The majority of the Portuguese Canadian population in Edmonton is from the Azores Islands, and most of these have come from São Miguel. Since the Azorean immigrants usually have little formal education, they find employment in manual jobs. Many work as section hands for the Canadian National Railway. These workers are often located in areas far from the city from May until October and may be unemployed during the winter; as in many other Portuguese communities, the seasonal workers use their free time to improve their houses. Other men work on construction sites in rough carpentry or in landscape gardening. Some work in nurseries or in market gardening on the fringes of the city. Still others are employed as janitors or cleaners of public or industrial buildings. The women also find work cleaning, either by the day or on a regular employment basis. Some are employed in the garment industry; some work in meat-packing or chicken-processing plants.

Successful entrepreneurs in the community include two real estate agents, one of whom also owns a retail store; a firm of travel agents, the owner of which also runs a driving school; bakery owners, a medical doctor, an industrial chemist, two draughtsmen, and a life insurance agent. Success in entrepreneurial activity is explained by the local Portuguese people as a matter of single-minded determination and hard work. But we have observed that an all-consuming passion to succeed can also be a detriment to community cohesion and service. As one man remarked, "They think only of their own selves, their homes, their own families, *not* the community." Another possible factor in success was expressed by a

Portuguese immigrant in the remark, "It's just a matter of contacts . . . knowing the people from back home, like my brother-in-law, he says to me come and get your [union] ticket.'"[7]

The propensity to work with others from the homeland is common in ethnic communities and has frequently been observed among the Portuguese in Canada. One young man remarks:

> Where my father works 75% to 80% are Portuguese. My uncles work there and also my best friends, or they went through there. You won't find people going out finding a job where there is no Portuguese person around. My dad and uncle brought their relatives out [to work with them] . . . . Many men will go up north for two or three years at a time. They will make $20,000 or $30,000 and then return and buy a home and have money in the bank too. The older brother might go with the father; the mother and younger children never go, because the woman would feel isolated and is usually shy . . . .
>
> [On arrival in Canada] most of the men lack education, but a kid of 14 or 15 [already] has a trade. (My cousin can fix refrigerators.) [Others] can do cement work or mechanical repairs . . . . Many of these men can lay tile but instead they lay [railway] tracks. They are afraid to go through the apprenticeship boards. Most guys would have to write an exam in English and know the [technical] terms. (My uncle could be making much money in automotive mechanics, but he works in a tannery.) To plumbers I say "get your ticket" but they reply, "no speak English." My brother-in-law is a qualified mechanic. People said to him, "You're going to have to learn English," and he did. He got his ticket and he can fix anything. He fixes transmissions and a number of Portuguese people work there now with him.

When some of the men enter a secure job, they are afraid to make a change. One man who was trained in the homeland as a mechanic was asked why he did not get back into his own trade and make considerably more money. He replied with an old Portuguese proverb, "*Saves onde estás a não sabes onde váis*" (You know where you are and you don't know where you are going). His son is critical, but the older man replies that he cannot leave his job now and go back to school. When the children were younger, it appeared to be taking too great a chance.

Some of the Portuguese Canadians in Edmonton claim to be living under the shadow of the Italians as they do frequently elsewhere in Canada. One young man stated:

> The Italians stick to themselves and to their own society; they live together and have their own stores. They are not as ambitious as the Portuguese, the young [Italian] men like to put on a new jacket and stand on the street corners; their ways of living are different, their way of thinking is different.

100

Two of the more articulate of the Portuguese young men in Edmonton are cousins who came to Canada as children and speak Portuguese in the home and English outside. The father of one arrived in Edmonton in 1957 and began working for the railway as a track-layer outside Edmonton. In 1958, he brought his wife and five children out from the Azores, but frequently they saw him only once a month. Another child was born in Edmonton.

The track-layer felt that he was not able to spend enough time with his family, since his work took him away for extended periods. He looked around for employment near his home and found a job in the chemical processing section of a tannery. He is still working in the same plant. Two years later, he brought his brother from Ponta Delgada in São Miguel. His son remarked:

> Right in Edmonton I have six families of relatives. In our block alone, my brother-in-law lives upstairs, my aunt is to the left, there are two families of friends to the left and another two families of friends across the street. In 1959 or '60, when we moved here we were the only Portuguese persons [on the street]. Now there are many families nearby. Most of the Portuguese like to buy a duplex. We had three families living in our place. We made it into a duplex, we have two kitchens and the downstairs is big enough to fit two families into it and they have five children.

The other cousin, currently (1973) employed as a life insurance agent, came to Canada with his parents via Curação, an island in the Dutch West Indies off the Venezuelan coast. It has large oil refineries and a profitable fishing industry. When the large multi-national oil corporations moved there, many Azoreans and Madeirans were attracted to the island. For this Portuguese family, however, their stay in Curação was only a brief interlude before they emigrated once again, this time to Canada, where they expect to remain permanently. Very few immigrants have come to Canada via Curação, but more have arrived from the Venezuelan Portuguese colony nearby.

There is a Portuguese bakery in Edmonton owned by a Portuguese and his nephew. The first man came to Edmonton in 1960 and later went to work at an asbestos company in British Columbia. In 1964, he returned to Edmonton, where he resumed his own trade as a carpenter. In 1973, he opened the bakery in partnership with his nephew, whom he had sponsored as an immigrant to Canada. The nephew is the baker, and his uncle makes the delivery rounds. The former recalls his trip to Canada:

> When I landed in Montreal, I saw snow for the first time. I was afraid to come off the plane. Supposedly, I was to take the plane to Watson Lake in the Yukon, where my uncle would be waiting for me. I was to change planes at Vancouver, but I made a mistake and waited at Vancouver for two days. I was lost for two whole days! In a store a

101

Portuguese person sent me to "immigration" and someone there who speaks Spanish phoned my uncle.

There is a grocery store in the Portuguese district which serves many needs of the local residents. Large sacks of beans and nuts cram the aisles. Pictures of the homeland decorate the walls, and posters advertise events of interest to the local Portuguese Canadians. The owner sells records imported from Portugal, newspapers from Lisbon, and magazines and books in Portuguese. He came to Edmonton in 1963. He had intended to locate in Montreal but had a friend in Edmonton, so opted to join him. In Portugal, he used to work for the government, but in Alberta he was first employed in the construction industry. He came as a single man and visited the homeland twice during his first ten years in Canada. In 1971 he invited a woman from Lisbon to come to Edmonton to marry him, and she now assists him in the store. This shop serves as an information centre for the local Portuguese Canadians; businessmen leave their calling cards on the counter and advertise their products and services there.

Driving is making a difference to the lifestyle of Portuguese women in this city. There is a Portuguese driving school in the area that provides lessons to both men and women. The women who learn to drive are much freer than they were before. In some cases, they are enabled to work in jobs outside the Portuguese area. As in other parts of Canada, often they own more real estate assets than the people for whom they work.

One resident of Edmonton stated that when he arrived in the city a decade ago he spent an entire year trying to find out where he could learn English in his spare time. Now, he said, the new arrivals have an established community where they can make enquiries and receive assistance.

British Columbia

Portuguese immigrants have been drawn to British Columbia by the availability of jobs and the benign climate in the southern parts of the province. It is estimated that in June, 1973, there were at least 25,500 Portuguese in six areas of major concentration (See table, p. 103).

Other centres, such as Castlegar and Revelstoke, have settlements of several hundred Portuguese Canadians. Because of early employment patterns, where the immigrants were scattered on farms or put to work on railway maintenance and extension, smaller clusters of families and young men sprang up in many other towns across the province.

It has been estimated that in Vancouver 80% of the Portuguese men work in the construction industry. As in other large cities across Canada, many are employed as cement finishers, tile layers, and stonemasons, where on-the-job training is available to persons of limited formal education. The men also find employment as janitors. Both men and women work in hospitals or factories, frequently as semi-skilled workers.

At first glance, it seems puzzling that comparatively few Portuguese men, many of whom have come from fishing villages and have had experience as seamen, are employed on the fishing boats and in other maritime

Southwest	Greater Vancouver	15,000
	Victoria	1,000
Northwest	Kitimat and Terrace	2,000
	Prince Rupert	1,000
	Prince George	2,000
Southcentral	Okanagan Valley, especially Osoyoos, Oliver, and Penticton	4,500

pursuits. The answer lies in legislation, introduced some years ago, directed at keeping Japanese interests out of Canadian coastal fishing. In an article dealing with the possible sale of Cassiar Packing Company Limited and the ensuing interchange of ideas between the British Columbia provincial government and the federal government on the subject, Environment Minister Jack Davis stated "that the right to fish in Canadian waters was going to 'remain in the hands of Canadians.'"[8] When only Canadians can be employed in the fishing industry, for at least the first five years that they are in Canada and until they obtain Canadian citizenship, immigrants have to find alternative employment. By the end of this period, many men think it is too late to change their occupation.

Within the British Columbian Portuguese communities, there is specialization of occupation from one location to another. In Kitimat, the men originally came to obtain employment in the construction of the Alcan plant there. When the plant was completed, many applied for work as unskilled labourers in the smelter. Now, many of these same men are skilled labourers, and some are foremen. In nearby Terrace, a service town for the surrounding area, the Portuguese Canadians work in the sawmill or in the surrounding bush as loggers. Others are employed in pulp and paper mills in Prince George and Castlegar. In Prince Rupert, there are also large numbers of Portuguese in the fish canneries.

The Okanagan Valley has attracted Portuguese families, especially the fruit-farming areas in the south around Oliver and Osoyoos. Few were full-time fruit farmers previously but some had owned fruit trees on their property in the homeland. The city of Victoria on Vancouver Island, with its mild winters, lures Portuguese immigrants to landscaping and gardening vocations. The settling of these various area of British Columbia by

103

Portuguese immigrants is recounted in the pages that follow through the stories of some of the first arrivals in the province.

SOUTHERN COASTAL REGION

Vancouver and Victoria: The first Portuguese person to settle in the Greater Vancouver area of British Columbia, Captain Antonio G. Quintal, came there by accident. He tells his own story:

It was August, 1939 that the "Yacht Reverie" arrived in Funchal, the capital harbour of Madeira Island. She was skippered by the Reverend John Antle and a young English lad, his only crew member. It had been a rough crossing from Plymouth, England and the boy had decided at this point, to return home. Mr. Antle was to remain in port until he could find someone willing to sail with him to British Columbia. When I heard of this opportunity for travel and adventure, I immediately offered my services, and I was accepted [although without pay. I was age 21 at the time].

My mother, of course, was very much opposed to my leaving home for a foreign land, especially since the Second World War was now in progress and she feared she would never see me again. However, my father was very much in favour of my taking advantage of such a unique opportunity which, no doubt, would give me a different way of life and would help me to decide my future occupation.

During the preparations for the voyage, I heard many other comments and opinions from my friends and neighbours, most of whom had a healthy respect for the sea, which was heightened by its ever-present mystery and [by] superstitions. In their minds I was crazy to believe that we could possibly survive such a sea venture on such a poorly fitted thirty-six foot sailboat with a broken-down engine and shabby sails [and which was not even equipped with a radio receiver]. I was also reminded that British Columbia was somewhere at the end of North America in Alaska and that I would freeze to death upon arrival, if I had not already drowned on the way.

Nevertheless, [although I had] been unable to obtain a passport for myself, we set sail at the end of September, 1939. The Atlantic crossing was one of both storm and calm, as Nature would have it. I spent much of the time mending the sails and doing the usual chores aboard ship. It was not possible to carry on long conversations in order to pass the time because of our language [problem. Mr. Antle could speak only English, and I spoke only Portuguese]. There was no other source of entertainment. At times, in order to supplement our food supply, I caught turtles and various kinds of fish. On a clear night I [used to study] the stars.

During our voyage we had visited the West Indies [and passed through the Panama Canal. We spent some time visiting] the ports along the Pacific Coast from California to Washington. At the end of one year, we arrived in Victoria, British Columbia, on a beautiful September day in 1940.

The immigration officer immediately asked for my passport and when I was unable to produce one, he did not know what to do, but said that I would probably have to return to Madeira. I found this to be a very gloomy prospect, indeed. But from Victoria, we sailed to Vancouver and at the Immigration office here, I applied for immigration to Canada. I was asked if I would be willing to fight for Canada, and I replied in a very definite affirmative. I was permitted to remain for a six-month probation period and during that time I could work at any job I could find. In June 1941, I received a letter from Ottawa granting permanent residence.

Almost immediately I was successful in obtaining a job as deck-hand on a tugboat towing logs from up north. [The following year], still having the sailing fever, I signed on at Vancouver in 1941, for the ship, *City of Alberni*, which was loading lumber for Australia, but when she was about to sail, they found that I had no passport and so I had to remain behind. However, I continued to work on the tugs during the war as first mate. I was called for the armed services in 1942, but was told, much to my chagrin, that I would have to stay with the tugs as that work was essential to the war effort.

In 1944, I applied for Canadian Citizenship ahead of time because I had been told that it sometimes took a year to be completed. In 1946, I went to navigation school and completed the course but I could not take the necessary examinations because I had not yet been granted citizenship. I wrote to Ottawa, explaining my plight and in early 1947 I went before Judge Boyd and swore allegiance to Canada and the Queen. Citizenship [was] granted!

I went back to navigation school for the examinations and obtained two certificates at the same time – the master's certificate for tugboats and the first mate's certificate for Home Trade vessels.

After completing six months as master of tugboats, I began working for the Standard Oil Company of B.C. as deck officer, but in 1951 went back to navigation school and obtained my master's certificate for Home Trade vessels. I served as master of the Standard tankers from 1951 until 1956, when I wrote and passed the examinations for pilots. I am still active in this capacity.

The next Portuguese immigrants appeared in Vancouver in 1954 and consisted of seven men from São Miguel, in the Azores. At first, they began to work on farms in Ontario, but [soon] they heard that there were better opportunities in Vancouver. Their greatest disappointment when they arrived here was that no one could speak Portuguese. It was on a Saturday when the office was closed, that I had to go to the Shipping Master's office in the Immigration Building in order to clear the ship for sea. There I learned that these seven men were on the top floor of the building, and I thought at the time that they must be from some ship, and so I went up to meet them and they were certainly very glad to see me. I promised to do everything I could to help them find work until they could get to Kitimat where the aluminum industry was just opening up and the town was being established.

Many more Portuguese from the east were to follow the first group and most of them had my address and knew that I would help them get to Kitimat. For a long time there were more Portuguese in that town than any other nationality. [Every] time that I was in Vancouver between assignments, there were always several [Portuguese immigrants] waiting for me to assist them in making their applications for work in Kitimat. Today there are many thousands of Portuguese in Vancouver.

An early post-war immigrant to settle in Vancouver came from Goose Bay, Labrador, on a vacation. He liked the west coast and in 1956, when his job in the east terminated, he decided to settle there, together with five or six other Portuguese men. He had had a wide range of experience in construction, both in Canada and overseas, and was soon able to find a job as a cement finisher. He continued in this occupation until his recent retirement.

He had initially arrived in Canada in 1952 as a visitor from Venezuela. "I arrived in Toronto just to travel and go directly to Montreal. I came as tourist – not immigrant – so it was difficult to get [a] job." He worked for a month or two in Montreal, then went to Sept-Iles and later Labrador. His wife came from Portugal in 1957, and all his children were born in Canada. He has four sons and two daughters. All the sons are in Vancouver. One works in cement finishing; another is employed as a gyprock filler. Another son and one of the daughters own a restaurant business worth over $100,000. Like many of the early Portuguese-Canadian settlers, he is satisfied with life in Canada.

His nephew and a partner own and operate a Portuguese department store located in an "ethnic neighbourhood" in downtown Vancouver. In the same block there are a Chinese fruit and vegetable store, a Dutch cheese and meat shop, a Spanish bakery, and an English shop. The store is large, with a supermarket specializing in Portuguese imports on the ground floor and furniture and appliances upstairs. It is more than a store: it is a news centre and a purveyor of the artifacts of the Portuguese cultural tradition. It sells copies of the Portuguese language paper, *O Mensageiro*, printed in Vancouver. Advertisements of programmes that are of interest to Portuguese persons, printed in their own language, are prominently displayed; they announce both church-oriented and secular programmes. Sports newspapers, women's magazines, other publications and records from the homeland are available. The supermarket offers an abundance of imported fish of many different types. The store began in 1966 as a food importing business, supplying frozen fish, canned fish, olive oil, dry beans of various types, and all manner of delicatessen items from Portugal.

Although only twenty-two years of age when he arrived in Canada, one owner had already migrated to Brazil, where he worked as a bartender for five years. In 1959, he came to Canada to join his parents, who had just arrived from Portugal. All were sponsored by their uncle. The young man had several years of experience in the construction business as well as working on the railway between the time he arrived in Canada and 1966 when he began working for himself. He laughs now about his initial experience in pick and shovel jobs for the railway about 140 miles from Vancouver. He had smooth hands and was not used to manual labour after his work as a bartender. The other men used to tease him about his bleeding blisters until he developed calluses on his hands like the rest of the work gang.

The food importing business flourished as the Portuguese population of Vancouver grew year by year. In 1969, the two business partners had expanded and opened a small corner store. The next step was to buy the property where the department store now stands and to erect the building which houses both the importing company and the department store.

The store operators know almost 90% of the Portuguese persons living in Vancouver, and suggest that about 30% come from the Azores and Madeira, and the rest from the mainland. (Other persons place the percentage as more nearly 50% from the islands.) The people of the community know where to find the manager as he sits in his open office at the head of the stairs in the department store. The store itself is strategically located in the heart of the Portuguese commercial district. There are many businessmen serving the Portuguese community. For example, another arrival in Canada via Venezuela had opened an import business before the main stream of immigrants arrived on the west coast. He is reputed to have come as a tourist and later applied to remain in Canada.

Also in the heart of the commercial district are a Portuguese real estate agency and an insurance agency. The owner of the realty company tells the story of his migration:

> I was customs officer in Faial [one of the islands of the Azores group] at the time of the volcano in 1957-58. My brother was here in Canada, so I came too. At the beginning it was very difficult as I couldn't speak any English. Imagine – brought rubber boots for the snow in July! At first I worked for Canadian Pacific in the Fraser Valley. That was in 1954. Then in March 1961, I went to work as a labourer in construction. In January 1963, I took off to school and did Grade 10 in a rush. The course was finished in four months. At Vancouver Vocational Institute I was admitted to a bookkeeping course the same year, but after completing it I couldn't get a job. I had typed over 200 letters of application for work. At home there was a wife and

two children to feed. I went to work in a sawmill until September when I enrolled in a real estate licensing course.

This building and business are owned by my partner and myself. We commenced in 1964. I started working as a salesman for Rutherford McCrae and was there two-and-a-half years. Then I worked for Klein Brothers Realty for a year. At that time Mr. Holt invited my partner and me to join him in this company. Mr. Holt has since passed away. In 1966, I enrolled in a university course in Urban Land Economics at the University of British Columbia. It was a three year diploma course. Now I am a member of the Canadian Real Estate Council of British Columbia and also a member of the Real Estate Institute of Canada.

On his office walls are certificates indicating that he is a member of the "Million Dollar Club" achieved in two-and-a-half years through Multiple Listing Services and also a member of the "Quarter Million Club" achieved in each of seven consecutive years in Vancouver. Many of his clients are Portuguese. He concludes:

I love it here; this is very contrary to the beginning. I used to know two-thirds of the people, but now the community is growing so fast. Last year we built this building and now I am an administrator. People are steadily arriving from Portugal. I no longer know as many of the new ones.

A man working in a Portuguese-owned travel agency (1973) a few blocks away is also editor of a Portuguese-language newspaper, the *Sentinela*. The travel agency serves many functions in the local Portuguese community, such as filling out government application forms, offering translation services, and interpreting for new arrivals. He first came to Canada from the Azores in 1964. He arrived in Montreal, worked in Kingston for a while, then finally settled in Vancouver in February 1972. He gives the following account of his employment in Canada:

When I arrived in Montreal I already knew French. I learned it in Portugal [which has many French tourists]. When I first came I was working in a restaurant as a waiter. Then I went to Kingston with the idea of working in the nylon plant there. Later I joined the insurance industry and took some evening classes at Queen's University in economics. In February 1972, I was transferred to Vancouver with my insurance company. Recently I resigned to join this travel agency. I'm from the Azores – Santa Maria Island. I was in the travel business and knew English there.

A prominent couple in the Portuguese community jointly edit the Portuguese-language newspaper *O Mensageiro*. It has a subscription list of about 1,000. The man works for a real estate company which employs several other Portuguese Canadians. He was attracted to Vancouver through a Canadian banker whom he met in Germany where he worked and he met and married a German wife. When he applied for immigration through the Canadian embassy, they suggested either Vancouver or Toronto as a destination. He had been working for a newspaper in Germany and was interested in starting one in Vancouver. In 1970, he began working in the real estate business because the newspaper circulation was not large enough to enable him to devote full time to it and support himself. Thus, his wife does much of the work on the paper. Because working hours with the real estate company are flexible, he is able to continue his association with the paper and with various Portuguese clubs and associations.

In 1956, the first group of about a dozen Portuguese immigrants arrived in Victoria from São Miguel Island in the Azores. One of them met a Canadian couple who spoke Portuguese and who arranged for him to have an interview with the owner of the city's famous Butchart Gardens. He was offered a job there and began work at the Gardens in July, 1956. He is still working there. In the summer of 1973, there were fifteen Portuguese men and women employed by the Gardens.[9] Gardening is one of the occupational specializations of Portuguese now in many communities in Canada. Even when working for construction companies many are employed in the landscaping sections of these firms.

NORTHERN BRITISH COLUMBIA
Kitimat: Kitimat in northern British Columbia seems an unlikely place for the establishment of a sizable Portuguese community. It came about in a way explained by one of the first Portuguese immigrants to arrive in Canada in the post-war period. He tells his own story:

> On May 14th 1953, there were eighteen people who arrived by boat from São Miguel in the Azores. One hundred were also on board from the Mainland. All of us were single men. We were taken to Montreal by train. "Immigration" took me to Valleyfield to look for work. But they couldn't find work for all of us so "Immigration" took me back to Montreal. I met a man – a Canadian – and he told me about a job working for a small shop where they make bracelets. I work there some time until work gets slack. Then I worked for the ____ Hotel in Montreal. While there I made a Canadian friend who works for the Bank of Montreal. He was moved to B.C. He told me there were plenty of jobs in B.C., but I would have to speak English there. I talked to my Portuguese friends and asked them to come with me to B.C., but they were scared of speaking English. I went alone, all by myself and arrived in the west on 16th of June 1955, by train. It was a very heavy rain when I arrived. A man in the train woke me up and said, "We are in Kitimat." I called a taxi and they took us to camp at the wharf, then he drove us to the hotel. There was no place – everything was full! We had to sleep outside in the rain. In the morning the taxi driver drove us to the employment office. I got a job after

filling out an application and being given a medical. Two or three guys from Portugal had already come there the previous week.

The first time I am in Kitimat it seemed like everyone is speaking English. (Really it was French, Italian and German – but the sentences sounded just one long jumbled word – they were all the same to me.)

When the Portuguese first came to this part of the country there was no one to help us. The cost of living was very high here. The first time the company shut down, after eight years of being in Canada I went back to Portugal to marry.

Today, the man is employed in the warehouse department of Alcan after a number of years of working in the plant.

Another early settler in Kitimat was born in the north of Portugal in Minho province, and then went to Lisbon where he worked as a baker. He decided to apply for immigration to Canada, and while he was making out the application, he struck up a conversation with another man who was similarly applying. They became friends and kept in touch. Altogether, seven men immigrated at the same time, coming to Montreal from various locations on the mainland. The baker had been learning English while awaiting confirmation of his passage to Canada, and it came as a considerable shock when he found out that in six weeks he would be going to French-speaking Canada. He and his friends were told to change to learning French, but they did not learn very much in the time remaining. When he reached Montreal, he went to live with a Portuguese couple.

At first, as for other immigrants, life in Canada presented a cultural shock for him. It was difficult to find work with limited knowledge of English and even less of French. Wages were low and led, quite naturally, to much disappointment. At first, he located a job as a baker, earning 50¢ an hour. Then he found a second job as a dishwasher, to do in his spare time and so supplement his income. But it was lonely working without being able to communicate, and he found French difficult to learn.

The friend he had met in the Lisbon office of Canadian Immigration left Montreal to work in Kitimat. The original seven from Portugal remained together in Montreal. Not long afterwards, the friend sent a telegram asking three of them to come to join him. They could not decide which three should go, and in the end they all packed up and went by train.

The journey across Canada was tedious, and en route the men wondered about the wisdom of such a venture. There was a wait of several hours in Jasper for the train to Kitimat; and while the group was wandering around the town to pass the time, they met ten other Portuguese men similarly strolling along the street. In the course of conversation, they told where they were going and why, and all ten men said that they would also join them. The baker had only $7 left when he reached Kitimat; the cost of the journey had exhausted his meagre savings.

When eventually the group of seventeen reached the construction site and applied for work, he acted as the translator for the other men. Consequently, his application was processed last. They were then seated in an outer office of the construction company. One by one they were called in; and as each man came out, he reported, "I'm hired." His spirits sank as man after man returned. He wondered what he would do if he was not offered a job. He sat there nervously fingering the seven dollar bills in his pocket, then at last his name was called, and he found that he too was hired. In fact he was the unofficial interpreter for the group. They were put to work in a gang building the pot lines for the Alcan smelter.

At one time during the construction, there were between 500 and 700 men from Portugal in Kitimat employed in the construction industry. They felt great pride in their work: they were building not only a new plant but a new city. Wages were regarded as excellent, and they looked forward to building a secure future for themselves and eventually having others from the homeland join them. A stereotype developed of the Portuguese as strong willing labourers. It is small wonder that some local people now say, "If it hadn't been for the Portuguese, there would not be a Kitimat today."

The former baker is now (1973) a foreman in Alcan plant and has men of many national origins working under him. Comparing those who come today with the early arrivals, he comments:

> When we first came as immigrants, we had no one to refer to, no one to help us. Now there are many people ready to assist the new arrivals. We were fighting for employment in those early days, but now people are not as eager. Things back home have changed – the standard of living is higher there now – the men have more in their pockets nowadays so they are more relaxed about finding a job. The Portuguese are known as reliable and good workers. Many leave because of the weather here. They have established themselves in Toronto and Montreal.

In his spare time he coaches a Canadian lacrosse team. In 1972, it won the B.C. championship in Burnaby.

In the period when he was in the process of establishing himself in the West, others "back East" were hearing via letters and personal contacts that many jobs were available in remote Kitimat for those who would work hard. For example, an Azorean worker in a Kingston nursery in 1960 received a letter from his brother-in-law, who had immigrated five years earlier, which began, "I hope you come to Kitimat . . . . " It went on to describe the hourly pay, $2.36 an hour, which was almost double the nursery rate of $1.25. It told of vacancies. On his present salary it was difficult to support a wife and several children in Portugal, and at the same time save money to buy a house. If he brought his family to Canada now, he would never have enough to purchase their own home; yet it was three long years since he had seen his children. He was tempted to pack up and go to Kitimat, but there was the problem of telling the owners of the nursery that he was leaving. He recalled their kindness when he first arrived:

> When they were very busy, they would ask me to work overtime. They gave me a good supper, and I stayed some nights till ten instead of five. They paid me overtime and took me home by car. There aren't many employers like that.

On the other hand, if he took the job in Kitimat, he would soon be able to bring his family there to a new home. At last, he decided: he ought to take the job in Kitimat. He hoped at least that his brother-in-law's reference would be all he needed. He would go the next day. It would be easier to leave without saying goodbye to his employers; perhaps he could leave them a note. They would surely understand that he had to look after the interests of his family first.

He bought his train ticket, then he remembered that his brother-in-law had said there were several vacancies. He decided to ask two friends if they would like to come along. They would be company for him on the trip.

The journey was a long one, longer than he had realized. The trio brought food with them so that they would not have to buy much on the train. As each day passed, the man thought of the money he was losing by not working. There would be no savings this week, no pay cheque on Friday. He was worried about what would happen if others should arrive first and take the vacant jobs; but he dared not discuss his concern with his friends – if things did not work out they would certainly blame him for telling them there was plenty of work. Then again, none of them had enough money to make a return trip to Ontario, so whatever happened they would be compelled to stay in British Columbia. When the trio finally arrived at their destination, they were relieved to find there were jobs in Kitimat for all of them. Now, many years later, he is still there, working at a responsible job in the smelting plant. His wife and five children joined him two years after he reached the West.

One event had a profound effect upon the Portuguese community in Kitimat. On the 13th of July, 1970, a strike commenced at the Alcan plant. It lasted 105 days. At this time there were 314 Portuguese workers out of a total hourly-paid work force of 1,900.[10] As the strike appeared to be leading into a prolonged period of non-employment, some of the Portuguese workers decided that this was the time to move to other parts of the country, as did many others from the plant. Many relocated in the Okanagan Valley.

Terrace: The town of Terrace in northwestern British Columbia is known as "the hub" because it is the service centre for the nearby logging operations. It is also at the crossroads of the highway that extends from Prince George in the interior to Prince Rupert on the coast and the north-south route that provides access to the thriving community of Kitimat. In

1973, Terrace had a population of 18,000, and further development is planned through government sponsored programs.

The first group of Portuguese men to arrive at Terrace came to work on the Canadian National Railway as section hands. About 90% in the area are from the Azores. Most of the men came West with the idea of making some money and then returning to the homeland. The majority, however, have stayed in Canada, although not necessarily in the northwest. They now own their homes and have steady jobs in the town. In Terrace itself, many are employed by the sawmills.

Terrace has a Portuguese grocery store which serves as a focal point for Portuguese immigrants in the vast area between Prince Rupert and Prince George. The local Portuguese Canadians come here to shop for imported foods and records, and at the same time obtain news of people in their community. From time to time, the grocery store owner visits the outlying communities in his truck, which is loaded with imported delicacies, such as Portuguese canned octopus, sardines, and other seafood.

A worker in the grocery store arrived in 1957 and took a job as watchman at the Canadian National shops in Terrace. Later, he learned to do all sorts of odd jobs, such as fueling the deisel units, and separating and coupling the trains. Next, he worked in logging near Twin River before returning to Terrace.

He had always thought of emigrating, since the age of fourteen or fifteen. He had relatives in California and thought that there might be a possibility of being sponsored. He finally was able to come to Canada when he was thirty-three, sponsored by his brother, who was in the first group of Portuguese to come to Terrace. He said, "Now I wouldn't go to the States for anything – they don't have anything that we have not got here and we have a lot they don't – other than good weather!"

The Portuguese community in Terrace has grown largely through the efforts and initiative of a construction contractor and restaurant owner in the town. He has been in Terrace since 1964. The large block of offices and stores he owns is situated on the main street of the town, and his restaurant occupies a prominent place in the same block. He worked both in construction and in a pulp mill before turning to the restaurant business. He came to Canada from São Miguel and began working as a janitor in a hotel in Ocean Falls, British Columbia. He was soon promoted to sandwich-maker, third cook, second cook, and eventually assistant chef. He also worked as a butcher and baker at various times.

He decided to leave and find employment in Vancouver, where he obtained a position in the University Club. After six months, he was offered a job by a catering company and subsequently became a catering manager in Calgary and at Lake Louise. The company then sent him to open a hotel and camp in Terrace. Later, his employer wanted to transfer him to Edmonton, but his wife, a Canadian, did not like the idea and they remained in Terrace.

When the Blue Gables restaurant became available soon after, they leased it and he left the catering company. Later, he bought the rest of the block in which the restaurant was located – it consisted of a second-hand store. He renovated the building and then began buying and renovating other buildings as he was able. In 1964, when he started in Terrace, he had one employee in addition to himself and his wife and lived in a one-room apartment. Now he employs twenty-five persons and lives in a large home. His contracting company, which employs six bricklayers and ten carpenters, has built nine houses in the town. Frequently, he buys old buildings, renovates them, and then leases them. The restaurant, which includes a thriving catering business, began with thirty-five seats, and now can accommodate 175 persons at a sitting.

He attributes his success in large measure to extremely hard work. His usual workday is 8 a.m. to 1 a.m. the next day. He commented:

> My wife complains, "Work, work, that's all you think of," [but] if I pass away I want to prove that I did well for Canada. I work seven days a week and I feel guilty about it. I would like to spend time with my family. But I am trying to prove myself – I'm not trying to become a millionaire – many immigrants have done a lot for this country.

Initially, he had to borrow a large sum from the Industrial Development Bank of Canada. Soon he will be renting them office space in one of his buildings. He has tremendous faith in his ability to provide jobs to people who really want to work. He has three brothers in Canada who are employed in woodworking plants or on the docks. They prefer security to the risks involved in going into business for themselves.

He was only able to attend school to the Grade Four level in São Miguel, but he has always been interested in learning whatever he could from various sources. He has taken courses by correspondence, including one in hotel management, and he later taught cooking in a series of television programmes. He is involved in the local Kinsmen organization and assists with children's camps and minor league hockey.

Since he has been in Terrace he has brought a total of forty Portuguese to Canada. Many of these persons were employed by him, and he found work elsewhere for those he could not employ himself. When people from the homeland encountered difficulties in this part of British Columbia they often sought him out. All the people he has brought to Canada now have their own homes, many of them built with his assistance. The homes were worth between $25,000 and $35,000 (1973) at local market prices – that is, they were slightly above average in Terrace. He has been known to mortgage houses without interest to recent Portuguese immigrants. His philosophy is that "Canada is as good as you make it yourself; it's how you get along with other people that counts."

Another person who assisted Portuguese immigrants in Terrace arrived in Canada in 1955, coming with several others to work in the bush near Fort Fraser. (His brother-in-law, also Portuguese, had a job hauling logs from the bush to the local sawmill.) He had earlier applied for work when he heard that one of the railways was looking for a carpenter, although he knew little about carpentry. He said he had tools and skill, and explained his lack of references on his recent arrival in the country. Afterwards, the foreman could see that he did not know the trade, but he was kept on as a carpenter's assistant. Later he worked on power lines in Terrace, in Vanderhoof and for eight years in the Alcan plant in Kitimat.

After this varied experience of heavy work in various parts of British Columbia he returned to Terrace to become a salesman for men's clothing, a job that was well suited to his Portuguese training as a tailor. In the early 1970s he ran a driving school. He not only teaches driving but arranges for the learners to finance their car purchases. He also helps local Portuguese who request his assistance with completing their income tax forms. He has given advice on house purchases and acts as an interpreter at the bank to arrange for mortgage loans. When relatives overseas wish to join immigrants already established he helps fill out the application forms – the "carta de chamada" or letter which "calls" someone from Portugal, as the Portuguese know it. During the period when visitors could apply for landed immigrant status he took people to Prince Rupert for interviews at the immigration office and served as their interpreter.

Not all the Portuguese immigrants in Terrace have achieved the prosperity and prominence of the successful men mentioned above. Many work for modest wages in the local lumber plants or in service industries in the town. Nevertheless, the large majority of the married men are purchasing houses. Some come to the area because of the employment opportunities and do not plan to settle there. They intend to stay long enough to save the money to buy a house in one of the large cities or to make a downpayment on a farm in the Okanagan Valley, and then they will move on. There is, however, a substantial core of permanent residents among the largely transient population.

SOUTH-CENTRAL BRITISH COLUMBIA

The Okanagan Valley: Although the Canadian government's immigration program was intended to bring Portuguese farmers to Canada in the 1950s, it is only in the Okanagan Valley that their hopes have been realized on any scale. Portuguese families are concentrated in the countryside surrounding Osoyoos and Oliver. The Valley is irrigated, and fruit and dairy farming flourish on its hillsides and along the lakeshore. Also, it is increasingly becoming a tourist area. In 1970, the Oliver-Osoyoos region had 106,000 tourists, and it is anticipated that this will increase to 147,900 by 1980:

> The Oliver-Osoyoos regional population increased by 27.6% to 8,600 in 1971 due primarily to tourist industry development and an influx of retired people. The Penticton and Vernon regional populations grew by 32.3% and 39.7% respectively due to expansion in tourism and some manufacturing and associated retail and service trades.[11]

115

The encroachment of residential areas into farming regions has provoked serious considerations of the future of the area:

> Agriculture as represented in the small family farm also has a social value to the life style of the Okanagan that should not be overlooked – British Columbia does not have enormous amounts of arable land and therefore for future production it would be best to protect good land now before it is covered up with concrete, etc.[12]

In the late 1960s and 1970s, there has been an influx of retired persons into the Valley, and now it is considered a prime area for retirement.

The balmy winters and hot summers which have brought tourists and retired people to the area have also attracted Portuguese immigrants from other parts of Canada. The first Portuguese workers were allocated to farm work in the area in 1955 to alleviate the shortage of hired help, especially in the harvest season. One such person told us of his arrival and settlement in the Valley.

He claims to have been among the first group of twelve Portuguese to come to the Okanagan Valley in 1955. Initially, he was employed by a dairy farm in Oliver. Shortly afterwards, he found a job in a fruit-packing house, where he still works. Prior to emigrating, he had been a policeman in the Algarve region of Portugal. Now, in addition to working in the packing house, he also owns and works a small orchard. In 1956, a year after his arrival, he brought his wife and son to join him. Later, he sponsored his brother-in-law. He speaks with feeling of the early days, when there was a sense of helplessness among the Portuguese men before they were able to speak English.

Most of the other men who came with the first group also own their own farms, although a few returned home to stay. On the farms, they grow cherries, peaches, plums, apples, grapes, pears, apricots, and walnuts. The majority of the men came from the fruit-growing area to the north of Lisbon, although they were not necessarily full-time farmers before coming to Canada. On the highway near Oliver, there is a gas station and variety store that sells Portuguese foods and other imported items. Farther south, in the area surrounding Osoyoos, there are about ninety Portuguese-Canadian families, the majority of whom have purchased orchards. Driving southwards from Penticton, one notices that German, English, and Irish names gradually give way to Portuguese names such as Moreira, de Melo, Sousa, Fernandes, and Ferreira.

The owner of several pieces of orchard property in the Osoyoos district was one of the original Portuguese immigrants who arrived in Canada in 1953. He took the train from Halifax to Quebec, where he worked on a dairy farm for a few days. Then he went to Toronto, washed dishes for a short time, and eventually obtained a job in the construction industry. By 1955, he worked in a factory, when he received word from a friend in Kitimat, B. C. that there were good jobs available there. He was reluctant to leave by himself and asked a friend to go with him; they left that very day.

He worked for five years in Kitimat "for the Municipality" but disliked the climate. In the summer of 1959, during his annual vacation, he visited the Okanagan Valley. The day he arrived in Osoyoos, he decided that this was where he should live and at once bought an orchard. It was not practical to move there immediately, as it was the end of August and the growing season was almost over; so he returned to his job in Kitimat and in February of the next year came back with his family to the Okanagan Valley. He has stayed there ever since. He proudly relates:

> I was the first to buy a farm; there were a few Portuguese around but they were working for someone else. Even when I worked hard they were very jealous and said, "Your place is not very good." Later on they bought places too, but they were still jealous and each says his is the best farm. I have worked harder than anyone else, so many, many long hours.

Some of his land was once swamp. He cut the brush during the winter, then dug drainage ditches twelve feet deep and laid drainage tile and pipe. There are eight of these parallel rows of pipe in his field.

He also owns twenty-five acres of cherry orchards in Osoyoos and another ten acres in Oliver. He gave thirty acres to his son-in-law. His large family assists him in working his extensive holdings. He has four married children, in addition to three at home. He has seen many changes since he landed in Canada more than twenty years ago. His father was a farmer near Funchal on the island of Madeira. When he first came to Canada, he could not speak a word of English or French, and he started working for $60 a month. He speaks of having to walk miles to church in the early days. His daughter relates stories she has heard him tell of the many initial hardships and struggles. Although of simple peasant stock and limited formal education, he has the proud independent spirit and initiative that is characteristic of many of the early Portuguese immigrants.

Most of his children are either in farming or in the automotive body repair business, but one daughter is married to a Portuguese who owns and operates a general store and gas bar. The store sells a variety of items of interest to the local Portuguese-Canadian community: imported china, paintings on velvet, religious pictures, and records of favourite artists from the homeland. The store owner came to Penticton in 1959. He says:

> We came from São Mateo on Terceira. I was 14 years old. Now I am 27. We were supposed to go to the United States to join my godfather. But he moved to Canada. We came out to join him. We were well-to-do in Portugal. We came because my family wanted to prevent us from having to join the army . . . . Wages were very low in the area. The men who came out were able to save quite a bit of money though, [eventually] buying everyone else out . . . . I was in Kitimat for two

months but it rained all the time. Then, for a year I worked on a farm with my father-in-law. He gave me a chance to buy this place [pointing to the store]. We put all our earnings into it. Soon, I hope to sell and go back into farming. We will buy in Osoyoos.

Many Portuguese men went to Kitimat to make money and then get out. Some never left that town. A few came down here – they couldn't take it and went back. Most that remained here are from Beira Baixa on the Mainland.

I'm Canadian, but I'm still very proud to be Portuguese.

He is also active in a radio program over CKOO, which serves both Oliver and Osoyoos. He broadcasts for an hour a week, giving information, sports, and news of Portugal, interspersed with music. He first gives the commentary in Portuguese and then translates for his English-speaking audience. When the Portuguese community needs a spokesman he frequently is called upon to be the representative of the younger generation in the Valley. He is active in community fund-raising drives such as the Crippled Children's Fund and the March of Dimes. Dances are organized among the Portuguese Canadians to raise money for their causes.

Another resident also came to Canada in 1953 in the earliest wave of immigration. Like many others, he first worked on a farm and then was employed by the railway, where he remained for eight months. He spent a period of time in the logging industry and subsequently became a supervisor on a logging boom. He left that job to come to the Okanagan Valley for a visit, and he purchased land in the Valley in 1965. Several Portuguese men had already bought orchards in the area.

His brother operated (1973) a fruit stand on the highway near Oliver. He came first to British Columbia in 1959. He spent one week picking potatoes on a farm near Victoria, then he too worked for the railway for a year. Subsequently, he got a job in a gold mine in northern Ontario, where he spent the next eight years. He was the only Portuguese man in the area, and so he moved to Toronto. For some time, he worked in a fruit store on Eglinton Avenue, driving the station wagon for deliveries. Then he moved West to join his brother, who was already in Oliver. Together, they purchased the orchard. They then brought their father from Portugal to help them to operate it.

Occasionally, one passes a closed fruit stand, where the owner is too busy to attend it. In one case there was no one left at home to sell the fruit: the man was working in his orchards, his wife was employed in the packing house, his son worked in an automotive body shop, and his daughter also worked in town.

One outstanding resident of the Okanagan Portuguese community is known by some of the English-speaking people of the region as 'the Portuguese king.' He was one of the very early settlers who came to work for Louis Hart, who owned extensive orchards. As he became established, he brought many members of his extended family to the Valley. His daughter and son-in-law operate a large hamburger stand on the outskirts of town. He is reputed to be the wealthiest man in the Portuguese community and is frequently regarded as the spokesman for the group. He has extensive land holdings in the area.

In the first generation, the Portuguese immigrants were eager to use their surnames on their property or enterprise. Thus, the fruitstands in the Okanagan Valley often bore titles such as Ferriera Fruit Stand and DeMelo's Fruits. In the second generation, the Christian name becomes anglicized, so that João puts up a sign reading Jack's Restaurant; Antonio calls his fruit stand Tony's Fruits; José is translated into Joe's Gas Bar. [13]

The process of revitalizing the fruit-growing farms in the Valley is an interesting one. In the early 1960s many farms were falling into disrepair because of the problems of attracting suitable day labour to the region for the harvest season. The area was at that time being worked by people of British, German, or Hungarian background. When the Portuguese entered the region in sizable numbers in the 1960s, they purchased the farms which were uneconomical for other groups to run. The Portuguese Canadians used their own families, which were frequently quite large, to harvest the crop and hence converted fruit farming into a profitable business. But as the children became adults, they began to want more leisure, like their Canadian friends. They saw no need to work a fourteen or sixteen-hour day. Now, among young married couples, the wife is frequently reluctant to work for very long hours beside her husband, in addition to looking after a young family. Some of the young people desire much more education than their parents received. Often they want to have a small business for themselves, which helps them to be independent of the parents. Sometimes a fruit stand has to be closed because there are no young people in the family who are willing to run it.

One way of getting around the problem of seasonal labour is to sponsor relatives from Portugal to work during the harvest months on the farm. The relatives obtain a trip, and probably some money too, for their months in Canada. It has been alleged by local business people in the Valley that the Portuguese-Canadian residents

> work all day in the [fruit] packing plant, and then come home to work during the evening in their orchards. They cannot do all the work themselves so they invite men over from Portugal who work for much less than local wages. At the end of the season they return to Portugal – it is unfair competition.

Another said:

> The Portuguese men came originally almost exclusively as orchard workers and were very well accepted here. They operate their farms with a closely-knit family – the members do almost all of their own work. This is changing as operations become larger – so they are having to hire like everyone else.

119

Many local farmers complain of problems obtaining orchard help to pick the cherry crop during the summer. One man lamented that a couple of young transient workers from Eastern Canada earned $160 in two days recently and then left. The owner was angry that they would not remain until the harvest was completely picked.

At present, the Portuguese owner-farmers in the Okanagan Valley are keeping valuable fruitlands in production. The future utilization of the area remains a question. What will happen after a generation? Will a new group of immigrants have to be imported to work the farms as family farms? Often to pay off the mortgages on the farm several members of the family have full-time jobs in nearby towns.

As noted, the current owners bought their farms when the former owners were ready to abandon the land. There are many cases of Portuguese Canadians who purchased a farm in the 1960s for $30,000 which is now worth $200,000. As the value of property has increased in the region, the Portuguese have bid against one another to acquire more land. Speculation in land has occurred as tourist accommodation is built and as housing developments cater to the interests of the increasingly large numbers of retired persons seeking homes in the Valley. But as the provincial government is now questioning the wisdom of using scarce farmland for housing, there may not be a ready market for the land which immigrants have purchased to sell for non-agricultural development.

Castlegar. Castlegar is typical of many smaller towns scattered in the interior of British Columbia. The Canadian Pacific Railway played a large part in the coming of Portuguese immigrants to the area. Men from the Azores were first attracted by the offer of steady employment by an agency for the CPR which commenced recruiting there in 1955:

> Eighty-nine immigrants flew from the Azores at their own expense and arrived in Montreal in the year 1956. Some found work in Montreal with the CPR while others were sent to various parts of the country including British Columbia. One group arrived at Nelson, a large CPR centre, in the middle of the winter and found there was no work for them with the CPR. They then applied for work with Sawmills in Nelson, Castlegar and Nakusp.[14]

The personnel manager of a sawmill in Castlegar received several applications for employment in 1956/1957. The company placed four Portuguese families in another of their sawmills located at Nakusp. By 1959 they were able to expand their work force in Castlegar and started to employ Portuguese men in the local sawmill. In 1974, out of a workforce of 400 men, 80 were Portuguese immigrants, attracted by relatively high wages and the prospect of steady employment. The same company also employs 300 workers in a large pulp mill and 400 loggers in the woods, but there are no Portuguese immigrants in these sectors of the work force. Sawmill employment has become a Portuguese specialty in the area.

The local community is served by a general store and a bakery. As yet the Portuguese immigrants are seldom active in community affairs other than through the Catholic Church.

REGIONAL DIFFERENCES – A COMPARISON

Portuguese areas of settlement in Canada are located from coast to coast, and from isolated northern outposts to southern border cities. This section of the study has presented material relating to the major areas of concentration. It should, however, be recognized that Portuguese persons live and work in many other regions which have not been studied here. There is scarcely any area of the country where at least one or two persons of Portuguese background do not live. But the major concentrations of Portuguese Canadians are to be found in our largest cities – Toronto, first and foremost, followed by Montreal and then Vancouver. These areas of settlement give every indication of becoming larger, as present residents draw relatives and friends from the homeland and compatriots living in the smaller centres come to work and reside in the flourishing communities of "urban villagers"[15] in our largest cosmopolitan centres. (The concept of "urban villagers" is discussed at length in the chapter on the family which follows.)

The largest settlements offer a full range of services in the Portuguese language as well as English and/or French. In Breton's terminology they are "institutionally complete;"[16] that is, they provide almost a full range of essential services within the community and in Portuguese. The major settlements are also of sufficient size to be able to subdivide into several communities on the basis of interest and background. They split, first, according to region of origin – Azoreans, Mainlanders, Madeirans – and then according to the educational level of the leaders. Often, well-educated, highly literate, middle-class leaders question the leadership of less educated though often highly intelligent men of peasant background.

The smaller communities demonstrate cohesiveness to present a united front to outsiders and to gain recognition in their local municipality or city. It is frequently in the medium-sized cities where divisiveness is greatest.[17] As we noted earlier, Calgary and Edmonton reflect this lack of unity. In part, it may be due to the fact that there were no established leaders in these communities prior to the arrival of large numbers of immigrants in the 1950s. Also, there is an absence of well-educated Portuguese in these cities who might provide leadership, as compared with the larger cities. Winnipeg, for example, has a few highly educated professionals to provide leadership. Some communities – again, those of Calgary and Edmonton in particular – are split into church-oriented and anti-clerical factions. In others, such as London, Ontario, the Portuguese work without conflict both in the church and in secular organizations.

Some areas have attracted immigrants from particular regions of Portugal. A few settlements, such as Streetsville, Wheatley, and Leamington, have concentrations of Portuguese from Aguadato in the Azores Islands and from Nazaré in the mainland Portugal. In the Prairie provinces, continental Portuguese are in the majority in northern communities and isolated construction sites, while Azoreans remain in the more southernly cities and towns. Toronto has a concentration of Madeirans; but some cities, such as London, have few or no immigrants from this island.

Regional origins of the Portuguese immigrants also are reflected in their occupational preferences. Throughout the country, the mainlanders usually opt for entering the unionized construction industry, while Azoreans often prefer to enter janitorial work where jobs are steadier, though rates of remuneration are lower.[18] Leamington and Wheatley in southern Ontario are unique as an area where the majority of the men are engaged in the fishing industry. Typically, the men arrive alone and work seasonally; then each winter, many of them return to Portugal to join their families.

Areas vary by the degree of participation of married women in the labour market. In some areas, such as St. John's, Newfoundland, the married women seldom work but in Galt and Kitchener, Ontario, many women work in light industry. Opportunity for the employment of married women may play a large part in these regional differences.

The Portuguese immigrants are more likely to assimilate to English-speaking than to French-speaking Canada.[19] Also close affinity to Italian communities is common to many settlements. Portuguese relationships with other ethnic groups are discussed at length in Anderson's *Networks of Contact,* Chapter IX.

Little methodical research has hitherto been undertaken on Portuguese settlements throughout Canada. Only in Toronto have serious studies of these communities been completed and published. Several studies are currently (1975) underway in Montreal. In other areas research, if conducted, remains unpublished or has been largely intuitive, without extensive data collection and analysis. The material contained in this and the preceding chapter is a preliminary attempt to rectify this situation and to provide a point of departure for further studies.[20]

NOTES

1. Our account of the Prairie Provinces regrettably excludes Saskatchewan. According to recent census data, there are only 210 Portuguese-speaking persons in the entire province; and we were unable, given time and resource constraints, to seek out these individuals for inclusion in this study.

2. Robert K. Merton, *Social Theory and Social Structure* (Glencoe, Illinois, 1968), Chap. x.

3. A. Peters, "The Portuguese Community – In Winnipeg," *Manitoba Modern Language Bulletin*, VIII, 2 (January 1974).
4. Other research studies have shown a high degree of conflict and parochialism among Portuguese in the homeland. See, for example, Bernard J. Siegel, "Conflict, Parochialism and Social Differentiation in Portuguese Society," *Journal of Conflict Resolution*, V (1961), 35-42.
5. Jose Cutileiro, *A Portuguese Rural Society* (Oxford: Clarendon Press, 1971), p. 71.
6. There is the international airport on Santa Maria and an American airbase at Lajes on Terceira Island. The nine islands in the Azores group are connected by a local air service also.
7. See Anderson, *Networks of Contact.*
8. "Ottawa Asked to Halt Fish Packing Firm Sale," *The Province*, Vancouver, June 23, 1973. For further information on the Portuguese in Vancouver see also "Algumas observações Sobre a minoria portuguesa de Vancouver," *Sentinela*, May 30, 1976.
9. W. C. Dodsworth, Manager, The Butchart Gardens Ltd.,Letter, August 21, 1973, Victoria, B. C.
10. Letter, Aluminum Company of Canada Limited, Kitimat, February 1, 1974.
11. *Economic Growth in the Okanagan Basin to 1980*, Canada-British Columbia Basin Agreement, Preliminary Study Data-Bulletin No. 9 (Kelowna, n.d., c. 1973), Fig. 3.
12. *Okanagan Alternatives*, The Okanagan Basin Study's Public Involvement Program, White Paper No. 2 (Penticton, n.d., c. 1972), p. 2.
13. Anderson, "The Channel Facilitators Model of Migration," pp. 39-40. Elsewhere, particularly in the Maritime Provinces, in the third and later generations it is the surname which becomes anglicized. The process of the change of surnames in a Portuguese community has also been observed in California. See also Hans Leder, "Cultural Persistance in a Portuguese-American Community" (Ph.D. dissertation, Stanford, Anthropology, 1968).
14. R. Rivers and Aires J. F. Cordeiro, report, Castlegar, January 4, 1974. We are indebted to Cordeiro and Rivers for research conducted in this area.
15. See Herbert J. Gans, *The Urban Villagers: Group and Class in the Life of Italian Americans* (Glencoe, Ill.: The Free Press, 1962), and chapter 6 for an expansion of this theme.
16. Raymond Breton, "Institutional Completeness of Ethnic Communities and the Personal Relations of Immigrants," in Bernard R. Blishen *et al.* (eds.), *Canadian Society: Sociological Perspectives*, third ed. (Toronto: MacMillan, 1968).
17. See also Estellie M. Smith, "An Ethnic enclave in a New England fishing village" (Brockport, N.Y., State University of New York, Anthropology, 1973 [mimeo] suggested that the occupational organization of the workers, which is influenced by the stability of the resource base, can influence

123

cohesiveness or divisiveness of an ethnic community. In the settlements we looked at, however, several displayed a similar range of occupations among the Portuguese but differing levels of integration. Clearly, more research is needed along these lines.

18. Anderson, *Networks of Contact.*
19. This has been demonstrated in Romão's study, "Le processus de migration."
20. For a comparison with Portuguese-American communities see Francis M. Rogers, *The Island Portuguese: In their Islands and in America* (Beverley Hills, Calif.,: Sage Publications, 1974), and "The Portuguese of Southwestern New England: Suggestions for Research," *Luso-Brazilian Review,* 11, 1 (Summer, 1974). For comparison with Portuguese communities in France see Bernard Granotier, *Les travailleurs immigrés en France* . . . édition revue 1973 . . . Paris, Maspero, 1973. For the study of a community see Maria Beatriz Rocha Trindade, *Immigrés portugais: observation psycho-sociologique d'un groupe de portugais dans la banlieue parisienne (Orsay),* Lisbon, Instituto superior de ciências sociais e política ultramarina, 1973.

PART THREE:

Major Institutions of the Portuguese-Canadian Communities

SIX

The Family

> Almost all the immigrants have accentuated that the family is
> the one thing most important to them, and . . . that they should
> be united.[1]

The centrality of the family and the priorities accorded it are well known
in areas of Portuguese settlement across Canada. The importance said to
be given to the family is not always reflected in the behaviour patterns of
the Portuguese community. For example, there has often been considerable delay in bringing members of the nuclear family to Canada.[2] As
noted in Chapter 3, in the early 1950s the men usually came first. They
were assigned work in isolated locations, or took temporary employment
and migrated frequently from one part of the country to another. Sometimes as much as ten to twelve years would elapse before the wife and
children came to Canada. For many families, however, the period of separation was much shorter, a matter of two to four years. Some men were
enjoying bachelor life, others wished to make a large down payment on a
home before bringing the family to Canada.

In Portugal, the family is often regarded as an entity in itself. One
immigrant in Montreal said:

> The family is the complement of myself, my activities are integrated
> in the family and each member of the family makes up a part of the
> circle.[3]

The majority in a group of immigrants in Montreal emphasized the importance of the family as a whole, though some believed that the individuals within the family were more important.

Some social anthropologists have described the attitude towards the
family in one area of Southern Europe as "amoral familism." According
to one author, an amoral familist acts on the rule, "Maximize the material
short-run advantages of the nuclear family; assume that all others will do

127

likewise.''[4] This attitude seems to be present among some Portuguese immigrant families from isolated peasant villages.

Contact of Portuguese-Canadian households with the extended family in Portugal is frequent. In Romão's Montreal sample, "more than half the families correspond on a weekly or biweekly basis."[5] We do not have comparable data on other ethnic groups of similar educational background, but suffice it to say that there is extensive communication with kin in the homeland.

CHANGES IN FAMILY RELATIONSHIPS

At the time of migration, the closest relationship in the family for the man was with his father and his brothers, rather than his wife or sweetheart left in the homeland. Among the working class it is usual for the men to visit in the pool hall or the tavern during the winter. In warm weather they cluster on street corners or visit together outside church after the service on a Sunday morning. This pattern of segregation of the sexes has been accentuated in Canada. The men who arrived in the early 1950s usually came alone. They frequently lived in boarding houses with a group of other Portuguese men and were also cut off from female workers in their places of employment. Many worked with railway track crews in isolated locations, or in heavy construction. Frequently they wrote home urging brothers and cousins to join them in Canada.

Meanwhile, in the homeland the women who had husbands in Canada found consolation in each other's company. They shared news of their menfolk overseas and commiserated with each other in times of loneliness. They also came to be mutually dependent in times of crisis. In many villages in continental Portugal and the Azores being alone was not a new experience for the women, for fishing on the Grand Banks or seasonal migration was the men's way of life. These village women were willing to forego companionship for a few years so that eventually they could have a much higher standard of living, especially for their children. On the other hand, women from the larger cities on the mainland were often reluctant to endure prolonged periods of isolation from their husbands. This in part explains the pattern of men from fishing towns and villages volunteering for the more highly remunerated jobs in isolated northern locations.

While close bonds remain among members of the same sex of the first generation bonds are also formed outside of the immediate family through godparentage arrangements. When children are baptized in the Catholic Church, godparents (*compadre* and *comadre*) are appointed for the child. They can be relatives or good friends of the family. Sometimes it is a proxy for a godparent in the homeland who stands with the couple in the church service, but more frequently another immigrant is chosen. Among mainland families, but not those from the Azores Islands, the parents of the godparents are also referred to by the title *compadres*. As one immigrant viewed the situation: "The families become related – they become like family." Godparents may also be chosen for the wedding, but usually a married couple is chosen, whereas a child's godparent may be single. Godparentage is an important aspect of extending the close bonds between families.

Families in the homeland emphasized respect for the household head. Respect for the father of the family continues to be evident in the comments of many Portuguese immigrants. Respect for the aged also is expected of children, particularly in families who have emigrated from the Azores Islands. But as a society becomes industrialized, this attitude frequently changes:

> People become obsolete before their time in our assembly line culture. We no longer grow old gracefully. Years of experience are not always valued. Instead of using the wisdom of age to help solve our problems, we have turned the aged themselves into a problem. Our preoccupation with youth has made us forget that, often, people considered "too old" have the youngest ideas of all.[6]

The North American denigration of the usefulness of the elderly contrasts with the way in which children have been brought up in the homeland. Romão, who studied the Portuguese in Montreal, reports:

> In the Portuguese family children are raised under severe discipline and to respect older persons .... Two thirds [of those interviewed] said that the children did not have respect for their elders .... The father loses some of his authority, because the man used to be the only one consulted about a decision, now there is more frequently consultation between the man and his wife.[7]

While the immigrant men tend to blame the changing structure of the family on contact with native-born Canadians,[8] this explanation is too simplistic. Several factors appear to be involved, including the changing attitudes of persons in the homeland; the long years of separation in which the wife has had to learn to get along without assistance and direction from her husband and during which the children have been without the presence, authority, and discipline of a father; and the financial situation in Canada, which frequently requires the mother to be employed outside the home if aspirations in the new land are to become a reality.

Change is taking place rapidly in Portugal itself. For example, there has been a substantial shift in attitudes towards the role of women, as evidenced by the government's recent recognition of women in politics.[9] In fact, there is deep appreciation of a wife as a companion as well as in other roles. Traditionally, she has exercised considerable influence on family decision-making, as documented by Cutileiro:

> In recent years when migration and emigration became new factors for change in this society, women were of paramount importance in the decisions taken by those who eventually emigrated or decided to

stay. On hearing of successful migrants from other concelhos, wives often insisted that their husbands should go, although they themselves stayed behind, at least during their husbands' first few seasons as field hands.[10]

At the same time, there is a strong feeling that a woman should be supportive of her husband rather than independent. One man we interviewed stated:

> Some people say that the Canadian wives are their husband's bosses – they have different bank accounts and do everything separate; they have their own money, etcetera. In my house we have everything together, the money is together, not mine, not hers, but ours. My wife worked for ten years to help me out. She got paid the third of the month when I got paid. She would sign her cheque and give it to me.

Ninety per cent of the men in the Montreal study seemed to feel that "a woman's place is in the home" and preferred to have a wife who was not working. Yet half of the spouses of those interviewed were working full time, and the remainder had part-time employment. They were, for the most part, "household helps" or charwomen, operators of sewing machines, dressmakers, nurses, or nursing aides.[11]

Women themselves are reassessing their position in the family. Those who were left on their own in Portugal for several years and struggled to maintain a growing family experienced considerable independence then. When they rejoin their husbands, they may not wish to resume the status of a totally dependent wife. They can earn their own money in Canada, even though they usually hand it over to their husbands. Some women are learning to drive, and the automobile gives them additional freedom.

Social agencies across the country report that they have complaints from Portuguese women of receiving beatings from their husbands. Often, the reason given by the husband is that the wife is becoming too independent. Word is spreading among the women, however, that in Canada they are protected by law from assault by a husband.

Although in Portugal none of the men had assisted with housekeeping chores, in the Montreal sample almost half of the men stated that they now helped in the home. Indeed, in all communities across Canada, we noticed that substantial numbers of men were shopping in the Portuguese grocery stores and fish markets. Of course, many of the early settlers were forced to learn to shop and cook for themselves when they first arrived, and this was a role they had never been required to perform in the homeland. Many Portuguese food markets have become social centres for the men, providing an informal news and information service.

In the Montreal families, Romão observed that "with immigration came a diminishing of the intensity of family life or of contacts with the extended family."[12] Since earning a living in Canada absorbs so much time and energy of both the parents, it is small wonder that this has

130

happened. In some ways, however, the Montreal sample cannot be taken as typical of Portuguese settlements across Canada. The Montreal Portuguese have few relatives in that city; as Romão points out, "it would appear that a large number of immigrants are acculturated to the English side in spite of all the initial disposition toward French language and culture."[13] In most instances, the relatives of Montreal-based immigrants live in other English-speaking provinces.

Outside the province of Quebec, it appears that the majority of Portuguese families have some relatives living nearby. Data from the current study indicate, however, that many immigrant families spend their holidays visiting kin in other parts of Canada and in the United States. Persons living in Central and Eastern Canada seem likely to have kin in New England and those in western Canada are frequently related to persons living in Californian Portuguese communities. Thus, the lines of communication tend to run north and south across the continent.

Moreover, it appears that many extended Portuguese families are reconstituted on this continent. Early pioneers frequently relate that they have encouraged all their own relatives and those of their spouses to come to Canada. Occasionally, it is thought to be disadvantageous to have one's relatives close: "too frequent contact with the family causes problems."[14] This is particularly true of relationships between different generations in a family. Young married couples often complain of the tension created between themselves and their parents' generation by the desire for proximity. Parents and relatives offer all sorts of inducements for the young couple to live near them, sometimes in rent-free accommodation. While the first generation is a centripetal force trying to draw the scattered extended family together again in Canada, the second generation is a centrifugal force attempting to place some living space between older members of the kin group and themselves.

This tension has been exacerbated by the problems created by migration both among the parents themselves and between a long-absent father and his offspring. While two-thirds of the families interviewed in Montreal said that immigration did not affect the family, the remaining one-third attributed most misunderstandings and tensions within the family to the adverse effects of migration.[15]

In summary, it appears that the patriarchal family of immigrants is moving slowly toward the egalitarian type of family idealized by many native-born Canadians. Children are particularly influential in this process, for they exert strong pressures on the family for change. Parents, kin, and the older members of the Portuguese community try to resist these pressures and attempt to arrest the changes. The response of some children as they reach adulthood and marry is to move a few miles away from their kin, but only a few become alienated from the family.

Because of the telephone gossip network much of life is in public view and there is very little privacy in the local community. Within the nuclear family, in the extended family, and also in the local Portuguese community, life is lived in a "goldfish bowl." Many Portuguese are urban villagers living in insulated communities, often within a cosmopolitan setting.

Gans's term *urban villagers*[16] describes immigrants from relatively-isolated village backgrounds who live in a small community of their own within a North American city. Usually they have their own stores, associations and other informal meeting places. Frequently they work for others of their own ethnic group who speak their own language. Often contact with the wider community is minimal. The nomination and sponsorship features of Canadian immigration policy in the formative years of establishment of the Portuguese in Canada has favoured the growth of many large family groupings of close and distant relatives. It is for this reason that Portuguese Canadians are often regarded by outsiders as clannish. It is significant that when an outsider asks about the size of a particular Portuguese settlement in a city the reply of an immigrant, even though he may have been in Canada for twenty years, is usually given in terms of the number of families, rather than the number of individuals. The family is a circle; and among first generation immigrants, the family as a unit is more important than the individual.

DATING AND MARRIAGE

Young Portuguese women in Canada are often chaperoned wherever they go. This is one of the primary causes of friction among young people and their parents. A young bank teller related that she dared not accept an invitation to have a cup of coffee with one of the young men she knew from high school because she was afraid of what her parents would say and do if they were to find out. A small proportion of the young women do rebel against parental dominance, but in doing so they also reject the entire Portuguese-Canadian community of first generation immigrants. The majority acquiesce to parental demands, although in some cases with a certain amount of bitterness and fatalism.

One young man in his late teens commented:

> In the Portuguese way of life you are restricted in many things. Parents like to see you home early. They are over-protective, I guess. But you take it bit by bit, you come home ten minutes late each evening for a month, then a bit later, and a bit later. Eventually, you come home when you are ready.
>
> It is hard to break away from your family. I would find it hard to up and leave. You realize your parents are disciplining you for your own good.
>
> My sister had an awful time. She dated Mario for five years in secret. Dad didn't let him in the door until he'd talked to him [about marriage]. She went through hell, then she was married when she was 21 . . . .
>
> A girl argues with her father until his foot's down and his arms are

waving. Then, that's it – if Dad says you can't do it, you won't unless you pack your clothes. My oldest brother, he left a few times. Once he headed out to Miami, but was sending back money to help us. He tried to make it on his own and then came back. In most cases sons leave when they get married, or they have come over here when in their early twenties without their parents.

There is so much respect in a Portuguese family. Many of us never smoke in front of Dad, that would show a young man's father had no control over him, in part it's fear too. My father is buying me cigarettes though. I sign and cash my cheque and hand it over to my father who gives me back what I need.

My parents change – every year they learn something new.[17]

Although young men are allowed considerable freedom, parents still show concern for them. One successful entrepreneur recounted that he went into business for himself, after a career in the construction industry, so that his adolescent son "would have something to keep him busy," fearing idleness as a source of mischief.

The problems of chaperoning young women and the consequences for both sexes are in evidence at ethnic association dances,[18] where girls are escorted by their parents. The young men prefer to go to non-ethnic dances, so that they will not come under the watchful eye of parents. They also prefer to take non-Portuguese girls to these dances. As a result, second generation men are more likely to marry outside their ethnic group than are second generation women. If the latter marry first generation men, their problems are compounded by their desire for a companionate marriage, while their husbands assume a patriarchal role.

In the early days, before the special service agencies had Portuguese workers and interpreters, these same young people, who were children at the time, often had to translate for their parents. During this process, the seeds of rebellion were often sown. The children picked up the local language quickly and could withhold information from parents if they wished. They were privy to all kinds of secrets from which they would normally have been excluded. They translated for their mothers at the doctor's office and for their fathers at the lawyer's office. Disciplining the children became much more difficult as parents found themselves dependent on them for certain services and for their discretion outside the family. Children who had translated for parents often became aware at an early age of potential problems in the marriage relationship or with the social services which would not normally have been discussed with them.

An older daughter often has had a much stricter upbringing than the younger one in a family: she has been the one to break new ground, and by the time her sister has reached adolescence, parents have become accustomed to Canadian ways and expectations. One young secretary in Western Canada remarked:

Portuguese parents do not understand Canadian ways, especially about dating – they are really strict. My younger sister is getting more freedom than I did – younger kids tell their parents off – older kids don't – we weren't brought up like that! My parents returned from Portugal a while ago and found that ways were different there too now . . . .

The vast majority of young women continue to give their pay cheques to their fathers, even when they are in their mid-twenties. They know, however, that if they marry they will be given furniture and sometimes a down payment on a house to the approximate value of the money they have turned over to their parents. We cannot yet judge whether those who do not marry are compensated later for their contribution to the family, for Portuguese communities have been established in Canada for barely twenty years.

The large majority of young people marry within the Portuguese community but gradually draw away from the ways of their parents. As in many other ethnic groups, members of the second generation emphasize that they will not bring up their children by their parents' traditions – they will be Canadian. The Portuguese are too recently settled in Canada to predict patterns of assimilation in the third generation as yet.[19]

For Portuguese in Canada some marriages are still arranged in the homeland, as they were in the early days of migration to Canada. One single pioneer decided it was time to marry; but because he was out of touch with suitable women in the home town, he advertised in the town newspaper for a wife. He received thirty-four replies. Sometimes an older woman in the community will act as a liaison or matchmaker between young men in Canada and young women in the homeland. School teachers with many Portuguese students in their classes note that each year one or two of the girls are taken out of school to marry a young man in a match initiated by their parents. Of course, the girls sometimes object, as they see the freedom of choice that their Canadian peers enjoy; more often they acquiese, pleased they do not have to endure the roulette of romantic attachment in the competitive marriage marketplace.[20]

Marriage by proxy was common among the early pioneers of the Portuguese communities in Canada. In these cases, the wedding was legalized while the husband was in Canada and the wife in Portugal; she was then allowed to enter the country, and often another Portuguese-style wedding took place shortly after her arrival. Now it more common for a man to return to Portugal, marry there, and bring his bride back with him. Also, more couples are emigrating jointly to this country than in the 1950s and 1960s.

The strength of the marriage bond and the closeness between relatives in the larger family setting has been a stabilizing factor within Portuguese communities. On the other hand, there has often been friction between family groupings. However, this factor is well known in rural and small town Portugal from which most of the immigrants came.[21] Assimilation is resisted by these close-knit families.[22]

NOTES

1. Romão, "Le Processus de Migration," p. 158 (translated by the authors).
2. See Chapters 4 and 5.
3. Romão, "Le Processus de Migration," p. 159.
4. Edward C. Banfield, *The Moral Basis of a Backward Society* (New York: The Free Press, 1968), p. 83. Nuclear family is the immediate family. By contrast the extended family includes more distant relatives such as grandparents and cousins, in fact anyone who is recognized by the immigrants as kin.
5. Romão, "Le Processus de Migration," p. 162.
6. *National Geographic*, Vol. 146, No. 2 (August, 1974). Back cover.
7. Romão, "Le Processus de Migration," pp. 164, 167, 168.
8. Further research is necessary to gather statistical data on this aspect of social change and acculturation.
9. Carmen Deben, "Women Fight for Rights in Portugal," *Toronto Star*, July 6, 1974.
10. José Cutileiro, *A Portuguese Rural Society* (Oxford: Clarendon Press, 1971), p. 106.
11. Romão, "Le Processus de Migration," pp. 163-164.
12. *Ibid.*, p. 167.
13. *Ibid.*, p. 171.
14. *Ibid.*, p. 161.
15. *Ibid.*, p. 160.
16. See Herbert Gans, *Urban Villagers: Group and Class in the Life of Italian Americans* (New York: The Free Press of Glencoe, 1962); and Rex Lucas, *Minetown, Milltown, Railtown: Life in Canadian Communities of Single Industry* (Toronto: University of Toronto, 1971).
17. A second generation comment from the Prairie Provinces.
18. See Cutileiro, *A Portuguese Rural Society*, p. 94, for an explanation of the function of dances in rural Portugal.
19. For a general discussion of this topic one viewpoint is presented in Robert Klymasz, "The Ethnic Folk Festival in North America Today," (paper presented to the Canadian Association for American Studies, Toronto, October, 1972).
20. See Sheila Copps, "A Marriage has been Arranged," and "Joe Wed Cidalia by Proxy," Hamilton, *The Spectator*, August 4, 1973.
21. See José Cutileiro, *A Portuguese Rural Society* (Oxford: Clarendon Press, 1971).
22. Maria Isabel Barreno, Maria Teresa Horta, Maria Velho da Costa, *The Three Marias: New Portuguese Letters*, trans. Helen R. Lane. (New York: Doubleday, 1975), is indicative of a new militancy among a small minority of women in the homeland.

SEVEN

Education

The majority of adult Portuguese immigrants to Canada between 1953 and 1973 had an average of four years of formal education in their homeland.[1] Schooling in Portugal generally begins at the age of seven. Thus, many of the immigrants, particularly those who came in the early 1950s, had been at school until they were ten or eleven and then entered the labour force.

This relatively low educational achievement of Portuguese emigrants follows a long trend. In 1912, for example, 65.9% of the migrants from continental Portugal were illiterate.[2] Few labourer or artisan families could afford to send their children for more than the free schooling provided by the state; and while the seminaries did provide some opportunities, as a general rule working class children were not expected to go to school after the age of twelve, but to contribute to the family economy instead.

Ferguson found that in the early 1960s the average length of formal education for Portuguese immigrants in Toronto was 3.7 years for men and 2.8 years for women. Many of the immigrants came from the Azores Islands where education beyond grade 4 level was not available when the immigrants in her sample were of school age.[3] Several years later, Anderson's study of working class Portuguese men did not show much elevation in the educational level of a sample of over 200 working class males.[4]

Among Portuguese Canadians, it is not generally believed that extensive education is necessary to adjust well to Canada. Many members of the Portuguese community are aware, however, that their children must be provided with a good education if they are to move upward socially. There is no clear class basis for parents' encouragement of their children to continue their studies, for in many cases they do not consider education beyond elementary school to be necessary in order to find employment. But it is also true that in Canada there is neither the tradition of nor the demand for young boys to fill positions as busboys, bellhops, errand and delivery boys and café attendants, such as exists in Portugal. Girls in

136

Portugal are almost never involved in such employment, but they are expected to take part early in looking after their brothers and sisters and helping their mothers. In Portugal, both boys and girls are expected to assume adult responsibilities earlier than is usual in Canada. Portuguese parents find themselves confronting a longer and a different education for their children than they received. Often, it seems to be much less disciplined than the rote learning they recall from their school in Portugal.

As education in Canada is provided under provincial and local jurisdiction, it is in areas with a local concentration of Portuguese that studies must be made, estimating their place in the public, separate, and private schools. In Western Canada, particularly, communities are more scattered than in Ontario and Quebec. The Portuguese constitute only one among many groups in Catholic and public schools; and outside the major urban centres, classes tend to have lower concentrations of New Canadian children. In Toronto, however, where there is the highest concentration of Portuguese-speaking people in Canada, and in Montreal, there are many separate and public schools that enrol large numbers of children from Portuguese homes.

The whole history of education and ethnicity in Canadian life is a complex one which calls for much research, and it falls outside the scope of this study to investigate it fully. One of the basic issues is the extent to which children of Portuguese background enter the Catholic or public school system. The level of piety in the home is important in this choice, as well as assumptions about moral conditions prevalent in the schools. There is a strong tendency, especially on the part of Azorean parents, to send their children, and particularly the girls, to Catholic schools. This is in no sense automatic, however; many parents send their children to a public school for at least part of their education. Moreover, it should be remembered that there is a strong anti-clerical current in Portuguese history.

In Quebec, parents are also faced with the question of integrating their children into the French or the English educational system. The parents of Portuguese children in that province tend to assimilate into French-speaking circles; but at the same time, through the 1960s, there was a tendency for the young to identify with the English-speaking community. Parents, particularly those with little education, want their children to learn English. It has been estimated that in 1974 about 70% of the children from Portuguese homes in Montreal attended English-language Catholic elementary schools and 30% attended French-language schools. In the fluid linguistic situation of Montreal, particularly in the Portuguese area, which is on the boundary-line between French and English-speaking communities, a large number of parents and children are trilingual; typically, they use all three languages constantly. Portuguese students are to be found in French and English CEGEPs (Collège d'Enseignement Général et Professionnel) and universities of the Montreal area. A number of those who have received secondary education in Portugal, where they learnt French, enter the French-language universities in Quebec.

The first school in Toronto to have a significant concentration of Portuguese children was Saint Patrick. The school grew rapidly between 1954 and 1960, and soon the majority of its students were from Portuguese families. The steady westward drift in Toronto from the initial Portuguese reception area was marked by a changing balance of cultural backgrounds in the schools along College Street west from Spadina. In this area, the ratio of Italian to Portuguese children fell during the 1960s until there was a Portuguese majority.

Sometimes, after attending school in English for a few years and speaking English in the home, children forget how to speak Portuguese. They are therefore sent to Portuguese schools, held on Saturdays or after regular school hours. There they relearn the language and study the history and geography of their parents' homeland.

Parents often feel that, should they return to Portugal, their children must possess the certificates of Portuguese studies issued through the consular offices, after the students have written and passed supervised examinations sent from the homeland. Accordingly, in the larger Canadian cities, special schools have been established for Portuguese education. The first of these began informally. The Associação Portuguesa do Canadá in Montreal first organized small classes in 1958 for the children of members, beginning with some fifty pupils. The classes have continued, with fluctuating attendance, and in 1974 about 150 pupils were enrolled. The first large Portuguese-language school in Montreal was organized by the Church of Santa Cruz in 1971. In that year, approximately sixty children attended on Saturday mornings; by 1974 there were eleven teachers and 350 students. The primary grades of the Portuguese curriculum are taught, and the school receives financial assistance, books, and certification from the Portuguese government. Another Montreal school is the Escola do Atlântico (Atlantic School – a reference to the sponsoring bank), which also has operated on Saturday mornings since 1971 and receives official Portuguese government assistance. About 300 pupils are enrolled. In Quebec City, the local Portuguese club has operated a small school since 1973, but it receives no subsidy. There are Portuguese schools in Ottawa, London, Hamilton, Winnipeg and Vancouver – indeed, wherever the community becomes sufficiently numerous to demand such arrangements.

In 1968, Mario Cipriano started a Saturday school in Vancouver. He was a teacher in the school for the first three years until three qualified teachers arrived from Portugal. The Portuguese government sends an outline of the courses annually and gives examinations through the consul in Vancouver so that if families should return to Portugal the children will have recognized credentials for the years of study in Canada. When the students are working towards preparation for examinations, advanced classes meet for two or three hours two days per week, in addition to attending Saturday classes. In 1972, the school enrolled a total of 100 children.

The most elaborate supplementary school system has emerged in Toronto. The most important is the Escola Mista Oficial de Português de Toronto. This is organized by the First Portuguese Canadian Club. Its classes are held in the buildings of Ryerson Public School, and the first six years of the Portuguese curriculum are taught. The school was founded in October, 1964, with 18 pupils and a teacher giving Saturday classes. In November, 1965, there were 94 pupils, 2 teachers and classes on Mondays, Thursdays and Saturdays. In 1974 there were 600 pupils and 12 teachers. Books and financial aid were contributed by official agencies in Portugal. A second, privately-operated school system held classes daily after regular school hours in classrooms of three local public schools, teaching the first four years of the Portuguese curriculum. There is a third school, organized by the main parish in the city, teaching about 60 children in the first 4 years of the Portuguese curriculum. The parents pay to send children to these classes. In December, 1973, fees paid in Toronto per child for the academic year ranged from $65 to $120. Acting through the consulate, the Portuguese government sometimes provided financial aid to these schools, and has sometimes given recognition in the form of certification of the grades attained by each child. There have also been some further schools started by private individuals.

Young children usually make a satisfactory entry into the Canadian school system. By the age of five, they have often picked up English from television and can translate for their parents. If, however, the children enter a Canadian school having already taken several years of their education in Portugal, they are at a disadvantage. Frequently, they lag considerably until they conquer the language. Some children have been extremely embarrassed in the past because they were placed with children several years their junior. In the 1970s, efforts are being made in most parts of Canada to keep the children with their own age group while they are learning the language. For many of these children, however, school is still not a pleasant experience. According to one study, if they are in a classroom with others from Portugal, they tend to sit together when given the opportunity to do so.[5] While this may hinder the assimilation of English, it has the advantage of reducing the culture shock.

Many older children who have come to Canada with their parents left school at the age of ten or twelve. Some boys worked for a couple of years in Portugal, and the girls may also have been out of school for some time. Suddenly they find themselves in a foreign environment, being treated as children once more. Even worse, from their perspective, is the humiliation of being placed in a class with much younger children. In the eyes of the Portuguese adolescents, their Canadian peers are babies in experience of the everyday world, for all their book knowledge. It is these boys and girls who are most likely to rebel against being in Canada and to announce their intention of returning to their homeland. Whether or not they actually will return is another question. Some may remain marginal to both cultures. The homeland that they remembered as teenagers is changing, and they also have changed since arriving here. They have taken on ways of life which are Canadian, often so gradually that they are completely unaware of the changes.

Moreover, when they left Portugal, they were usually from working class families. Their parents were anxious for them to have more education than was possible in the homeland. During the extended education period in Canada they often develop middle class values and attitudes. Thus, they could find themselves marginal in respect to social class on their return. In the homeland, they would probably find themselves labelled as Canadian.[6] A study currently underway in the Azores Islands may soon provide further insight into the situations of the returned migrants.[7]

A few of the better-educated Portuguese men have brought some of their younger brothers to Canada, and have encouraged them to continue their education and enter skilled trades. The young men who come on this basis have their successful older brothers as models and also have the opportunity to escape heavy-handed parental discipline. In these circumstances the young Portuguese tend to make a faster and more successful adjustment to the school and social environment than do those who immigrate with their parents.

School is a socializing experience for both the children and the parents. It is most frequently in the school that children become aware of differences between themselves and their Canadian peers, particularly with respect to parental discipline. In Montreal and Toronto the socializing influence of Canadian children is more apparent in suburbs, where relatively few Portuguese reside, than in downtown areas of high concentration.[8]

The influence of school upon children gradually filters back to parents over a period of years and has a Canadianizing effect upon them. Frequently, the process is slowed if the mother of the family works outside the home. Moreover, Portuguese fathers seldom have the time to become involved in their children's schooling. Communication between teachers and Portuguese parents is often impeded by the language problem, and the children must act as intermediaries. Recently, however, second generation Portuguese men and women have begun to enter the school system as teachers. In the largest urban centres, a few highly regarded Portuguese-trained teachers are employed as consultants to schools with a high proportion of Portuguese students.

Some second generation young people are also entering the universities across Canada, from Montreal to Vancouver. They are enrolled in a variety of courses, ranging from history and romance languages to computer science, forestry, and law. Many are in vocational schools and a few in post-secondary technical colleges, preparing to enter a variety of skilled occupations. Their parents, meanwhile, attempt to keep abreast by learning English in evening classes. Usually, though, their progress is hampered by the difficulty of simultaneously earning a living, keeping up a home, and raising a family. The drop-out rate tends to be high, especially among women.

Little attention has been paid in this study to Portuguese professional and managerial personnel and their children, because these represent an extremely small minority among the total immigrant arrivals. In this ethnic group the nature and timing of the immigrant process precluded recruitment of middle class persons in significant numbers. The few well-educated Portuguese who have immigrated usually arrive with some knowledge of English or French, or both. They encourage their children to obtain a good education and to prepare themselves to enter business or a profession.

As the second generation of immigrants comes to maturity and draws on the experience of a Canadian education, new leadership potential will be available to the Portuguese communities. Whether it will be welcomed and utilized or perceived as threat remains to be seen.[9]

NOTES

1. Compulsory education for all Portuguese was set at three years by a law passed in 1898; in 1960 it was increased to four years; and in 1967 it was extended to six years. There has been some difficulty in fully implementing these reforms, especially in the most remote areas, where there is a shortage of teachers and facilities; but by 1972, six years' compulsory schooling was enforced throughout European Portugal. In 1973, in some larger cities, a pilot project of eight years' primary schooling is under way. In 1967, only 1.4% of Portugal's gross national product was being applied to primary and secondary education, as compared to 8.3% in Canada. In 1968, Portugal's illiteracy rate was over 30%, the highest in Europe. (Source: "Public expenditure on Education," United Nations Educational, Scientific and Cultural Organization, *Statistical Yearbook . . . 1972* (Paris: Unesco, 1973)

2. Carqueja, *O povo português*, p. 404.

3. Edith Ferguson, *Newcomers in Transition* (Toronto: The International Institute of Metropolitan Toronto, 1964), p. 42.

4. Anderson, *Networks of Contact*, p. 56. See also E.N. Wright, "Student's Background and Its Relationship to Class and Programme in School," (The Every Student Survey), #91. (Toronto: The Board of Education for the City of Toronto, Research Department, December, 1970).

5. H. Tuitt, "Portuguese" (unpublished paper, Waterloo Lutheran University, 1972). A study of education in a Southern Ontario community.

6. A government study is currently addressing itself to the question of self-identification of immigrants.

141

7. Department of Anthropology, Brown University, Providence, Rhode Island.
8. These generalizations require additional research, but this is beyond the scope of the present study.
9. As this volume goes to press we have just obtained a copy of Francis M. Rogers, *Americans of Portuguese Descent: A Lesson in Differentiation*, Sage Research Papers in the Social Sciences, Studies in Religion and Ethnicity Series, No. 90-013 (Beverley Hills and London: Sage Publications, 1974). Professor Rogers gives an excellent outline of the school system in Portugal and its North American equivalent (pp. 61-64).

EIGHT

The Church

Roman Catholicism is an integral component of Portuguese popular traditions because of a long national history in which no other religion had a large number of followers. In the social life of rural Portugal religious beliefs, ceremonials, confraternities and devotions were interwoven with many aspects of life. Nowhere was this more true than among the cod fishermen of the White Fleet: the men said a "Hail Mary" on deck at midday, and the traditional phrase from the captain for the launching of dories was "Go . . . in praise of Our Lord Jesus Christ." The men of the White Fleet donated a grotto of Our Lady of Fatima to the Basilica of St. John's, Newfoundland, in the 1960s and went there to attend services during their shore leaves. Catholicism was part of such annual communal events as the *romarias* (pilgrimages) which were especially popular in Northern Portugal and which are, in some senses, recreated by families who drive long hours to attend *festas* (religious festivals) held in Canadian and New England cities and towns.

The sacred and profane were never neatly compartmentalized in the lives of Portuguese Catholics and the same has remained true in Canada. Community picnics, fairs, dances and the opportunities to meet old friends and neighbours are frequently associated with religious festivals. In many Portuguese-Canadian homes statuettes and religious pictures are displayed, showing Our Lady of Fatima, Saint Anthony of Lisbon, the Infant Jesus, and the Crown surmounted by a dove, representing the particularly Azorean devotion to the Holy Spirit. Even secular social clubs may organize processions, dances and convivial meetings to coincide with the observation of religious feastdays, particularly those of the *Santos Populares*, the "Popular" saints: St. Anthony, St. Peter and St. John.

These activities are important affirmations of the place of religion in community life. The largest *festas* and religious processions in Canadian cities have often passed relatively unnoticed in the media showing that the organizers saw them more as vital to their community identity than as public amusements, by contrast with the way in which some other ethnic groups present their cultural, religious and folkloric activities. Some processions through city streets, like that in Kingston in early May to mark the appearance of Our Lady of Fatima or that of the Christ of the Miracles (*Senhor Santo Christo dos Milagres*) in Toronto, may receive wider notice.

The latter has become the largest Portuguese Catholic religious ceremony in North America. The original Christ of the Miracles statue is housed in a chapel of Ponta Delgada, the largest town in São Miguel. In 1963, a Toronto priest arranged for a copy of the statue to be sent to St. Mary's Church, Toronto, from Braga in Northern Portugal. Later he arranged for a second copy to be brought to Montreal. In both cities the statues and their altars have become the focus of much local devotion. The procession is held on the fifth Sunday after Easter: the statue is carried through the streets of the Portuguese area close to the parish church by men wearing red capes (*opas*), preceded by a procession of children in costume, bands and contingents from various community organizations. In 1974 ninety thousand people attended the procession and subsequent celebrations in Trinity Park, coming from as far afield as Bermuda, Fall River and New Bedford in New England, and outlying parts of Ontario. Almost equally popular is the early August celebration in Toronto of the *Senhor da Pedra* (Lord on the Stone after His Scourging), a devotion especially associated with the town of Vila Franca on São Miguel.

Other *festas* have less publicity. The Madeiran devotion to the patron of that island, Our Lady of the Mount (*Nossa Senhora do Monte*), is connected with the establishment of Madeira Park outside Toronto in 1963-1964. A shrine was built on the site. Decorated with lights and flowers, the statue provides a focal point for the annual festival in honour of the spiritual protectress of the island and of all Madeiran families. An outdoor Mass (*missa campal*) is said in Portuguese, sometimes by a Madeiran priest if one is available. There is usually a procession and a rosary is recited.[1]

The largest of the *festas* and processions are the most visible manifestations of Portuguese religious life in Canada. However, in the almost quarter of a century since the arrival of the first major post-war immigration of Portuguese, numerous religious institutions have been established, and most predated secular associations. In Toronto the first Portuguese-language services were said in 1955 at St. Michael's Cathedral by an American Franciscan Father who had worked previously in Brazil. In 1957 a Madeiran priest came to the city to assist English-speaking priests in pastoral work with the Portuguese. He worked first from St. Michael's Cathedral and then moved to the "Hungarian" church – that of St. Elizabeth – which in due course was replaced by St. Mary's as the first Portuguese parish in Toronto. Other priests joined him. By 1963 there were two priests from the Azores and two from mainland Portugal meeting the needs of the congregation. With the steady increase in the size of the Portuguese population other churches were becoming popular, like Mount Carmel, formerly heavily Italian speaking. Two more Portuguese parishes were set up: Saint Agnes (1970) and Santa Cruz (1974). Masses were said in Portuguese in other Catholic churches in the city, and at one of these, St. Helen's, the congregation in the mid-1970s was almost 80% Portuguese. By 1975 thirteen Portuguese priests were serving the needs in the City of Toronto proper.

Religious services in Portuguese in Montreal began later than those in Toronto and Vancouver. The *Luso-Canadiano* of November, 1959, cited these prior examples and the work of the Portuguese clergy in the United States in calling for a Portuguese priest in Montreal. A French-Canadian priest first served the community, having learned the language during previous pastoral duties. By March, 1965, one of the Toronto priests from St. Mary's was asked to move to Montreal and he served as parish priest of the Santa Cruz Church, established in a former Jewish community centre's remodelled gymnasium. Portuguese Catholics in the city also attended French and English-language services.

During the first ten years of heavy immigration after 1952 the Portuguese communities often lacked regular pastoral care in their own language, but it is notable that there was a rapid increase in the 1960s of the numbers of Portuguese priests in Canada. In Ottawa, Hamilton, London, Winnipeg, Edmonton, Calgary, Vancouver and other cities the clergy played an important part in organizing social and recreational services. A number of Portuguese nuns were also active in the communities.

Among the smaller Portuguese settlements priests often play a very important part as community leaders. They are asked for advice on a wide variety of problems. During the early stages of Portuguese emigration to Canada the priests often found heavy demands on them to travel "circuits"; for example, one priest went from Vancouver to Victoria, and another between 1960 and 1962 served a scattered congregation of 5,000 families in the area of Osoyoos, Oliver and Penticton. Others went from Ottawa to the Portuguese congregation in Kingston (St. Mary's Cathedral), or from Hamilton to Galt. It is not possible nor intended to give here a capsule history of each Portuguese congregation in the country, but the following examples show something of the place of religious activities in Portuguese community life.

An excellent example of the growth of a Portuguese parish in Canada is the Missão Católica Portuguesa in Vancouver, which was the first Portuguese-Canadian organization in the city. The first Portuguese congregation in the city had been established canonically with an Italian priest. Portuguese Mass was said at two different churches: Saint Paul's and Saint Patrick's. In 1965, weekly collections were enough to pay for the priest's rent and subsistence. A Brazilian priest from São Paulo came to Vancouver through the agency of an organization called Assistência aos Emigrantes Católicos, and he travelled periodically to Victoria, Kitimat, Terrace, and Ocean Falls to hear confessions and to say Mass for the Portuguese communities in these outlying areas. In 1967, the congregation had raised $30,000 to buy a church, but at the last minute the incumbents changed their minds about selling. The money raised was offered back to the donors, but many refused to take it. In 1968, $17,500 remained in the bank, and plans were launched by the Missão to build its own church. After long negotiations for bank loans, support from the bishopric, further fund-raising campaigns, and the donation of many hours of labour by members of the community, the new church of Nossa Senhora de Fatima was consecrated in November, 1969.

During his stay in Vancouver, the Brazilian father remained an important stimulus in the community. While the church was being built, he multiplied appeals for more donations, labour, and co-operation. He frequently wrote in Vancouver's Portuguese newspaper, *O Mensageiro*, about the need for community effort:

> Let us unite for all that brings about the spiritual and social progress of the Portuguese Community. With the cooperation of all we can give to our community a glorious name: a united, religious and patriotic community.[2]

He often chided his congregation for its obsession with material success:

> It can be said in passing that many Portuguese, like moreover many immigrants arriving in this country, exchange religious devotion for the devotion to the dollar. As money enters into the house religion leaves.[3]

In Catechism classes, in the columns of *O Mensageiro*, in a half-hour Saturday radio show, he defended traditional Portuguese religious values while presenting them as a defence against the strains of adjusting to Canadian life. At the same time, he encouraged the learning of English and helped to establish English-language classes. Again he wrote in *O Mensageiro*:

> ... 95% of the Portuguese do not know English – nothing or something equivalent to nothing .... All feel the necessity of knowing English, but how many truly interest themselves in learning this language .... Without it we shall always be on the margin of Canadian society without being able to read a newspaper, without being able to defend our rights. How many people suffer in the hospitals, courts, on trips, etc. because they do not know English? But they prefer to suffer rather than learn.[4]

Within the structure of the parish organization, the priest encouraged classes for couples contemplating marriage. The parish also looked to the social needs of the Portuguese community of Vancouver and arranged excursions, dances, festivals, and charter flights to Portugal. The Sunday announcement sheet, entitled *Voz da Paróquia Portuguesa* (Voice of the Portuguese Parish) contained advertisements for services and businesses of interest to Portuguese. Another publication, *Encontro* (meeting) was a mimeographed magazine which carried articles on religion, announcements of baptisms, engagements, weddings as well as poems, photographs of community interest and coming events. In Vancouver in the mid 1970s the church played an active part in the life of the parishioners. At the same time there were many Portuguese who did not attend Mass regularly but only on special occasions. Equally there were those who actively dissociated themselves from church activities.

Another example of the development of a Portuguese congregation is that of the approximately 1,000 families in Oakville, Ontario (1975). A Portuguese priest has said Portuguese masses at St. James church since 1968 as well as being involved in a daily radio programme and a newspaper, *A Voz Portuguesa*, which provides news of community interest. Almost three-quarters of the families in the congregation came from the Azores, and among them there is a predominance of migrants from the island of Pico. Besides Mass there is a *festa* of the Bom Jesus during the second weekend in August, this being a devotion both on Pico and Northern Portugal.

One special feature of Portuguese Catholicism introduced into Canada is the *Irmandade* (confraternity), a religious association in a form which greatly declined in numbers in mainland Portugal in the years since World War II but still flourished in the Azores and to a lesser extent in Madeira. The *Irmandade*'s main function is to organize annual celebrations in honour of a particular devotion, although the most important throughout the Azores is that of the Holy Spirit. In the islands a number of members of the brotherhood are selected to keep in their homes the symbol of the Holy Spirit: a *coroa* (silver crown) topped with a dove, and a silver sceptre, also decorated by a dove. In the full Azorean tradition the man who received the crown was an *Imperador* (literally "Emperor"), who on the announced feast day offered meat, bread, wine and entertainment to the poor, neighbours and guests, the actual distribution of food being made by a child under fourteen, usually a boy and often called the *menino santo* (Holy Boy). Each island has distinctive differences in the ritual and customs associated with this ceremony.

In a Canadian urban setting the traditions have been modified in a way which retains the essential characteristics of the Azorean ceremonials. In the Toronto Portuguese parish of St. Agnes some 700 heads of families, or single men and women, belong to the *Irmandade do Espirito Santo* out of a congregation of some 7,000 (1975). The church has nine silver *coroas* which are distributed after Sunday Mass to the members of the *Irmandade* who have requested the honour and who have been selected by the officers of the association. The first recipient of the *coroa* after Easter is considered especially honoured. During the weeks between Easter and Pentecost a number of families are thus able to keep the *coroa* in their home for a week during which time the room where it is kept is specially decorated, rosaries and prayers are recited there, and friends, relatives and guests come to visit the fortunate home. The officers of the *Irmandade* also try to ensure a

147

geographical spread throughout the city among those who have the *coroas* in their homes. In this way, although modified, the Azorean tradition which involves bringing a revered religious symbol into the home and combining this with social celebrations continues in Canada.

There are other *Irmandades* involved in different ceremonies. In Oakville the *Irmandade do Bom Jesus* is responsible for arranging the annual celebration of this devotion in August, and also provides a form of funeral insurance. Members attend the Mass for their dead fellows wearing their regalia. In St. Mary's parish, Toronto, there are various *Irmandades* which meet annually to organize *festas*. The processions, the special celebrations and the complex structure of the associations are highly typical of the religious life of the Azores. Not surprisingly, congregations with many Azorean members once established in Canada wished again to set up those traditions in the new land.

The history of Portuguese-Canadian Catholicism is too recent yet to provide answers to questions about what continuity can be found in the religious life in Canada with the traditions of the areas in Portugal from which families originated. The importance of parish organizations in community life often appears to be in direct relation to the size and Portuguese regional origins of the congregations. Any conclusions reached on such a complex issue are highly tentative and await further probing by students of the sociology of religion as well as by historians. However, Boulard and Remy in France have emphasized the predominant importance of regional traditions in explaining the level of practice in both rural and urban settings. Neither age, sex, nor the socio-professional composition of a group compares in importance with the long-established religious behaviour of areas. It would be well in consequence to be able to compare both the variety of levels of Catholic practice across Canada with those of the areas of Portugal from which migrants come in order to establish the problems to be investigated. Portugal has long-displayed sharp regional differences between areas north of the Tagus, and even more so north of the Douro, where Catholicism was practised much more assiduously than in the centre and south. The Atlantic islands of the Azores and Madeira have often been described as profoundly religious societies since their settlement. One writer said of Madeira:

> Just as the intricate network of the vine grows like a ubiquitous roof uniting the settler's house with his crops, so here is his religion the link binding the most isolated inhabitant to his fellow. Its role in the life of the island is a dominant one both spiritually and socially, and the church is not only a house of worship but a meeting place where a heated argument may be heard as often as a friendly conversation.[6]

The Azores have been often described as very devout, not least so by people from the islands. One priest quoted to us a saying about the islands:

> In Portugal (Azores) I see more stars during one night than in

Canada during the whole year. That is because in Portugal God stays closer to the people.

To our knowledge no studies have yet been undertaken to show if, and how, migrant families in Canada maintain the religious traditions of their areas of origin. At a speculative level it is sometimes said that men, in particular, although regular worshippers in the village or small-town context of the homeland no longer attend Mass in Canada. Less drastically, others are said to stop attending church during periods when they are isolated from their families, as many early migrants were, but that once their home life is reconstituted they return to former habits. Equally we do not yet know whether Canadian-born children will display the differences in levels of observance which characterized the Portuguese regional origins of their families. In all such matters we need statistical study of religious practice over time. It is well known that questionnaires on matters of faith often produce idealistic answers, those which the respondent would like to give, rather than an exact picture of social reality. The whole question of the place of Catholicism in Portuguese community life raises many possibilities for research.

Some Portuguese families in Canada have been attracted by Protestant and fundamentalist religions. *A Igreja Evangelica Portuguesa* in Toronto, for example, holds services and for a time ran television and radio broadcasts to attract converts. It commands minority interest and has strong Brazilian connections. Olivet Baptist Church in Toronto has recently appointed a Portuguese-speaking youth worker.[7] Some United Church and Anglican congregations have attracted Portuguese. It is not possible to say whether enough Portuguese have turned away from Catholic observance to begin some other type of worship for any general conclusion to be formulated in the absence of studies of the subject.

There are a great many agnostics among the Portuguese in Canada. There is also a strong anti-clerical current. The latter can be ascribed on the one hand to criticisms often voiced about the part played by the clergy in "running" different communities. Over the years some Portuguese newspapers in Canada have used innuendo and sarcasm to attack members of the clergy. There is also a generalized level of rumour which questions the integrity of some priests, especially in the larger cities. The second major source of anti-clerical feeling derives from recent Portuguese history. In some quarters the church is said to be looked on as a "form of government." Opponents of the Portuguese government which was overthrown in April, 1974, sometimes accused leading members of the hierarchy of not being sufficiently impartial and of throwing their weight in support of colonial wars and a repressive regime. From this point of view opposition to the activities of the Portuguese clergy was another facet of opposition to the *Estado Novo*.

The future development of Portuguese Catholic institutions in Canada will show whether the community becomes more closely identified with

149

Canadian Church responses rather than those of the homeland. Canadian churchmen do not seem to display any opposition to the particular rituals favoured by some Portuguese congregations, and the existence of Portuguese parishes appears to be mostly a result of language. Not all Canadian observers are as well informed as they might be about Portuguese Church organization. For example, one man suggested "Here, instead of the Church running them, they run the Church." Whatever the accuracy of the first part of the remark his point presumably was that an ethnic church organized within a Canadian social context, with fewer local pressures for conformism, produced a more associationally-based religious life. The sociologists Glock and Stark have shown this has happened elsewhere in North America.[8] However, it is necessary for us to turn now to the development of secular associations in the Portuguese-Canadian community.

NOTES

1. The development of this park is described in more detail in Chapter 9.
2. *O Mensageiro*, May 24, 1968.
3. *Ibid.*, September 27, 1968.
4. *Ibid.*, March 7, 1969.
5. Augusto Querido, "Eléments pour une sociologie du conformisme catholique au Portugal," *Archives de sociologie des religions*, 7 (1959), 144-151.
6. W. Heinzelmann, *Madeira, Portugal* (Basle, 1971), p. 29.
7. "Olivet welcomes new Youth Worker," *The Canadian Baptist*, December, 1974, p. 26.
8. Charles Y. Glock and Rodney Stark, *Religion and Society in Tension*, (Chicago, 1965). See especially Chapter 9, "Religion and integration of Society."

PART FOUR:

Organizations and Identity

NINE

Social and Community Organizations

Portuguese communities appear to outsiders to be cohesive but when viewed from within they are seen to be differentiated on the basis of social class, Old Country politics and religious or secularized perspectives. Regional differences are often divisive. The *Luso-Canadiano* of January, 1959, described a screening at the Montreal Portuguese Association of films of both the Portuguese community in Kitimat and the Azorean island of São Miguel, a show which was well attended by both Azoreans and continentals. The newspaper published a letter which called for both groups to continue to come to the club since previously Azoreans rarely attended:

> I am convinced that if everybody united in a single group and in a single spirit of fraternity, rivalry and paltry prejudices would cease to exist . . . . My dearest wish is that the *Luso-Canadiano* will continue to try and dissipate the barrier of mistrust and misunderstandings that sometimes arise between continentals and Azoreans.

Similar calls for unity have been made by prominent individuals in Portuguese communities across Canada.

Like most Europeans, the Portuguese have a strongly established tradition of class distinctions. Emigration is usually a more or less conscious attempt to escape the economic consequences of a class system. The motives behind the decision to migrate are often expressed in economic terms: higher wages, better housing, more possessions. At the same time, the relative "openness" of Canadian society is seen as an equally desirable complement to the economic advantages it offers, and some immigrants militantly reject Old Country social attitudes. There is nothing peculiarly Portuguese in this; it is part of the European emigrant experience. After financial or professional success, however, there is often a tendency, especially on the part of the first generation, to 'translate' this back into a style of life, or attitudes, based on the Old Country class system. No longer faced with insecurity or concerned about survival or success in the new

153

country, the immigrants again define social advance in Portuguese terms. Others make a final rejection of their native language and culture. The first tendency is more prevalent among the Portuguese, and community leaders see themselves as Portuguese rather than Canadians. The total Canadian community has a complex set of class, religious, cultural, and linguistic relationships which varies from one part of the country to the other. The perceptive immigrant soon begins to analyze his place within it.

Class divisions are very pronounced among the Portuguese. Any community traditionally defers to the better-educated *gente de gravata* (people wearing neckties) and to men of talent for leadership. In as new an immigrant community as the Portuguese, those first established in Canada were naturally looked to for advice and aid by those who followed. They were the new *competências de aldea*, the men of ability in a village, and in one sense the early Portuguese communities had something of the character of a village united by language and kinship. As noted in Chapter 3, friends, relatives, and new arrivals were guided to places of employment which had already accepted Portuguese workers, and they were advised about where to shop and find accommodation. The first arrivals had necessarily learned French or English quickly under the acute stress of linguistic isolation. The first shopkeepers, travel agents, and real estate salesmen found their prosperity deriving from their ability to provide a bridge between newer arrivals and Canadian society. This favoured position gave them a prominence which made them *de facto* community spokesmen: many of this early generation owe their rapid increase in prosperity to the services they provided to subsequent Portuguese immigrants.

There is also a hierarchy among those who are prominent in the principal centres. Montreal, Toronto, Winnipeg, and Vancouver are cities with substantial Portuguese communities, and they also have Portuguese consulates. The main holidays of the Portuguese year are marked by receptions, banquets, or cocktail parties, and the invitation lists to these affairs are a kind of *Who's Who* of this community. The Portuguese clergy, the editors of the Portuguese newspapers, the principal businessmen, and some interested non-Portuguese are invited to such occasions.

An important component in this hierarchy is the economically successful businessmen of the community. In Toronto, for example, the owner of an electronics factory and the owner of a food import and canning business have very high social ranking, as do the managers and senior staff of the four Portuguese banks (Totta e Açores, Banco do Atlântico, Pinto e Sotto Mayor, and Banco Intercontinental Português) and the owners of successful real estate companies and travel agencies. Professional people – doctors and lawyers – comprise another important group. Outside this somewhat traditional hierarchy is a generally younger group of community leaders, some of whom were acknowledged opponents of the Portuguese government prior to 1974 and some who see themselves as more "Canadianized," more modern and progressive in their outlook than the

Portuguese "establishment." This description of the more important leaders among the Portuguese is misleading insofar as it is generalized and glosses over the complexities of individual relationships; but it provides a rough guide to understanding the ways in which the social clubs function.

The Portuguese are a sociable people, and clubs and meeting places play an important part in establishing community solidarity and social life. Each major community tries to establish a social club: in broad terms, when there is a concentration of 100 Portuguese-speaking families, community organizations emerge. The clubs hold dances, picnics, and entertainments which provide an opportunity for social interaction and for courtship. Games are organized for the children; the men have an opportunity to discuss work and job possibilities, sports, and other topics of interest; and the women proudly show off their families.

While the clubs are a vital part of community social life, they do not direct it; paradoxically, they provide a focus for the strong individualism of their members. Conflicts of personality, rivalry for office, and other clashes are common and many clubs are rocked by accusations of improper use of funds or regional favouritisms. In the view of one Canadian reporter,[1] the very multiplicity of Portuguese-Canadian organizations proves the parochial outlook of the community. But this is to over-simplify. Any significant community organization that develops among the Portuguese as they become fully integrated into Canadian life must reflect the atmosphere and traditions of the social clubs. They provide a vehicle for bridging generational and cultural differences, and they serve to organize educational, sporting and recreational activities. All of these aspects are considered below.

The first major Portuguese club formed in Canada which still exists in the 1970s was the Associação Portuguesa do Canadà (Portuguese Association of Canada) in Montreal. Its aims were to provide a social centre for Portuguese immigrants, to advise on integration into Canadian society, and to preserve Portuguese culture in the new land. The initiative derived from a Christmas show of movies of Portugal which was provided by the Portuguese consulate in the mid-1950s. About 200 families attended, and they decided on that occasion to establish an association. Founded on January 7, 1956, the club has flourished. Now it proudly describes itself as "the oldest Portuguese collective association in Canada." The club also produced a news bulletin for members and subsequently became associated with the founding of a Portuguese newspaper in Montreal, *O Luso-Canadiano* (The Portuguese Canadian).[2]

From its inception, the APC found itself at loggerheads with the Portuguese consul in Montreal, who wanted the club to endorse the views of the Lisbon government. The association was frequently asked to keep the consulate informed of developments within the club; and in mid-1956, it was characterized in a letter from the consul as a Communist organization. Complaints were made to the Portuguese ambassador in Ottawa and the Portuguese authorities, but they fell on deaf ears. Matters came to

155

a head in 1957, when the consul was implicated in a swindle involving a Portuguese club and was recalled by Lisbon. The new consul took a more conciliatory view of the APC than did his predecessor.

In 1958, Henrique Tavares Bello, the editor of the *Luso-Canadiano*, was elected as executive president of the club. A number of figures within the Montreal Portuguese community bitterly contested his policies in both these offices. He was criticized on the one hand by those who wished the association to become more profit oriented, and on the other by those who felt that the acceptance by the club of a financial donation from the Portuguese Ministry of Foreign Affairs was improper. These criticisms caused many members to leave the club and resulted in the resignation of the executive committee of the association, in a show of solidarity, in the spring of 1959. After new elections, Alcides Quaresma de Moura became president. He was sympathetic to the views of the former executive, but the period of strife had weakened the club. Tavares Bello continued to edit the *Luso-Canadiano*, but he turned away from the association. Early in 1961, he founded a new club in Montreal, the Portuguese-Canadian Club, which was intended to be a social, cultural, and recreational group without political, religious, or racial connections. About the same time, he founded a political club called the Casa dos Portuguêses, which subsequently evolved into the present Portuguese-Canadian Democratic Movement.

These developments caused a break – or, more accurately, a pause – in the continuity of the association. In 1961, a number of former members reactivated the association, and the new club rules specifically forbade members to use the APC for political purposes. The present club (which occupies a building on St. Urbain Street that was formerly a synagogue) includes a permanent office, library, stage, meeting hall, and social centre. The club is in use most weekends and some weekdays for various meetings, dinners, and language classes in French, English, and Portuguese, as well as entertainments and social events. By 1974, there were approximately 300 paid members and a further 400 in a looser association with the club.

Among the activities organized through the club are theatrical, sporting, musical, and folkloric events. The theatrical group (*Grupo Cenico*) has presented Portuguese-language plays performed by amateurs. The APC has a soccer team, the Luso-Stars, which is actively supported by the younger members and participates in matches with other local and national teams. Musical activities centre on a band – the *Filarmonica Portuguesa* – involving some seventy musicians in 1974. Music classes are given to those interested in learning to play an instrument. The club also supports a folkloric group, called *Sol de Portugal* (Sun of Portugal), which performs the dances and music of the Ribatejo district of Portugal. In 1969, the group danced at Terre des Hommes in Montreal during a week of engagements. It also has performed at the Montreal Museum of Fine Arts and participates in numerous Portuguese celebrations.

The APC and the Clube Português de Montreal, which is more purely social in its activities, are the major community centres for the Portuguese residents of Montreal. Other organizations also provide social activities, such as the Portuguese Democratic Movement (discussed below) and also the parish of Santa Cruz. The two main clubs participate in Portugal Day celebrations, and have organized *festas* for such popular events as the June celebrations of São João, which are marked by costumed processions. The Clube Português de Montreal also has a folkloric group, founded by Antonio Lourenço and others in 1964, which gives displays of the folklore of the Minho region of Portugal. Another organization, the Centro Português de Referencia e promoção social (Portuguese Centre of Information and Social Advancement), holds monthly meetings attended by some eighty persons and acts as a clearing house for community activities in other associations throughout the Montreal area.[3]

There are Portuguese clubs in other communities in Quebec. In 1974, these were located primarily in Quebec City, Sainte Thérèse, and Hull-Ottawa. In smaller centres, where there is a Portuguese community but insufficient support for a fully-fledged club, social activities centre on the church or on an informal social life of celebrations and picnics.

In Toronto the First Portuguese Canadian Club was founded on September 23, 1956, on the initiative of a dozen men from mainland Portugal. It was first located on Nassau Street. It later included a credit union, and in 1974 there were 1,100 members. In 1972 the organization bought a large building and established a centre for a variety of community activities. The centre includes several halls, a lecture room, a bar, games rooms, offices, a display of trophies, and accommodation for the Portuguese school.

By 1969, as a result of informal discussions among themselves, some Portuguese in Toronto had decided that the community needed a central body which could represent and co-ordinate the various clubs in the city, such as the First Portuguese Canadian Club, Madeira House, Benfica House, and Nazaré Club. Accordingly, a group of professional people drew up the constitution of the Portuguese-Canadian Congress. The membership was composed of the officers of other Portuguese clubs. The Congress was intended as a community organization which would fight for the protection of Portuguese interests and the improvement of certain social and employment conditions that worked to their disadvantage. It was to serve as a "federal" organization, bringing together the other clubs into a united front while not infringing on their independence.

Some in the community opposed the emergence of the Congress. One spokesman denounced it as an organization in the control of "persons not involved in the community." He pointed out that only the Portuguese Democratic Association had affiliated with the Congress. The claim of the Congress to represent the community was unfounded, he said; instead, there should be a union of clubs, "because no organization wishes to place itself below another, but on an even footing." He went further in his attack on the Congress:

Firstly, the Congress is said to be for the Portuguese Community but already it is only for Portuguese, but also for Canadians. I don't know if you know that one of the persons who is a member of the Congress was expelled from Angola for making a campaign against Portugal, going so far if I am rightly informed as collecting money to buy armaments for killing Portuguese soldiers in Angola, and if this is the truth, I do not wish to associate with these people.[4]

In the same issue of the newspaper where these comments appeared, another writer suggested that the First Portuguese Canadian Club was the proper basis for a truly representative community organization.

The Congress was to suffer from this lack of support by other organizations. In 1971, in an attempt to provide a common ground for the community, the Congress tried to organize the Portugal Day celebrations in co-operation with the municipality of Toronto; but political and personality dissension brought about the resignation of the president, and the Congress found itself severely lacking in funds. Under the leadership of a local businessman and a child psychologist the Congress recovered some of its lost influence but by 1974 it was moribund.

Many other centres in Ontario have active local Portuguese associations which are organized around social events, soccer or folk dancing. In Kingston, for example, there are two soccer teams; and although they do not yet have their own club house, they play frequently in Ottawa, Hamilton, and Montreal. A folk dancing club is often requested to perform and has presented its traditional dances in Toronto as well as locally. It was organized in 1967 as part of the city's Centennial celebrations. In 1970, the community organized a Miss Portuguese Kingston beauty contest, and this has become an annual event.

Social services in Hamilton are rendered by COSTI (Italian Community Education Centre), which originally was formed to look after the needs of the Italian population. There is a Portuguese Information Centre located in a downtown school which provides an information booklet in Portuguese detailing all varieties of problems that recent arrivals might encounter. In 1973-1974, the centre handled an average of 150 inquiries per month.

The Kitchener Portuguese Club is very active, as illustrated by these descriptions in the local newspaper:

When the Kitchener Portuguese Club's 500 members moved from their Williamsburg Road farmhouse to a just-completed clubhouse on the same property, Dr. José de Mello Gouveia . . . Portuguese consul for this area, and his vice-consul, Marcelino de Almeida Moniz . . . , both of Toronto, were there to congratulate club president, Alfredo da Silva, 123 Second St. Club members did most of the work on the building.[6]

About 1,500 Portuguese attended Kitchener's first Holy Spirit Festival, a spring religious and social event over the weekend.

A bazaar, a draw, folk dancing, two dances, a parade, an outdoor mass and a free dinner highlighted the weekend. About 1,000 loaves of bread, 800 pounds of meat and 200 gallons of home-made wine were consumed at the dinner Sunday.

The festival was held at the Kitchener Portuguese Club on Williamsburg Road in honor of the 11th Century queen of Portugal who gave meat and bread to all her people on Pentecost Sunday.

The queen chosen for the K-W festival was Grace da Silva, 15, 271 West Heights Drive, Kitchener. She led the parade carrying the traditional symbol of the Holy Spirit, an eight-pound Portuguese sterling silver crown.

Participating were delegations from other Portuguese clubs in Southern Ontario.[7]

On an occasion such as this, the association joins with the church in sponsoring the festival; but on other occasions, its social events are organized apart from religious activities. The club also holds dances each Saturday. Many in the community enjoy films of the homeland which are shown from time to time. The Portuguese Eagles soccer team is also an important part of the community.

Among the many other Portuguese clubs in Ontario can be numbered the London Portuguese Club, founded in 1968, which offers a range of cultural activities and since 1972 has provided a Portuguese school. The club owns land on Falcon Street, and its executive meets in a small house on this lot. The club has about 150 members but welcomes everyone from the Portuguese community who wishes to attend its social events. These take place once every two weeks on the average. Dances are held and cultural programmes presented. These take place either in the church basement or in a rented hall. The club also publishes a *Boletim Informativo*. The Portuguese Club has its own soccer team, which plays in the second division of the Ontario league. It competes against teams from other ethnic groups and, according to one informant, does not play serious games against teams from other Portuguese communities.

The Wheatley Soccer Club is very active and has a small clubhouse situated at the rear of the home of the president. They play matches on Sundays in neighbouring towns and cities, such as London, Kitchener, Windsor, and Chatham. Their league consists of other Portuguese teams, as well as some Italian and German teams. The Wheatley club fields both junior and senior teams, and all the members are Portuguese. The Wheatley Portuguese-Canadian Club meets from time to time in a rented hall for social events.

In Western Canada there are prominent Portuguese associations in Winnipeg, Edmonton, Calgary and Vancouver, in addition to those in smaller centres like Kitimat. The Winnipeg association sponsors social events, folkloric dancing and also soccer teams. The Edmonton Portuguese association assists recent arrivals in the city. It also sponsors a soccer team that plays in Calgary from time to time. Some of the teenage boys attend the Boys Club of Edmonton. Here they mix with young people of many ethnic groups and number among their friends boys of Italian, Indian, or Chinese descent. Many of the Portuguese boys consider themselves more Canadian than Portuguese if they have received most of their schooling in Canada. Often they have difficulty conversing in Portuguese with persons from outside their region (for example, a boy whose parents came from the Azores may have difficulty understanding persons from continental Portugal or from Brazil). Sometimes they suspect that mainlanders deliberately use "fancy" language to prevent the islanders from understanding and thereby to assert their superiority.

Calgary's Luso Canadian Club is a centre for social events and Saturday evening dances. But it has frequently been the scene of leadership rivalries and dissension.

In British Columbia, it has been claimed by several prominent members that the associations do not play an important part in the life of Vancouver's large Portuguese community, for the members they claim are often only nominal, having once paid membership fees but seldom attending the meetings. The Portuguese Club of Vancouver has 250 members. It sponsors dances and a soccer team. Once a year it holds a dinner for members of the Portuguese community. The Lusitania Club is strictly a sports club and sponsors a soccer team which plays in the local leagues. Usually these games attract about 100 spectators from the Portuguese community. In 1970 an association was created for the purpose of sponsoring charter flights to the homeland. It had no influence in the social life of the community and has since ceased to operate.

To indicate how a social club can develop from a range of particular interests, we can cite the example of the Portuguese community in Kitimat, B.C. In the early 1960s, the community was fairly small. By 1968, there were only about 400 Portuguese families in Kitimat and Terrace combined. The development of the Luso-Canadian Association of Kitimat reflected the need for a social centre for the community. The association was formed in 1961 and has continued to expand. It serves to unite the Portuguese community by arranging social events such as dances and festivals. By the early 1970s, the members had requested a resident Portuguese-speaking priest, a need especially felt by the women with growing families. The existence of religious services in Portuguese is often felt to be part of the definition of a "true" community, and it is sufficiently specific and pragmatic to be widely agreed on. Up to the early 1970s it had not been possible to satisfy this request.

Regionality forms the basis for club membership in the largest areas of settlement for immigrants from the mainland. But the Azoreans, who comprise the largest single group among Portuguese Canadians, seem to have little interest in regional clubs as such. For them, the Church provides the principal focus. "Continentals" and Madeirans have shown more interest in starting clubs with regional affiliations: there are clubs for people from the Minho, Nazaré, Algarve, and Madeira in Toronto. A good example of the type of organization deriving from a regional identity is provided by the Madeirans. In 1963, ten years after the first arrival of Madeirans in Canada, discussions took place on a very informal basis about the possibility of celebrating the event. A plot of land near Toronto was rented from a Portuguese farmer, and a *festa*, including a Mass and dancing, was held which netted a profit of over $300. Five men from among the first group of Madeirans to arrive in Canada thought the success of the event augured well for a scheme to develop a special park where future festivals could be held. They organized a campaign to raise money from Madeiran immigrants throughout southern Ontario: $20 per family towards the capital cost, and $1 a month family membership to pay for the running costs of the park. In 1964 they purchased fifty acres to the south of Sutton, Ontario, and immediately launched another campaign to finance the clearing of the land and the development of facilities. Electrical equipment was installed and a soccer field, swimming creek, barbecue pits, picnic tables, and food stalls were put up. The focal point of Madeira Park – as we mentioned in Chapter 8 – is the shrine to Our Lady of the Mount.

Enough examples have been given to show the range of Portuguese community organizations. Wherever there is a concentration of Portuguese there are clubs, but they are often at loggerheads. Readers of Portuguese newspapers soon encounter letters and articles dealing with accusations of double dealing, or bad faith. Sometimes the grounds of these charges and counter-charges are political, sometimes financial, and sometimes personality clashes. In one of the longest established of the Toronto regional clubs in the 1970s there has been something of a generational split between older men who distrust younger successors' ability to carry on the club, and young people who are frustrated by their inability to effect change in the club. In this situation it is becoming difficult to find candidates for the club officers. At least one foreign sociologist (Siegel) has suggested that endemic disputes are a particularly prominent characteristic of Portuguese society.[8]

Have Portuguese clubs in Canada shared the same quality in the past? Many Portuguese in Canada lament the lack of unity of purpose in the struggle to protect Portuguese interests. One example of both aspects of this problem has already been given. The Portuguese-Canadian Congress, founded in 1969 in Toronto, was to represent thirty organizations of varying significance but which involved up to 50,000 Portuguese in the city. This effort to produce a "federal" structure for the clubs broke down as a result of personal disputes and political rancour. Such disputes diminish the possibility for effective community organization. Perhaps because of the recent arrival of significant numbers of Portuguese in this country it is not surprising that no umbrella organization has yet been established.

161

The Portuguese tend to look on the clubs not as a vehicle for political or community organization, but to provide them with recreation. There is widespread suspicion of any attempts to make the clubs serve broader political or social purposes. Professional people who take offices are accused of seeking more clients. Vague insinuations about corruption are often voiced. As a result, the younger and better educated members of the community have in the past often lost interest in the essentially familial and blue collar focus of even the largest clubs.

NOTES

1. *Toronto Star*, December 8, 1969.
2. We discuss the establishment and evolution of this publication in detail in Chapter 10.
3. *Novo Mundo*, February 28, 1973. See also *Portugal Em Montréal 1975*.
4. *Correio Português*, Easter Edition, 1971.
5. Serviço Central de Informação, Direção de Cidadania, "Servicos Principais para o Recem-Chegado a Hamilton" (Hamilton: Direção de Cidadania, Secretariado da Provinciae Ministerio da Cidadania, n.d.).
6. *Kitchener-Waterloo Record*, January 3 or 4, 1973.
7. "1,500 attend festival for Portuguese," *Kitchener-Waterloo Record*, June 17, 1974.
8. Bernard J. Siegel, "Conflict, Parochialism and Social Differentiation in Portuguese Society," *Journal of Conflict Resolution*, v (1961). See also José Cutileiro, *A Portuguese Rural Society* (Oxford: Clarendon Press, 1971).

TEN

Newspapers and Politics

PORTUGUESE NEWSPAPERS IN CANADA

The Portuguese community has been very enterprising in the publication of a range of newspapers in Canada. Their development has reflected the difficulties and aspirations of the group. This is particularly true of the first, *O Luso-Canadiano* (The Portuguese-Canadian), which started as a monthly publication of the Associação Portuguesa do Canadà in Montreal. Its editor, Henrique Tavares Bello, came to Canada in 1955 with his wife, sponsored by relatives who had arrived in 1951 and 1952. His first employment in Canada was in a secondary position in Montreal's Portuguese consulate. Tavares Bello soon began to show a keen concern for the condition of his fellow countrymen. In a letter to the Montreal *Star* in November, 1955, he complained of the working conditions and exploitation experienced by Portuguese agricultural workers. In 1956, he became a co-founder of the APC, and in October, 1958, he brought out the first issue of *O Luso-Canadiano*. In his first editorial, he wrote:

> Another aim that the Luso-Canadiano sets itself to realise is the implantation among our immigrants of solidarity and mutual understanding, and at the same time to cooperate for a more perfect assimilation and integration of the Portuguese immigrant to Canadian life.

There were four distinct phases in the life of the *Luso-Canadiano*. Between 1958 and 1960, it served as the official voice of the APC. Although the newspaper was intended to publicize the work and activities of the association, it was always the property of Tavares Bello. He was concerned with providing a window on Canadian culture and life, as well as purely Portuguese-Canadian concerns. The paper included articles on such subjects as Portuguese immigration and trade with Canada (October, 1958), Canadian native art (November, 1958), and Canadian geography (March, 1959). Various articles gave information on Canadian social

163

services and history. In his April, 1959, editorial, Tavares Bello reiterated the aims of the newspaper:

> The *Luso-Canadiano* is a Portuguese voice in Canada. Its objective is to maintain among the Portuguese living here the linkages of language and traditions, to cooperate in the strengthening of Luso-Canadian relations under all their forms, to show Canada and the most diverse aspects of its economy, industry, commerce, politics and culture in the Portuguese language thus facilitating a more rapid integration and knowledge of Canadian life to our immigrants.

The newspaper also kept abreast of events among Portuguese in other cities in Canada. A frequent theme was the need for the immigrants to overcome rivalries based on Portuguese regionalism and to create a strong and united community. The newspaper printed articles on different Portuguese groups, so that immigrants from other parts of Portugal could understand and better appreciate each other (June, December, 1959).

In comparison with its development after 1960, the first two years of the *Luso-Canadiano* could be described as apolitical. Critical discussion of the policies of the Lisbon government was at that time totally lacking. Tavares Bello had held highly hostile opinions towards the *Estado Novo* (see below) while living in Portugal and continued to do so in Canada, but until 1960 the *Luso-Canadiano* was published in Portugal and had to pass the official censors before it was exported to Canada. In May, 1960, the last edition of the newspaper under this dispensation appeared. Tavares Bello then brought in a Portuguese typographer and began to print the newspaper in Canada. The first edition of the "new" *Luso-Canadiano*, now bi-weekly, appeared on October 25, 1960. Its former objectives and the high calibre of writing were now complemented by a statement of democratic and liberal views and strong criticism of the policies of the Lisbon government. The editorial of the first new issue clearly defined the paper's political posture:

> We are declaredly anti-fascist because fascism . . . evokes a stage of human history in which those who serve it, or make use of it, try to thwart the march of Humanity. We are viscerally anti-Bolshevik because such an oppressive political system, so vexatious of liberty and human dignity, cannot be accepted by any conscientious man of integrity . . . . We are for a democracy of the type which exists in Canada and which so honourably respects the liberty of the individual (without however, being able to escape certain abuses) – our attitude is, for the moment, inclined for the [Portuguese] opposition, but with a total independence on our part. We are consciously and freely opponents, and not systematically destructive in the behest of others: we defend a cause which seems to us to be the cause of the Portuguese People, not that of particular individuals or groups.

The newspaper took the opportunity to compare the civil liberties of Portugal and Canada. For example, in 1965, when the Canadian federal elections coincided with the Portuguese national elections, the front page of the November 5 issue juxtaposed two contrasting articles: one on Canada was headed, "A free people goes to the polls," while the other, on Portugal, was headed, "What lies beyond the fascist elections." The paper subsequently carried critical articles on Portugal's African policy (November 15, 1960), excerpts from the banned writings of Portuguese writers such as Aquilino Ribeiro (December 1, 1960), and interviews with political opponents of the Salazar government such as Henrique Galvão and General Humberto Delgado (February 15, 1961). The new orientation of the newspaper displeased the Portuguese government, and it made various informal attempts to persuade Tavares Bello to end his criticisms.

After the edition of February 15, 1961, publication of the *Luso-Canadiano* was suspended until November 30, because – at the instigation of an individual who was in the pay of the Portuguese secret police (the PIDE) – the Portuguese typographer refused to continue to work for the paper. The interruption cost Tavares Bello heavy financial losses; but after a time of considerable difficulties, publication was again resumed. About this time, Tavares Bello launched a libel suit against a rival Montreal Portuguese newspaper, the *Voz de Portugal* (the Voice of Portugal), which opposed his political views. On June 4, 1965, the *Luso-Canadiano* announced that the court had judged that the comments in question were defamatory and false, and that he had been awarded $600 damages plus costs. The newspaper continued to print Canadian news aimed at helping Portuguese immigrants to integrate into the new country. It also continued to criticize the Lisbon government. Tavares Bello wrote in an editorial of March 10, 1962:

> One of the constant preoccupations of our newspaper is to interest the Portuguese in Canada in the problems of his new country in all its aspects: political, social, religious, cultural and economic. In other words the integration of the Portuguese immigrant into Canadian life is our touchstone . . . to encourage the true democratic spirit and to inform about the democratic system in which we live.

During this third stage of its existence, the newspaper had to refute rumours that it was receiving a subsidy from the Lisbon government (unlikely as such a possibility must have appeared) as well as the more banal accusation that it was sensationalist. In 1965, the newspaper became a weekly. This most prolific stage of the *Luso-Canadiano* came to an end with the death of Tavares Bello on December 13, 1967, after a long and painful struggle against cancer. The subsequent issue was edited by a political refugee from Portugal, who promised to continue the founder's efforts.

After Tavares Bello's death, publication of the newspaper continued for several years, largely through the efforts of his widow and two main collaborators, Dr. Domingos Costa Gomes and Rui Cunha Viana. In 1969, Costa Gomes returned to Portugal, and in the following year Cunha Viana also left the newspaper. Mrs. Tavares Bello continued publication for another year and a half, but the last issue of the *Luso-Canadiano* appeared in May, 1971.

The *Luso-Canadiano* was unusual among the Canadian Portuguese newspapers published in the 1960s in that it opposed the policies of the Lisbon government of those years. One highly educated Portuguese immigrant has described this paper as the best objective reporting produced in Portuguese in Canada. Other newspapers, in Montreal and elsewhere, did not openly disagree or, on the contrary, pledged support for the Portuguese armed struggle against African liberation movements and for the *Estado Novo*.

As noted earlier, while Tavares Bello was still editor of the *Luso-Canadiano*, a group of Montreal Portuguese who disapproved of his political views established another newspaper, *A Voz de Portugal*. Twenty men subscribed about $100 each to the working capital, and one of them became the editor. Following a dispute over the management of the new paper one of the associates started a third newspaper, *O Lusitano*. In 1972, after the termination of the *Luso-Canadiano*, another newspaper began publication in Montreal, the *Tribuna Portuguesa*.

The first Portuguese newspaper to be established in Toronto was *O Correio Português*, founded and edited by Antonio Ribeiro and his wife. The second Toronto newspaper, *O Jornal Português*, was first edited by F. Pedrosa, who was born in Setubal. His father died when he was seven, and it was not possible for him to study beyond the primary level. He moved to Lisbon from Setubal, and he worked there for the electric company for fourteen years. He studied at night, and he also became acquainted with various journalists. He himself wrote articles for the Catholic Youth Magazine called *Juventude Operaria*, based on his holiday travels which took him through much of Europe. In 1964, he made application to come to Canada and after a six-month wait arrived in Hamilton, Ontario, in 1965. He stayed there for three years, living in the house of a Spanish family. At that time, there was no Portuguese club in Hamilton, although a number of Portuguese frequented a Spanish café.

Pedrosa was one of the founders of the Hamilton Portuguese Football Club, which was the first community organization outside the church among the 7,000 to 8,000 Portuguese in the city at that time. For two years he served as president of the club. Every weekend, he travelled to Toronto to buy magazines and books at the Portuguese bookshop on Nassau Street, and in 1968 he moved to Toronto. In Hamilton, he had met Father Antonio Cunha from Braga in Northern Portugal, and Antonio Alves, and the three men had decided that the Portuguese community should have a newspaper showing an interest in local activities and Canadian subjects without any pronounced political orientation. They established *O Jornal*

Português, and the first issue appeared on March 8, 1968. For the first issue, 3,500 copies were printed and the second went to 9,000. After some years, Pedrosa gave up the editorship of the newspaper. In his view, ethnic journals need the support of a political or commercial organization to survive, since the small revenue from sales and advertising and the pressure on a limited staff to produce a newspaper at a reasonable price make this almost impossible. Subsequently, the ownership of *O Jornal Português* passed to a company, Saudade Publications.

A third Toronto newspaper, *Novo Mundo* (New World), was established by Antonio J. Pina Fernandes, a native of the Algarve, who came to Canada after a career in governmental administration in Lisbon. This newspaper tried to reach a more literary audience, as well as providing interesting feature articles on the life experiences of various businessmen in Canada and reports from correspondents in London, Brampton, and Montreal. The first issue was published in April, 1970, and the last issue on December 15, 1973. In a front page editorial of the last issue, Fernandes gave his description of the difficulties encountered by his own newspaper, and of the ethnic press in general:

> *Novo Mundo* was born in April 1970, founded by six Portuguese full of enthusiasm and illusions, an enthusiasm which did not last long because the newspaper needed a lot of work, did not give profits and in order to be read had to be given away. Thus, disinterest and abandonment on the part of five of these enthusiasts. In order that the newspaper survived it was necessary to call on other friends both financially and with work. In the first year about twenty people were involved in the production and distribution of the newspaper. None of them received a salary or any financial compensation.

He went on to describe financial difficulties arising from the attempts to sell books, and the lack of support in the form of subscriptions. He also complained of the lack of governmental support:

> To guarantee to advertisers a minimum of readers who justify the placing of publicity we found ourselves obliged to maintain a free circulation, because the immigrant does not buy made-in-Canada [Portuguese] newspapers. They say that they are not worth it, and that they carry stale news. Others say they cannot read. These are the most sincere.

In conclusion, Fernandes announced that it was no longer possible to publish the newspaper. Despite its failure, *Novo Mundo* will be remembered for its determined effort to encourage Portuguese writing in Canada through its regular columnists and through analytical reports on community concerns.

The main newspapers are now published in Montreal and Toronto, since many of the more highly educated Portuguese reside in these cities. Others are published in Western Canada, but these are generally much less ambitious in scope. They contain local community news and some reprints from Portuguese newspapers.

The Portuguese community in Vancouver produced two newspapers in the 1960s. One of these, *Nosso Jornal*, lasted only two issues (October 10, 1969 and November 21, 1969). The paper appeared under the editorship of Marcelino Horta and the management of Mario Cipriano. The content of *Nosso Jornal* was largely made up of news clippings from Portuguese newspapers, translated articles from publications such as *Canadian Scene*, sports reports of events in the British Columbia Portuguese community and advertisements.

O Mensageiro, a member of the Canadian Ethnic Press Federation, is the second Vancouver Portuguese newspaper. First published on May 10, 1968, this bi-weekly was the first of its kind to appear in Western Canada. It has since been followed by *O Mundial* in Winnipeg. *O Mensageiro* has continued its publication to the time of writing (Autumn, 1974). The objective of the paper was outlined in its first editorial:

> The *Mensageiro's* principal aim is to be a means of contact between Portuguese, and to bring to their homes news from the distant motherland . . . . In its first edition the *Mensageiro* invites the Portuguese to unite and cooperate. Only with the cooperation of all is the publication of our periodical possible. We hope it will be useful and helpful for every Portuguese and, as is obvious, for the Canadian Portuguese community and especially that of B.C.

The best section of *O Mensageiro* was the space dedicated to the social, cultural, and religious events of the Portuguese community in Vancouver. From it, one can trace the development of the Portuguese in Vancouver from 1968 to 1974. A large number of clubs sprang up in Vancouver to unite the Portuguese of the city. Some of those were the Missão Católica Portuguesa, the Sociedade Portuguesa de Dança (The Portuguese Society of Dancing), the Portuguese Club of Vancouver (PCOV), the Canadian Portuguese Cultural Association of British Columbia, the Portuguese Theatre Group, and the Lusitania Club of Vancouver. There were also clubs outside Vancouver such as the Luso-Canadian Association of Kitimat, which kept close contacts with the Portuguese associations in Vancouver (in fact, the Luso-Canadian Association merged on May 1, 1970, with the PCOV). The strongest associations were the Missão, the PCOV, and the Lusitania Club of Vancouver. These three clubs have collaborated in organizing dances and festivals.

In Edmonton the Portuguese community is served by two newspapers: the *Boletim Formativo e Informative* (Bulletin of Opinion and Information) published by the Parish of our Lady of Fatima, and *O Despertar* (The Awakening), which was founded in 1972 with the objective of assisting the unification of the community and helping to provide Portuguese-speaking immigrants with information about Canada and the homeland.

Television and radio programmes in Portuguese also provide information, frequently serving several communities. For example, the Portuguese community in Hamilton has its own television program on the local station (Channel 11), aired on Sunday mornings from 9:30 to 10:00 under the name "Telejornal." The programme presents advertisements of stores and services, and the local priest gives a brief talk. The station reaches homes in the Golden Horseshoe and the Golden Triangle cities, as well as communities in New York State.

In Toronto a radio programme also reaches out to embrace many southern Ontario communities during the week. It is presented through CHIN (the Toronto multicultural station) as "Ecos de Portugal" from 6:00 to 8:30 in the mornings. The programme includes sports, news, and music from the homeland, as well as advertisements of job vacancies. A Calgary radio station, CJDV, offers a programme in Portuguese every Sunday between 11:00 and 12:00 noon in which are presented music from the homeland, sports, news, and other information of interest to the Portuguese community. The host of the programme is Portuguese and owns a local construction company. Radio and television programmes serve the ethnic settlements within a region and often present the viewpoints of a particular faction, either religious, political or social class.

POLITICS OF THE PORTUGUESE COMMUNITY

It is not the concern of this study to describe in detail the recent history and policies of Portugal. It may, however, be recalled that the troubled period of the Republic (1910-1926) was followed by a period of authoritarian government known as the *Estado Novo* (New State) headed by a former economics professor, Dr. Antonio de Oliveira Salazar. In 1968, Salazar was succeeded by Dr. Marcelo Caetano, a law professor, who remained the major figure in the Portuguese government until the *coup d'état* of April 25, 1974, carried out by the Portuguese armed forces. This brought about a rapid decolonization and sweeping social and economic change in Portugal. The Portuguese community in Canada was comprised of relatively young immigrants. Even the first major wave of newcomers in the early 1950s became adult under the *Estado Novo*. Very few of them had political memories of the period before 1926, and this became increasingly true with the passing of time.

The political life of the *Estado Novo* was characterized by state control of labour organizations, censorship of news media and publishing, a strong emphasis on public order and an exaltation of traditional morality and patriotism. One of the social consequences of the regime was that only those with access to foreign publications or to the intellectual life of the larger cities were well-informed politically. Before 1926, among the labourers and artisans of Portugal were men who had been leaders in small village campaigns for higher salaries and better working conditions, and in organizing electoral groups. It was precisely this type of worker who most heavily felt the repressive action of the *Estado Novo*. Despite the

169

efforts of clandestine opponents of the government it seems correct to suppose that the mass of the Portuguese population became less politically conscious than had been the case under the Republic. This was particularly true in the Azores archipelago and on Madeira where newspapers were small and concerned primarily with strictly local reporting. Newspapers from the mainland were not readily available and were more expensive. Political discussion was everywhere inhibited by fear of the security police and of the informers who were to be found at many levels of society.

Not surprisingly, the political activity that existed in the Portuguese-Canadian community between 1950 and 1974 was focused largely on the policies followed by the Lisbon government. There were sharp and often bitter disagreements over both domestic and overseas policy. In general, it can be said that the leaders of the Portuguese community, including the most economically successful individuals, either favoured or were not openly hostile to the Lisbon government. These families associated with the official functions at the consulates wrote in the newspapers or broadcast their support for the overseas policy of Lisbon, and often returned to Portugal on visits. By contrast, in Vancouver, Toronto and Montreal, there were others who actively disapproved of the *Estado Novo*. These men and women often perceived their life in Canada as a political exile as much as voluntary emigration. They described themselves as opponents of fascism, as they usually characterized the pre-1974 Lisbon governments. Their range of political viewpoints was broad, extending from the democratic centre to the extreme left, but they were united on two major points: an end to the *Estado Novo* and an end to Portuguese colonialism.

All of the Portuguese-language newspapers in Canada carried news of Portuguese politics. In Portuguese law, prior to April 25, 1974, the overseas territories in Africa and Asia were an integral part of a multiracial, pluricontinental Portuguese nation. This thesis was vigorously attacked by many states in the United Nations. Both French and English-language newspapers in Canada had often carried articles critical of Portugal since the outbreak of guerrilla warfare in parts of Angola (1961), Portuguese Guinea (1963), and Mozambique (1964). Only one Portuguese newspaper published in Canada was clearly hostile to the Portuguese presence in Africa and elsewhere: *O Luso-Canadiano* in Montreal. The other newspapers either avoided the subject or printed articles telling of the successes of Portuguese troops, both black and white, in fighting the insurrectionists. Also, particularly in the period 1970-1974, there was an increasing number of articles quoting favourable statements by visitors to Portuguese Africa.

The Portuguese community in Canada was divided on the matter of the African wars. As a result of the conscription laws many Portuguese Canadians had relatives on active duty. Others had fought in Africa before coming to Canada. Portuguese-Canadian newspapers repudiated allegations of atrocities by Portuguese troops and they were supported by many in the community. At the same time, some Portuguese men in Canada had left Portugal either to avoid conscription or to avoid fighting in the African wars. In 1972, for example, at a time when there was a Canadian movement in support of draft resisters against the Vietnam War, a conference held in Toronto included Portuguese draft resisters as a gesture of solidarity. The majority of those men settled in Montreal, for the usual pattern of clandestine emigration from Portugal by young men eligible for conscription was to go to France and there work and learn the language. Montreal thus became a logical choice of destination if those migrants had to move again in order to avoid French military service. The process of granting full independence to Portugal's African territories began with the recognition of the Republic of Guiné on August 26, 1974, and brought large-scale fighting between Portuguese troops and independence movements to an end. A reduction of the period of conscripted service was to follow.

The best known Portuguese political groupings in Canada from 1960 to 1974 were the Portuguese-Canadian democratic movements in Montreal. The Toronto organization was formed in 1959 by a group of immigrants from continental Portugal. That in Montreal emerged from the Casa dos Portugueses (House of the Portuguese) established in 1960 by Henrique Tavares Bello after he had left the APC. The membership of both of these organizations included the whole spectrum of opposition to the Lisbon government. Some members has been in some measure touched by the activities of the Portuguese Communist Party, which operated as an illegal organization, before their emigration to Canada. There were others whose opposition to the Salazar régime derived from socialist or liberal democratic principles. The membership in both organizations, which remained distinct despite their similar aims, was mainly of continental Portuguese of worker origin. Some were from service occupations – a barber and a travel agent – and others had a professional background as lawyers, teachers, or architects. The aim of both clubs was primarily to oppose the domestic policies of the *Estado Novo* and colonialism. With the increasing scale of fighting in the Portuguese African territories during the 1960s there was a desire to enlist Canadian opinion in bringing those wars to an end. By late 1972, as many as fifty active members met intermittently to discuss policy, both in Toronto and Montreal.

Political opposition to the Lisbon government was undertaken by only a minority of Portuguese-Canadians because of the fear of reprisals against relatives remaining in Portugal or because pride in their origin made support of a campaign against the government of the motherland repugnant to them. Even after immigrants had become Canadian citizens some were interrogated about their political activities during visits to Portugal. This seemed to confirm the widespread belief that informants of the Portuguese secret police existed within the Portuguese-Canadian community. In November, 1961, for example, it was charged that agents of the

PIDE (International Police for the Defense of the State) were working in Toronto. Informants were said to exist in Montreal. The members of the organizations in Montreal and Toronto tried to establish contact with like-thinking individuals in other countries and to publicize as much as possible the existence of an opposition to the Lisbon government through demonstrations, leaflets, and meetings. For example, a demonstration was held in 1971 at Toronto's City Hall during the Day of Portugal celebrations. Even before the ceremonies, objections to participation had caused the resignation of the Congress president. On the day itself, the Portuguese flag was hoisted to honour both the occasion and Portuguese Canadians; the mayor, William Dennison, and the Portuguese consul were among those present. They were surrounded by a group carrying placards, who handed out pamphlets denouncing the policy of the Caetano government. Both the mayor, who told the demonstrators that Old Country politics should not be exported, and the consul entered into an exchange with the demonstrators. On the following day, during a talk by a University of Toronto professor on the subject of Portuguese literature in connection with festivities arranged by the consulate, other demonstrators from the Portuguese Democratic Association and some non-Portuguese speaking individuals interrupted, shouting their opposition to the Portuguese government and its African policy. At the end of his speech, the professor invited the audience to read Portuguese literature both in the original and in translation, to which some people replied that since many Portuguese were illiterate this was impossible. Such demonstrations, letters to the Canadian press and discussion groups characterized the effort to organize opposition to the *Estado Novo*.

The change of government in Portugal following the "Revolution of the Carnations" of April, 1974, changed the political attitudes to be found within the Portuguese-Canadian community. Supporters of the major Portuguese political parties began to meet, especially in Montreal and Toronto, to debate the social and economic changes taking place in Portugal and the colonies. As a result, the loose grouping of opponents of the *Estado Novo* now fragmented into a wider spectrum of organized political groups.[1] Feelings began to run high, particularly among anti-communists, and the reports of attacks on the offices of the Communist Party in Northern Portugal during the summer of 1975 were paralleled by some shouting and scuffles in Toronto. This was reported in the Lisbon press.[2] On August 23, 1975, an anti-Communist demonstration which formed on Denison Square in Toronto moved through the Portuguese area with placards and attracted some 200 marchers.

As well as strong differences of opinion about the future orientation of Portuguese national policy, there was also an upsurge of feeling in favour of Azorean regional autonomy or even independence. Azoreans in Canada echoed criticism of the way in which the Lisbon government ruled the islands, and pamphlets circulated which stated that the archipelago has as much right to decolonization as had the former African colonies. Bumper stickers reading "The Azores are for the Azoreans" appeared in the Portuguese districts of Toronto and Montreal. Madeirans also expressed a desire for greater autonomy and invoked the special character of island society. Meetings were held in Montreal and Toronto calling for support of the Azorean independence movement. Differing viewpoints on social and economic developments inside Portugal, on the rapidity of the decolonization process which brought about the flight of many tens of thousands of settlers, and on the question of Azorean and Madeiran autonomy, heightened the divisions within the community.

Few Portuguese Canadians showed any interest in Canadian political life at the federal, provincial or local levels up to the 1970s. The voters' lists for 1958, 1964 and 1971 in areas of Toronto and Montreal with high densities of Portuguese residents show relatively few registered. To date (1975), there has been no significant initiative for provincial or municipal organization of Canadian Portuguese; indeed it seems true that few have joined riding associations or ratepayers groups.

Only rarely have individuals presented themselves as candidates for public office and they have tended to emphasize to Portuguese-speaking people their contacts with influential figures in the larger political structure. In some ways these men could be seen as presenting themselves in the guise of influence-brokers in a patronage system more than as political figures in a democratic tradition. One reason for this is that Portuguese voters do not appear to have a clear sense of a community vote. This was illustrated by the very low poll for an unsuccessful candidate for school board trustee in Toronto's Ward Four in 1972. He had arrived in Canada from Lisbon in 1955, settled in Toronto, and had been involved in a variety of community activities. Despite the fact that he was the only Portuguese candidate in an area with a very heavy concentration of children from Portuguese homes, he trailed several other candidates. Comparable situations elsewhere show the lack of a clear "Portuguese" vote supporting candidates who have a concern with Canadian-Portuguese issues.

In general, the Portuguese have not developed a strong political representation at any level of Canadian government – municipal, provincial, or federal – by the mid-1970s. This had consequences in the lack of a clear articulation of the problems confronting their community in Canada and in a weakly organized response to them. The most immediate problem confronting the Portuguese was the attitude of governments to emigration. Their concerns also affected the homeland which welcomed their remittances; the federal government and its consular and immigration services in Lisbon, Funchal and the Azores; and provincial programmes designed to help newcomers to adjust to Canadian life. There was also the question of community interests on a more varied level that required more vigorous defence if they were not to be lost by default.

NOTES

1. For a variety of political viewpoints current in the Toronto community see *O Correio Português*, 15, 30 June, 15 August 1975.
2. *O Século* (Lisbon) 11 August 1975. "Toronto é alvo de violência reaccionária."

ELEVEN

Cultural Identity

The Portuguese are intensely aware of their cultural identity but often find it difficult to define. It is summed up by one word: *Portuguesismo*. This refers to a complex of attitudes, customs, sensibilities, and values that make up the Portuguese lifestyle. Centred on the home for the most part, and extending from home to immediate relatives and close friends, it provides an attitude of mind. *Portuguesismo* can, of course, be seen as something to do with language, literature, and music; that is, it can be seen as a philosophical or artistic statement of ideas reflected in many aspects of life. Yet many Portuguese Canadians have little familiarity with the formal components of Lusitanian "high" culture, but are convinced of the importance of a Portuguese *maneira de ser* – way of being.

The character of any group of people, or their self-image, can be explained in a variety of ways. Determinist historians would say that such character results from the economic situation of each group. If this is the case, the character of the Portuguese in Canada will presumably change quite rapidly in the confrontation with an industrialized society. Traditional historians tend to appeal to amorphous concepts of large social units. More than one has seen the Portuguese as being of "Celtic" character – melancholy, sensitive, affectionate, and very imaginative. Historians less involved in all-embracing theories have looked at the social consequences of Portuguese geography and its influences: the discoveries are explained by reference to the "maritime vocation" of a country with long coastlines, counter balanced by the agricultural traditions of the hinterland peasantry. Even more important in defining the Portuguese character has been the course of a particular history: strongly regional as a result of geography, extremely stable within its frontiers, very international as a result of the establishment of a world empire and emigration. It is suggested that this has produced a population in which many people had some immediate experience of "overseas" and of different ways of doing things, just as the unifying link that held together this far-flung empire was a Portuguese sense of identity and language. The Portuguese Canadians in the shops of the *mercado de Augusta* in Toronto, Duluth St. East in Montreal, William Avenue in Winnipeg, and Commercial Avenue in Vancouver, are aware of themselves as part of a migration which has continued through centuries and to various countries. They define their *Portuguesismo* as the unifying factor.[1]

At the same time, this strength of identity may slow down the process of integration, particularly for the working class. In an article printed in *Novo Mundo*, Jaime Monteiro, an editorial writer for the Portuguese newspaper *O Setubalense*, observed:

> The Portuguese immigrants do not project themselves into the life of the countries which welcome them because they come from such low horizons that, when they have been able to amass a sum of money, they believe that they have arrived at the final triumph of life. However, without integration, which is not to say assimilation, not only the ethnic group as a minority but also the individual suffers from marginality and ignorance of the milieu where he lives, and in this case he is neither Portuguese nor Canadian.[2]

The same point was a major theme of the article, "Portugal in Toronto," by Joan Nankivell in the *Weekend Magazine* of August 11, 1973. Under the caption, "They never really left home: in Toronto 75,000 Portuguese have created a community that is as much Portugal as it is Canada," the article pointed to the self-contained nature of Portuguese life in Toronto.

Such criticisms are not new. Various ethnic groups in Canada have in the past been accused of making an insufficient effort to enter the mainstream of Canadian life. At the same time, the reasons are better understook by members of the group itself. Writing of the Polish community in Manitoba, Victor Turek has addressed the same problem:

> The rise and growth of ethnic communities on the outer fringes of the general life of this country ... has not been the result of the inborn clannishness of immigrants, but of the unavoidable consequence of too great social and cultural differences between the immigrants and the new world. By building up its own cultural entity ... the ethnic community in this country, like the ethnic communities of other national immigrant groups, has undoubtedly protracted the duration of the assimilation process, but at the same time has protected its members against the dangerous implications of maladjustment. These as we know are usually consequent on the direct impact of new environment on individual immigrants completely unprepared for such a radical change. Owing to the efforts of these ethnic communities, the enormous difference between the Polish peasants and Canadian society, that existed in the first moments of their mutual contacts did not break out into an obstacle to assimilation, full of stormy surprises, but

let itself be reduced, to a level of co-existence and a gradual integration into the fold of Canadian society.[3]

We do not wish to suggest that the development of the Canadian Polish community, essentially rural in its early stages, will show an exact parallel with the Canadian Portuguese, the major point stands that the "clannishness" of the community is an important and valuable transitional phase.

Breton suggests that ethnic communities which have a full range of services functioning in their own language, such as stores, travel agencies, employment opportunities and recreational facilities, will remain more segregated than other ethnic communities which do not have these services. The latter are forced to mingle with the wider community.[4]

The second generation in particular, and those immigrants who have the financial independence to obtain an education or are already sufficiently cosmopolitan in outlook, find themselves more able to participate entirely in both Portuguese life and the larger community. This viewpoint was expressed by a young student of chemical engineering at the University of Waterloo, in an article written in 1973 for a Toronto newspaper. Writing of the difficulties which confronted him as an Azorean immigrant to Canada, he said:

> I gave up the pretense of being "integrated." Instead, I want to select the best from both systems [that is, Portuguese and Canadian] and make as much use of each as possible.[5]

He went on to define his personal sense of the value of a Portuguese upbringing in the following terms:

> There is the whole notion of respect, self-discipline and duty, contrasting with many of the slacker forms of permissiveness that corrode the basis of North American society. On the other hand, there are those things which ought to be discarded altogether, such as unquestioned acceptance of authority and ideas, a deformed concept of religion and rotten social relationships. These are the well-known symptoms of the malaise that plagues the Portuguese nation in Europe, in the Atlantic Islands, and also unfortunately in Canada.[6]

The most obvious characteristic that unites the Portuguese differences in Canada is language. There are, however, clear regional differences between the speech of Northern, Central, and Southern Portugal, that of Madeirans, and especially that of the Azores. The offshore islands have remained in relative isolation from the metropolitan ways of speaking and have developed typical forms.

Language for the Portuguese is domesticated in a special way: a number of linguistic scholars have pointed out that it is quite difficult for the foreigner to learn to speak the language well, or to grasp its inflexions. The pronunciation, often quite closed and sibilant, makes the spoken language much less accessible than the written. To an extent less true of English or French, the ability to speak Portuguese defines the essence of the group.

As noted elsewhere, a major problem for New Canadians who speak neither French nor English is the language barrier. Sometimes, especially in the larger metropolitan cities like Montreal and Toronto, it may also be necessary to have familiarity with some other language which is found in particular trades. For example, in Toronto the construction industry is largely in the hands of Italians. Portuguese, speaking a language closely related to Italian, can with some difficulty both understand and be understood by Italian-speaking fellow workers. All employment is largely conditioned by communication, and there are distinct areas of employment available according to the ability to speak and write the relevant tongue.

Language and its complexities are thus a dominant factor in the community. Many Portuguese Canadians find it easier to work in jobs where Portuguese is the language of work. In this case, they come in contact with dialectic varieties within Portuguese, as it is spoken in Portugal proper ("the Continent"), in the Azores, and in Madeira. The names of shops may proclaim their owners' origin, as in the Padaria Aveirense (Aveiro bakery, named after a coastal town of metropolitan Portugal), the Salsicheria Madeirense (the Madeira sausage shop), or the Padaria Michaelense (bakery shop of São Miguel). As a consequence of this familial and linguistic situation, it is common to find working for the same company whole groups of adults who come from the same region and are either related or friends.

Outside his immediate range of possibilities for employment within the community, the Portuguese Canadian must deal with either English or French. It may be possible, within a highly specific vocabulary, to be efficient on the job without speaking either well. As an example, one can cite the owner of a pizzeria in Ottawa who was fully conversant with the mysteries of cheese, mushroom, sausage, and anchovy, but found more extensive discussions in English or French hard to follow. People in service jobs and other occupations involving contact with the public are keenly aware of the desirability of improving their grasp of English or French, and they may take one of the many language courses available to working adults across the country.

Many first generation immigrants have already experienced language difficulties before arriving in Canada. One man from a small village near Braga, in Northern Portugal, went to France without a passport in 1967. He paid 7,000 escudos ($280) to be conducted to France, and his wife later paid 6,000 escudos ($240). He lived in the Paris region for four years, during which time he learned some French and added a daughter to his family. Leaving his wife in France, he came to Toronto, where he roomed with a Portuguese family and began to work. In his after-work hours, he tried to learn functional English – from a phrase-book whose copyright predated World War I! Once established, he planned to bring his family to Ontario. This experience is not uncommon, as studies in France confirm.[7]

This constant emphasis for new arrivals on the language skills required to make the best use of employment opportunities has produced a corresponding sensitivity to Portuguese. The language and its poetry are the most important single element in Portuguese cultural pride. The record shops that serve the Portuguese in Canada bear witness to this heritage. "O Natal do emigrante," a song recorded in Canada, which sings of the difficulties of life and the nostalgia for Christmas at home, gives some indication of this.

The ability to speak the languages of Canada is one of the most prized skills in the community. Parents wish to break through the language barrier, but at the same time they wish to preserve the bond of spoken Portuguese in the family. At its most immediate, language is spoken in the kitchen and the dining room, but the children are often drawn strongly by English or French. This is the language of play between them and their playmates from other linguistic backgrounds. Often, children develop a kind of patois, using proper nouns in Portuguese mixed with English, or sometimes replying entirely in English to what is said to them in Portuguese. For the parents, this often gives a sense of alienation or diminishing contact with their children.

Historians of immigration have rarely looked closely at the way in which English or French is learned by immigrants.[8] The quaint turn of phrase in the new language is often memorable, and, as in the case of Yiddish speakers, may become permanent in certain North American expressions. For the Portuguese, there is a gradual linguistic ladder of assimilation which begins to appear very soon for the new arrival. He lives often among those who speak Portuguese but who are themselves using many new words which he has not heard at home. The people *vão aos stores* (go to the stores), *pagam os bills* (pay the bills), *usam o snowshovel* (use the snowshovel), and *apanham o streetcar* (take the streetcar). There is also a series of words which have been taken into the language, such as the usage of *chuva*, literally "rain," for a bridal shower. It remains to be seen whether any literary forms will emerge using this kind of vocabulary in the years to come; it is, however, already found in the various Portuguese-language newspapers.

The use of language is also related to social communication with people outside the Portuguese community. Particularly in dealing with strangers, the Portuguese have a reputation for politeness and courtesy. Sensitivity to every nuance of behaviour is keen, and the outsider may often be unaware that he or she has affronted this code. Aubrey Bell, an English expert on Portuguese literature, pointed this out: "Unhappily the Portuguese delicacy often meets with rougher manners in foreigners and shrinks as from a rebuff."[9] To members of a society where spoken forms of address at least prior to 1974 were still extremely variegated (*Vossência, Vossa mercê, O Senhor, Vôce, tu*, down to the jocular *E pa!* among men) to match a fairly

179

TABLE 20

LANGUAGE SPOKEN AT HOME, AFTER SIX MONTHS AND
TWO YEARS, BY RESPONDENT'S COUNTRY OF ORIGIN

(Portugal)

English		French		Other Mother Tongue	
6 mths	2 yrs	6 mths	2 yrs	6 mths	2 yrs
12%	18%	6%	3%	82%	79%

Source: *Three Years in Canada: First Report of the Longitudinal Survey on the Economic and Social Adaptation of Immigrants* (Canada Immigration and Population Study), Ottawa: Manpower and Immigration, 1974, p. 99.

TABLE 21

PERCENTAGE OF IMMIGRANTS WITH KNOWLEDGE OF
ENGLISH BY COUNTRY OF BIRTH

(Portugal)

Good or Perfect Knowledge of English

After 6 mths	After 2 years	After 3 years
5%	20%	23%

Source: *Three Years in Canada: First Report of the Longitudinal Survey on the Economic and Social Adaptation of Immigrants* (Canada Immigration and Population Study), Ottawa: Manpower and Immigration, 1974, p. 104.

complicated pattern of deference and regard, the casualness of Canadian speech, with the ubiquitous *tu* of French Canada and the first-name introductions of English Canadians, is something of a shock. Most language groups have problems in a new situation, but it is characteristic of many first generation Portuguese Canadians to emphasize the lack of "respect" in Canadian social usage, much as they may appreciate its relative openness. In an interview, a Toronto bus driver, brought up in Canada since his arrival as a child from Portugal, thought the principal difficulty of Canadian social life was a lack of respect shown by the young to the old.[10]

Food is an important part of the cultural identity of every social group. Portuguese cooking is highly varied, as might be expected from the wide variety of foods available in Portugal. The unifying factors are oil and wine. Portuguese olive oil, with a distinctive, slightly acrid taste, is mixed with onion and tomato paste as the basic sauce *refogado* of many meat and fish dishes. Family life is at its most intense around the meal table, and the Portuguese remain very faithful to the special foods that are associated with the region of origin and with festivals. Madeirans traditionally make the *bolo de mel* (honey cake) at Christmas, and many meals include the cornmeal gruel which is typical of that island. Azoreans have a variety of corn and fish dishes which are the specialty of each island in the archipelago. Particular grocery stores in the Portuguese communities cater to the special needs of the housewife cooking in each style.

The North American style of food preparation considered "Canadian" by Portuguese is obviously different from the foods of the Atlantic islands and Portugal. An early pamphlet for the benefit of Portuguese emigrants pointed out that they would find a great difference in Canada in the composition and method of cooking foods:

> Where the principal difference is to be found is in the fats, whereas in Portugal oil and and vegetable oils are mostly in use, in Canada they principally use fats of animal origin; butter and lard.[11]

One of the Portuguese contributions to Canadian life has been the development of restaurants that serve their distinctive foods. These range from the fairly modest establishments providing meals for single immigrants (the first Portuguese-owned business in Toronto was such a restaurant on Nassau Street opened in 1956), to the more elaborate or specialized restaurants. In Toronto, there are restaurants that specialize in chicken grilled in the Portuguese manner, and some that cook such famous dishes as *porco à tejano* (a combination of pork and clams) and the many forms of dried cod preparation. Wherever the Portuguese congregate, fish shops (*peixerias*), butchers (*talhos*), sausage shops (*salsicherias*), and groceries (*mercearias*) make their appearance.

Music in Portugal has been more of a popular art than an upper class accomplishment. This is a valuable addition in Canada, where folk singing has always been vital. The Portuguese have innumerable songs dealing with the human situations that arise in the town and country. Perhaps the most famous of these forms of singing is *fado*, a nostalgic and usually sad song sung to a guitar accompaniment. The word *fado* means fate. *Fado* is played on the radio programmes in Portuguese, singers perform at weekends in restaurants, and special evenings of *fado* are an event in social clubs. Plates of seafood, fried savouries of cod and minced meat, and glasses of wine are consumed by the appreciative audience as a series of *fado* is sung, ranging perhaps from such classic titles as "Lisboa Antiga," which describes the former splendours of the Portuguese capital, to the "fado do emigrante," which tells of the nostalgia of a person yearning for his distant family and loves. The arrival of a famous *fado* singer is always a notable occasion in the community. Amalia Rodrigues, one of the best-known performers of this art, has visited Canada a number of times. Her concerts were of great interest, not only to Portuguese, but to Canadians who have come to appreciate this sensuous and wistful music.

The Portuguese in Canada have formed a number of folklore groups or *ranchos*. The first in Canada was that established in 1964 by the Ottawa Portuguese Club. This group sang and danced "in pure *Minhoto* style" and in Montreal of that year made an appearance described in *O Lusitano* (October, 1964):

> It was the first time in the history of the Portuguese living in Canada that a group which represented one community went to another city to give a presentation of pure and healthy regionalism and folkloric fraternization.

In Montreal in 1964, Antonio Lourenço and others set up a folkloric group and gave performances at the Dorval Hilton, then at the folklore festival held at the Maurice Richard Arena. They performed at Expo '67, Laval University, and other places. A First Festival of Portuguese Folklore was held in Montreal in October, 1966, where groups from Ottawa, Kingston (*Rancho Tipico Português*), and Montreal appeared.[12] In Toronto, there are two folkloric groups: the *Rancho do Minho*, founded in 1969, and the *Rancho Folclorico de Nazaré*, founded in 1968. Other groups exist in Kitchener, Winnipeg, and Vancouver. Some of these groups have periods of inactivity, depending on local commitment, but they are a significant aspect of community life.

A celebrated form of Portuguese life is the bullfight. The Portuguese bullfight differs in several essentials from the better-known Spanish variety. One of these is that the bull is not killed in the ring, and in consequence is not so severely weakened by the assistants before the *espada* appears. The second is the appearance in the ring of the *forcados*, a file of men, the first of whom literally leaps onto the charging bull's horns and forces the head down, while the momentum of the charge is slowed by the successive impacts of the men behind. The last in the file is usually a fairly heavy man, whose particular task is to run around and catch the bull's tail. In May, 1973, a *tourado à Portuguesa* took place in Montreal and was widely reported in the Portuguese-language press.

Many Portuguese-Canadian men are very much interested in sports, particularly soccer, and all the Portuguese newspapers published in Canada and the radio and TV programmes carry features on the subject. The players and games in Portugal are followed avidly by supporters here. *A Bola*, the Portuguese sports newspaper published in Lisbon, has the largest circulation of any Portuguese-language publication in Canada. Benfica House in Toronto is a fan club for the famous team of that name in Portugal. In other cases, there is a distinct section of social clubs dealing with sports and arranging matches which take place right across Canada.

Portuguese cultural activity is not confined to the folk tradition in Canada. There are a number of book shops that sell novels, poetry, and other books and magazines published in Portugal and Brazil. The Toronto newspaper *Novo Mundo* published an original novel in serial form written by a member of the community, together with poetry from various contributors. In 1972, the same newspaper invited one of the best known contemporary novelists in Portugal, Fernando Namora, to tour the Portuguese communities in Eastern Canada. In his address at a banquet in his honour in Toronto, Namora stressed the importance for the Portuguese community of their language as a continuing link with their origins.

While many adult Portuguese Canadians received only a limited formal education in Portuguese, there is ground for anticipating that this interest in writers and playwrights will continue. A group of students at the University of Toronto, most of whom were of Portuguese origin, gave a memorable presentation of readings from the *Lusiadas* of Camões on the occasion of the four hundredth anniversary of its publication. The Portuguese press in the city recognizes the importance of such events. In November, 1972, the *Sociedade Procultura* held a program in Toronto, which included a play, a speech on the Portuguese part in the history of the discovery of Canada, and a brief recital of songs. About 200 people attended.

There are some differences of opinion about such clubs and associations. One spokesman for the community wrote in the *Toronto Star* that the "Portuguese community is young, poor, and has no time for phoney promoters"and criticized "cultural" activities as a cover for social pretensions.[13] Others welcome efforts to affirm cultural pride in Portuguese art and literature.

There is an increasing number of students of Portuguese culture at Canadian universities. Departments of Romance languages in a number of universities give courses in Portuguese language and literature, and the number of these seems to be increasing. Students of Portuguese background frequently attend these courses, either as electives or as parts of a major in language and literature. Portuguese university students in Toronto have established a club to reflect their cultural interests. Among Portuguese post-graduate students from Canadian universities, there are those who study Portuguese history or the Portuguese place in other aspects of the humanities.

NOTES

1. *Portuguesismo*: " . . . a Portuguese idiom or colloquialism; Portuguese mode of thought or feeling," in James L. Taylor, *A Portuguese-English Dictionary* (revised edition, London, 1963). For a fuller discussion of the ideas of a Portuguese "national character" see Francisco da Cunha Leão, *Ensaio de Psicologia portuguesa* (Lisbon, 1971).

2. *Novo Mundo*, January 30, 1973.

3. Victor Turek, *Poles in Manitoba*, Studies No. 5 (Toronto: Polish Research Institute in Canada, 1967), p. 245.

4. Raymond Breton, "Institutional Completeness of Ethnic Communities and the Personal Relations of Immigrants," in B. Blishen *et al.* (eds.), *Canadian Society: Sociological Perspectives* (3rd edition, Toronto: Mac-Millan, 1968).

5. *Novo Mundo*, May 15, 1973.

6. *Ibid.*

7. "L'Immigration Portugaise" *Hommes et Migrations: Études Sociales*, Vol. 105, 1966.

8. See Paul M. Migus (ed.), *Sounds Canadian: languages and cultures in multi-ethnic society*, Proceedings of the Canadian Ethnic Studies Association, 1971 (Toronto, 1974).

9. Aubrey Bell, *Portugal* (London, 1907), p. 11.

10. *Novo Mundo*, 30 June 1973. See also "The Family", chapter 6.

11. Portugal. Junta da Emigração, *Instrucções . . . Canada* (Lisbon, 1955).

12. *O Lusitano*, October, 1966.

13. *Toronto Star*, August 19, 1972.

PART FIVE:

Portuguese in Canada:
Past, Present and Future

TWELVE

Conclusions

Portuguese settlements in Canada have come of age – more than twenty-one years have passed since the earliest of the waves of immigrants came here to stay. Previously, for a period of nearly five centuries, they had been only visitors on our shores. Now they have arrived to stay. Initially they sometimes referred to their settlements in Canada as "colonies." Although scattered in Central and Western Canada, they resist assimilation through the barriers erected by language and by *Portuguesismo*. Now a younger generation of Portuguese Canadians is passing through the educational institutions and into the employment marketplace. They are the transitional generation, caught between the old country ways of their parents and Canadian lifestyles of their peers.

Members of the first generation frequently work in the construction industry and janitorial positions, and occasionally in factories. In certain areas of the country they are farmers or fishermen or lumbermen. Their wives, for the most part, are employed in janitorial or housekeeping jobs or work in canning or garment factories or in hospital kitchens. There are a few of the first generation who own stores, restaurants, travel agencies or construction contracting businesses. Only a very small proportion are in the professions; there has been little incentive for the most highly educated persons to emigrate. Therefore the Portuguese communities in Canada are heavily working class in orientation.

But the younger generation, many of whom have been born in Canada, have achieved a higher level of education than their parents, most of whom received only a few years of elementary education. The young people are reaching Grades 9 or 10 in high school. Many are taking vocational courses. The young men are entering skilled trades, carpentry and welding, or are taking training to become electricians or auto mechanics; the young women are entering hairdressing, secretarial work, clerical work in banks, or seeking careers in social work, nursing or teaching.

An area of life which is slower to change than many other aspects among the Portuguese immigrants is their family life.[1] As indicated in an earlier chapter, it is possible that the Portuguese family will approximate the French-Canadian rather than the English-Canadian family life style.

Since the very large majority of the immigrants come from working class backgrounds it is unlikely that there will be much growth in associational life, especially since conflict and divisiveness is pervasive in Portuguese communities.[2] It is too soon to examine the assimilation process for this ethnic group.

TABLE 22

SENSE OF BELONGING, BY COUNTRY OF ORIGIN

(Portugal)

At Home in Canada	Attached to Their Country of Origin	Undecided
64%	10%	26%

Source: *Three Years in Canada: First Report of the Longitudinal Survey on the Economic and Social Adaptation of Immigrants* (Canada Immigration and Population Study) Ottawa: Manpower and Immigration, 1974, p. 109.

The recency of Portuguese settlements in Canada has prevented the formation of umbrella organizations on a national level. The immigrants have been directing their energies to establishing themselves in the work force, purchasing homes and raising their families.

The political situation in the homeland since 1974 is changing rapidly. It is unlikely that Canada will receive many political exiles, since they will probably find other countries in Europe and South America more sympathetic to their outlook. But it is possible that Canada may receive some of the repatriates from the African colonies during the late 1970s.

The history of cultural groups is an integral part of the larger history of Canada. Moreover, it is a type of history which is formed here rather than brought from the homeland. However complete the traditional institutional framework imported by the community, the interaction with the larger Canadian society makes it different in form from a simple extension of the ways of the homeland. We hope that in future there will be many more studies of the Portuguese-Canadian communities in all their aspects.

We are especially hopeful that many Portuguese Canadians will realize the value of all the records of the development of their community, from family documents and the archives of businesses and recreational clubs, to the artistic and cultural accomplishments that have been realized in Canada. These are part of a heritage which must be preserved and handed on to the future, for the history of any group of Canadians is part of the history of all Canadians.

NOTES

1. Romão, "Le processus de migration."
2. Bernard J. Siegal, "Conflict, Parochialism and Social Differentiation in Portuguese Society," *Journal of Conflict Resolution*, v (1961). See also Cutileiro, "Crisis and Conflict," p. 69ff.

Bibliographies

GENERAL HISTORICAL BIBLIOGRAPHY TO 1950

Agostinho, José. "Les îles Açores et l'expansion vers l'Occident" in Portugal. *Bulletin de renseignementspolitiques,économiques et littéraires.* Lisbon, 1941, pp. 68-70.

Arruda, Manuel Monteiro Velho. *Coleção de documentos relativos ao descobrimento e povoamento dos Açores.* Ponta Delgada, 1932.

Avery, Donald. "Canadian immigration policy and the foreign navvy, 1896-1914." *Canadian Historical Association Papers, 1972.* Ottawa, 1973, pp. 135-156.

Bourinot, J.G. "Baccalaos on the old maps." *Royal Society of Canada. Proceedings: Appendix* v (1891), pp. 299-300.

Brazão, Eduardo. *The Corte-Real family and the new world.* Lisbon, 1965.

——. *La découverte de Terre-Neuve.* Montreal, 1964.

——. *Os descobrimentos portugueses nas histórias do Canadà.* Lisbon, 1969.

Buchanan, M.A. "Notes on Portuguese place-names in North-Eastern America." *Estudios Hispanicos. Homenaje a Archer M. Huntington.* Wellesley, Mass., 1952, pp. 99-104.

Campbell, Frank W. *Canada's Post Offices, 1755-1895.* Boston, 1972.

Campeau, L. "Découvertes portugaises en Amérique du Nord." *Revue de l'Histoire de l'Amérique française,* xx (1966), 171-227.

Canto, Ernesto de. "Os Côrte-Reais." *Archivo dos Açores.* 1882-84, iv, pp. 385-390.

——. "Quem deu o nome ao Labrador?" *Archivo dos Açores.* 1894, xii, pp. 355-371.

Cortesão, Jaime. "A viagem de Diogo de Teive e Pedro Vasquez de la Frontera ao Banco da Terra Nova em 1452." *Arquivo historico da marinha,* i 1 (Lisbon, 1933).

Costa, Abel Fontoura da. *A marinharia dos descobrimentos.* 2nd ed. Lisbon, 1939.

——. "Uma carta náutica portuguesa

anônima de circa 1471." *Publicação da Agencia geral das colónias.* Lisbon, 1940.

Duncan, Bentley. *Atlantic islands, Madeira, the Azores and the Cape Verdes in seventeenth century commerce and navigation.* Chicago, 1972.

Figueiredo, Fidelino de. "A colaboração portuguesa no descobrimento da America do norte." *Revista de História,* 15 (Lisbon, 1926), 241-263.

Freire, Antonio de Oliveira. *Descripçam corografica do reyno de Portugal.* Lisbon, 1739.

Gilbert, Humphrey (Sir). *The voyages and colonising enterprises of Sir Humphrey Gilbert.* 2 vols. London, 1950.

Groulx, Lionel. *La Découverte du Canada.* Montreal, 1966.

Hakluyt, Richard. *The principal navigations, voiages and discoveries of the English nation.* 2 vols. London, 1589, 1965.

Harrisse, Henry. *Les Corte-Real et leurs voyages au nouveau-monde d'après des documents.* Paris, 1883.

_____. *Découverte et évolution cartographique de Terre-neuve et des pays circonvoisins, 1497-1501-1769.* London, 1900.

Larsen, Sofus Kristian. *The discovery of North America twenty years before Columbus.* Copenhagen, 1924.

Layng, T. "Charting the course to Canada." *Congresso internacional de história dos descobrimentos.* Lisbon, 1961.

Lescarbot, Marc. *Histoire de la nouvelle France: 1608.* Toronto, 1907-14.

Lima, Manuel C. Baptista de. "Deux voyages portugais de découverte dans l'Atlantique occidental." *Bulletin des Études Portugaises.* 1946.

_____. "A ilha Terceira e a colonização do nordeste do continente Americano no século XVI." 18 (1960), 5-37.

Lisboa. Sociedade de geografia. *Colónias portuguesas no estrangeiro.* Lisbon, 1880.

Marie de l'Incarnation. *Words from New France: the selected letters.* Trans. and ed. by Joyce Marshall. Toronto, 1967.

Moogk, P.N. "The Craftsmen of New France." Unpublished Ph.D. dissertation, University of Toronto, 1973.

Morison, Samuel Eliot. *Portuguese voyages to America in the fifteenth century.* Harvard Historical Monographs, XIV. Cambridge, Mass., 1940.

Mota, Avelino Teixeira da. "Portuguese navigations in the north Atlantic in the fifteenth and sixteenth centuries." A paper delivered before the university on the occasion of the unveiling of the statue of Gaspar Corte-Real in Saint John's on 28 September 1965. St. John's, 1965.

Oleson, Trggvi. *Early voyages and northern approaches, 1000-1632.* Toronto, 1963.

Pap, Leo. "Portuguese pioneers and early immigrants in North America." *Actas: V coloquio internacional de estudos Luso-brasileiras: Coimbra, 1963.* Coimbra, 1965.

Patterson, George. "The Portuguese on the north-east coast of America and the first European attempt at colonization there. A lost chapter in American history." *Proceedings and Transactions of the Royal Society of Canada*, VIII. Montreal, 1891.

Quinn, David. *Sebastian Cabot and Bristol Exploration*. Bristol, 1968.

Ribeiro de Andrada, Antonio Carlos (1773-1845). *Cultura americana, que contem huma relação do terreno, clima, producção e agricultura das colónias britanicas no norte da America e nas Indias occidentais ... por hum Americano (?), traduzida da lingua ingleza pelo Antonio Carlos Ribeiro de Andrada*. Lisbon, 1799.

Roncière, C.G. de la. *Jacques Cartier et la découverte de la nouvelle France*. Paris, 1931.

Rosenberg, Stuart. *The Jewish community in Canada: a history*. Toronto, 1970.

Sauer, Carl O. *Sixteenth century North America*. Berkeley, 1971.

Tanguay, Cyprien. *Dictionnaire généalogique des familles canadiennes depuis la fondation de la colonie jusqu'à nos jours ...*, Québec, 1871-90. Vol. I, II, III.

Seary, E.R. *Place-names of the Avalon peninsula*. Toronto, 1971.

Szjkowski, Z. *Jews and the French Revolutions*. New York, 1970.

Trigozo, Sebastião Francisco de Mendo. "Ensaio sôbre os descobrimentos e comércio dos Portugueses em as terras setentrionaes da America," read in 1813. *Memorias de litteratura Portugueza, publicadas pela academia real des ciências de Lisboa*. 2nd ed. Vol. VIII. Lisbon, 1856, pp. 305-326.

Winter, Heinrich. "The pseudo-Labrador and the oblique meridian." *Imago Mundi*, II (1937), 61-73.

THE PORTUGUESE FISHING FLEET AND CANADA

Almeida, Gabriel. *Os Açores e a industria piscatoria*. Ponta Delgada, 1893.

Azambuja, Jacob Frederico Torlade Pereira de. *Memória sôbre a pesca do bacalhau*. Lisbon, 1835.

Gonçalves, Armando de. *L'économie maritime du Portugal*. Lisbon, 1934.

Lisbon, Gremio dos Armadores de Navios da pesca do bacalhau. *Conselhos a um pescador*. Lisbon, 1940.

Nascimento, Luis Gonzaga do. *As escolas de pesca e a sua importância na formação cultural do pescador*. Setubal, 1942.

Queiros, H. de. *A pesca do bacalhau*. Lisbon, 1940.

Ryan, Shannon. "Newfoundland Cod Fisheries." Unpublished M.A. thesis, Memorial University of Newfoundland, 1971.

Serpa, José de. *Opusculos açorianos ... I. A indústria piscatoria nas ilhas Fayal e Pico*. Coimbra, 1886.

Simões, Jorge. *Os grandes trabalhadores do mar: reportagens na Terra Nova e na Groenlândia*. Lisbon, 1942.

Villiers, Alan. *The Western Ocean. The Story of the North Atlantic.* London, 1957.

Villers, Alan John. *The Quest of the Schooner Argus: A Voyage to the Banks and Greenland.* London, 1951.

Warren, Mathew H. Lecture on Newfoundland and its fisheries with statistics before the Mechanic's Institute of St. John's, March 14, 1853. n.p., n.d.

Canada. National Film Board. "The White Ship." 1966. 14 min.

THE PORTUGUESE BACKGROUND TO EMIGRATION

Almeida, Carlos and Barreto, Antonio. *Capitalismo e emigração em Portugal.* Publicação da faculdade de geografia. Lisbon, 1970.

Antunes, M.L. Marinho. "Vinte anos de emigração portuguesa: alguns dados e commentarios." *Análise Social* VIII (1970), 299-385.

Barata, Oscar Soares. *Migrações e povoamento.* Lisbon, 1965.

_____. "O problema demográfico português." *Revista Militar,* II sér. 5 (1970), 386-409.

Bettencourt, José de Sousa. *O fénomeno da emigração portuguesa.* Luanda, 1961.

Boléo, José de Oliveira. "Colônias portuguesas em países estrangeiros." *História da expansão portuguesa no mundo,* III Lisbon, 1940, pp. 509-510.

Brans, R. *The Azores.* London, 1963.

Carqueja, Bento. *O povo português: aspectos sociais e econômicos.* Oporto, 1916.

Castles, Stephen, and Kosack, Godula. *Immigrant workers and class structure in Western Europe.* Oxford, 1973.

Emigração e despovoamento. (Coleção Actualidade Portuguesa, 12.) Lisbon, 1974.

Gonçalves, José Julio. *Portuguêses dispersos pelo mundo.* Lisbon, 1971, [i.e. 1973].

Granotier, Bernard. *Les travailleurs immigrés en France . . .* édition revue 1973, Paris, 1973.

Heinzelmann, W. *Madeira, Portugal.* Basle, 1971.

Laranjo, José Frederico. *Theoria geral da emigração e sua applicação a Portugal.* Coimbra, 1878.

Leloup, Yves. "L'émigration portugaise dans le monde et ses conséquences pour le Portugal." *Revue de géographie de Lyon* XLVII (1972), 59-76.

Navarro, Modesto. *Emigração e crise no nordeste transmontano.* Lisbon, 1973.

Pereira, Gil. "O distrito do Porto e a emigração." *Estudos politicos et sociais,* II, 2 (1964), 499-518.

Poinard, Michel. "L'émigration portugaise de 1960 à 1969." *Revue géographique des Pyrénées et du sudouest,* t. 42, fasc. 3 (1971), 293-304.

Portugal. Ministério dos Negócios Estrangeiros. *Emigração portugueza . . . documentos apresentados às Côrtes na sessao legislativa de 1874.* Lisbon, 1874.

Ramos da Costa, F. *Emigração: fatalidade irremediavel?* Lisbon, 1973.

Serrâo, Joel. *A emigração portuguesa.* Lisbon, 1971.

Trindade, Maria Beatriz Rocha. *Immigrés portugais: observation psychosociologique d'un groupe de portugais dans la banlieue parisienne:*

Orsay, Lisbon, Instituo superior de ciências sociais e politica ultramarina, 1973.

A BIBLIOGRAPHY OF PORTUGUESE IMMIGRATION TO CANADA SINCE 1953

Books and Monographs

Anderson, Grace M. *A Selected Bibliography on Portuguese Immigration.* Toronto, Ontario: Dept. of the Provincial Secretary and Citizenship, Queen's Park, 1970.

_____.*Networks of Contact: The Portuguese and Toronto.* Waterloo: Wilfrid Laurier University Press, 1974.

Brown, K., ed. *Those People.* Toronto: Inter-Agency Council for Services to Immigrants and Migrants (n.d., c. 1972).

Ferguson, Edith. *Newcomers and New Learning.* Toronto: The International Institute of Metropolitan Toronto, 1966.

_____. *Newcomers in Transition.* Toronto: The International Institute of Metropolitan Toronto, 1964.

Hamilton, John. *Portuguese in Transition.* Toronto: Toronto Board of Education, Research Dept., Dec. 1970.

Serviço Central de Informação, Direcão de Cidadania, "Serviços Principais para o Recem-Chegado a Hamilton" (Hamilton: Direção de Cidadania, Secretariado da Provincia e Ministério da Cidadania, n.d.).

Streeruwitz, M. *Portuguese Directory for the Metropolitan Area of Toronto.* Toronto: International Institute of Metropolitan Toronto, 1972.

Published Articles

Anderson, Grace M. "The Educational Ladder and Success." *The Journal of the American Portuguese Cultural Society.* New York (Fall, 1971).

194

Martins, Luis Augusto. "Emigração Portuguesa no Canadá." *Boletim.* Lisbon: Sociedade de Geografia de Lisboa, 89 (July-Sept., 1971), 7-9.

Norris, John, ed. "The Portuguese," in *Strangers Entertained: A History of the Ethnic Groups of British Columbia.* Vancouver: Centennial '71 Committee, 1971.

Peters, A. "The Portuguese Community in Winnipeg." *The Manitoba Modern Language Bulletin,* VIII, 2 (Jan. 1974).

"Portuguese," in *The Canadian Family Tree,* Centennial Edition 1867-1967. Ottawa, Queen's Printer, 1967.

Sunderland, Lynne. "Portuguese." *Ethnic Groups and Their Cultural Differences.* A Handbook for the Helping Professions. Calgary: Catholic Family Service, Nov., 1969.

Tavares, M. Custodio. "Canada; myth or reality?" *Novo Mundo,* Toronto, September 30, 1971, translated and summarized from Portuguese by the ethnic press analysis service, Department of the Secretary of State, in Howard Palmer, (ed.) *Immigration and the Rise of Multiculturalism,* Vancouver, Calgary, Toronto, Montreal, Copp Clarke Publishing, 1975.

In Press

Higgs, David, and Anderson, Grace M. "Portuguese" in *The Canadian Family Tree,* Revised Edition. Ottawa: Information Canada.

Mimeographed Articles

Anderson, Grace M. "Channels of Employment: The Portuguese in Toronto." Paper presented to the Canadian Sociology and Anthropology Association Annual Meeting, St. John's, Newfoundland. Mimeographed, Waterloo Lutheran University, 1971.

____. "Illegal Immigration: A Sociologically Unexplored Field." Paper presented to the American Sociological Association, Denver, Colorado. Mimeographed, Waterloo Lutheran University, 1971.

____. "Institutionally-oriented Networks." Paper presented to "Network Seminar II," The American Anthropological Association Annual Meeting in Mexico City, November 1974. Mimeographed. Wilfrid Laurier University.

Bieler, Caroline. "The Institutions of Portuguese-Canadian Integration in Toronto," and "Ethnicity and the Entrepreneur." Brown University, Anthropology, Spring 1973.

Kemp, Madeleine and Morisset,

195

Claude. "Enquête sur la population d'origine portugaise de Hull" Commission Scolaire, 1974.

Smith, Estellie M. "Portuguese Enclaves: The Invisible Minority." State University of New York at Brockport, 1973.

Theses

Anderson, Grace M. "The Channel Facilitators Model of Migration: A Model Tested Using Portuguese Blue-Collar Immigrants in Metropolitan Toronto." Ph.D. dissertation, University of Toronto, Sociology, 1971.

Bear, M.L. "A Study of the Program for New Canadians at St. Christopher House." M.S.W. thesis, University of Toronto, 1955.

Lipman, Marvin H. "Relocation and Family Life: A Study of the Social and Psychological Consequences of Urban Renewal." D.S.W. thesis, University of Toronto, 1968.

Rigby, Douglas. "Citizen Participation in Urban Renewal Planning: A Case Study of an Inner City Residents' Association." Ph.D. thesis, University of Waterloo, Planning Department, 1975.

Romão, Isabelle. "Le processus de migration, la mobilité professionnelle, la mobilité sociale et l'acculturation chez les ressortissants d'un groupe ethnique à Montréal." (Une étude clinique sur les Portugais à Montréal.) Unpublished M.A. thesis, Dept. of Sociology, Université de Montréal, 1972.

Theses in Preparation

Fernández, Ronald Louis. "The Logic of Ethnicity: A Study of the Montreal Portuguese." Ph.D. dissertation in progress, McGill University, Anthropology.

Rosa, Victor M. Pereira da. "Emigration et Dépendance: Les Portugais de Montréal et le Portugal." Ph.D. dissertation in progress, McGill University, Anthropology.

Research in Progress

Roskies, Ethel. "Life Change and Illness in Immigrants." Dépt. de Psychologie, Section Clinique, Université de Montréal.

Sources of Statistical Data – Portuguese

Anderson, Grace M. "The Channel Facilitators Model of Migration: A Model Tested Using Portuguese Blue-Collar Immigrants in Metropolitan Toronto." Ph.D. dissertation, University of Toronto, Sociology, 1971.

_____. "The Educational Ladder and Success." *The Journal of the American Portuguese Cultural Society*. New York (Fall, 1971).

_____. *Networks of Contact: The Portuguese and Toronto.* Waterloo: Wilfrid Laurier University Press, 1974.

Anuário Demográfico. Lisbon: Instituto Nacional de Estatistica. (Published annually).

Atunes, M.L. Marinho. "Vinte anos de emigração portuguesa: alguns dados e comentários." *Analise Social* VIII (1970).

"Comunidades Portuguesas." *Journal of the Union of Communities of Portuguese Culture.* Lisbon: Trimestral Publication.

Canada. Manpower and Immigration. *Immigration Statistics.* (Annual and quarterly publications.) Ottawa: Manpower and Immigration.

_____. Royal Commission on Bilingualism and Biculturalism. *Report of the Royal Commission on Bilingualism and Biculturalism*, Book IV, *The Cultural Contribution of Other Ethnic Groups*, Ottawa, October 23, 1969.

Canada. Manpower and Immigration. *Immigration and Population Study. Immigration Policy Perspectives.* (Green Paper on Immigration, Vol. 1.) Ottawa, Manpower and Immigration, 1974.

Canada. Manpower and Immigration. *The Immigration Program.* (Green Paper on Immigration, Vol. 2.) Ottawa: Manpower and Immigration, 1974.

Canada. Manpower and Immigration. *Immigration and Population Study: Immigration and Population Statistics.* (Green Paper on Immigration, Vol. 3.) Ottawa: Manpower and Immigration, 1974.

Canada. Manpower and Immigration. *Immigration and Population Study: Three Years in Canada: First Report of the Longitudinal Survey on the Economic and Social Adaptation of Immigrants.* (Green Paper on Immigration, Vol. 4.) Ottawa, Manpower and Immigration, 1974.

_____. Statistics Canada. Census of Canada, 1971. Ottawa: Statistics Canada. See especially Population: Ethnic Groups, Vol. 1, Part 3.

Ferguson, Edith. *Newcomers and New Learning 1964-1966.* Toronto: The International Institute of Metropolitan Toronto, 1966.

_____. *Newcomers in Transition, 1962-1964.* Toronto: The International Institute of Metropolitan Toronto, 1964.

Hawkins, Freda. *Canada and Immigration: Public Policy to Public Concern.* Montreal and London: McGill-Queen's University Press, 1972.

Martins, Luis Augusto. *Boletim, Sociedade de Geografia de Lisboa* Series 89, Nos. 7-9 (July-Sept. 1971).

O'Bryan, K.G.; J.G. Reitz; O.M.

Kuplowska. *Non-Official Languages: A Study in Canadian Multiculturalism.* Ottawa: Minister Responsible for Multiculturalism, 1975.

Pereira. "A emigração portuguesa no decénio de 1951-1960." *Estudos políticos e sociais,* XI, L (1964), 205-45.

Quebec. *The Position of the French Language in Québec. Book 3, The Ethnic Groups. The Gendron Report,* Vol. 3.) Québec: Government of Québec, Dec. 1972.

Richmond, Anthony. *Ethnic Segregation in Metropolitan Toronto.* Toronto: York University, Feb. 1972.

Rogers, Francis M. *Americans of Portuguese Descent: A Lesson in Differentiation.* Beverley Hills, Calif.: Sage, 1974.

Romão, Isabel. "Le processus de migration, la mobilité sociale et l'acculturation chez les ressortissants d'origine portugaise à Montréal." M.A. thesis, sociology, Université de Montréal, Sept. 1972.

Wright, E.N. *Students' Background and Its Relationship to Class and Programme in School.* (The Every Student Survey), #91. Toronto: The Board of Education for the City of Toronto, Research Department, December, 1970.

INDEX

DATE DUE	RETURNED